THE MODERNIST CRISIS
von Hügel

THE MODERNIST CRISIS: von Hügel

BY JOHN J. HEANEY

CORPUS BOOKS
Washington—Cleveland

Corpus Instrumentorum, Inc.
1330 Massachusetts Ave., N.W.
Washington, D.C. 20005

First Printing 1968

Library of Congress Catalog Card Number: 68–15780

PRINTED IN THE UNITED STATES OF AMERICA

PREFACE

The image of Friedrich von Hügel is like one of those trick pictures which changes perspective and shape as one takes various positions before it. Viewed from the right, it looks sinister, suggesting machination, plot, maneuver, dodge, finesse, imposture, and deception. Viewed from the left, from the angle of the Modernist, it looks spineless, revealing two-faced diplomacy and, perhaps, unconscious cowardice.

The interesting point about the literature on von Hügel, accordingly, is that neither the violent anti-Modernist, nor the thorough-going Modernist, dared to take seriously a view of von Hügel seen from only one perspective, although the scattered hints reveal the urge. It is as if everone sensed that there was some other perspective for which allowance had to be made to explain this amazing man. Everyone seeks a central position from which to view him truly. But this demands that one must not only view in perspective, but also examine the image up close. Once the ideal view is attained, its validity must be evaluated as objectively as possible.

Angelo Crespi, von Hügel's Italian philosopher friend, termed him "the greatest religious thinker after Newman," and others have said he was the greatest in England after Newman. The sweeping generalization in both these statements may well be challenged, but I personally feel that, if there is one area where his significance is preeminent, it is in the area of his grappling with the problem of authority. The Baron was not specifically a Scripture scholar; most of his scholarship in this field filtered to him through the minds of German liberal theologians, Loisy, and Protestant exegetes in Britain. A good bit of his early interest was in geology. While he read and analyzed all the great philosophers, he cannot be considered a world specialist in this domain, though many of his insights into the knowledge of God have permanent value. While he read widely and profoundly in mysticism, and produced his great life's work on the subject, *The Mystical Element of Religion*, he never confined himself exclusively to this study, and today one finds important works on the subject in which he is rarely mentioned.

He did, however, have a truly great mind and character, and he is unique in one sense. What Catholic layman of his time was more familiar with the combined contemporary, scientific scholarship in geology, Scripture, Church history, philosophy, mysticism and theology? Was there anyone so thoroughly familiar with the personnel who bore authority, and exercised jurisdiction in the Church? And, lastly, it is certain that few surpassed him in genuine religious conviction, loyalty to the Church, and conscious sincerity.

From this picture emerges the von Hügel of vital interest today, a highly intelligent Catholic layman, well versed in science, and grounded in faith, struggling with the pronouncements of the Church when they seemed at variance with the apparent conclusions of the critics; the von Hügel who was competent in so many fields, and who, over a period of twenty-five years, gradually synthesized a coherent religious philosophy on the nature of the Church.

Thus, Friedrich von Hügel is of rare importance because of his standing as a symbol of the Catholic struggling with the problem of authority and liberty. This question is of major importance in the Church today.

The method to be followed in this study will be both historical and theological. I will try to situate von Hügel in his period, and follow the issue of authority with as great fidelity to chronology as possible. My perspective, however, is also theological. Since the present subject is extremely complex, I have thought it best to include a theological evaluation in each chapter rather than to reserve this for the end. Since the Baron had a somewhat sharp debate with Blondel, and minor differences with other important figures like Tyrrell and Loisy, it seemed that these should be evaluated immediately lest the points at issue be forgotten by the time we reach the conclusion.

Whenever possible, I have cited correspondence from the original MS; when a letter has been published, I have included reference to the publication.

Fr. Henri de Lavalette, S.J., the selfless and hidden originator and supporter of the many works issuing from the Institut Catholique in Paris, cannot be left here without a word of deep gratitude for his overflowing generosity, humanity, and insight in helping to bring the present project through its first draft.

CONTENTS

CHAPTER ONE

VON HÜGEL'S EARLY BACKGROUND AND THE INTELLECTUAL CURRENTS OF THE TIME

A. NATIONAL CHARACTERISTICS AND FAMILY TRAITS

Baron Friedrich von Hügel was born in Florence, Italy, on May 5, 1852,[1] and lived there for seven and a half years. Though dimly sensed at the time, certain impressions still influenced him years later. In the early 1920's he wrote:

> I think myself back in Florence, from my birth there over seventy years ago up to seven and a half years of age, and I still see the big-headed, black crickets I used to lure with long straws out of their holes in the light green Cascine in spring; or again the black and red leaflice so frequent in the Boboli Gardens.

The Baron had a life-long absorbing interest in the concrete, and this quotation reveals that it had made an early appearance. This interest was further fed by the family taste for scientific fact. His father, Baron Carl von Hügel, whose chief pursuit was diplomacy, became an authority in horticulture. His maternal grandfather, Benjamin Outram, was a prominent engineer. His brother, Anatole, became director of the Museum of Archeology and Ethnology at Cambridge. This seemingly unimportant love for the concrete will be, in later life, as the Baron saw it, at the root of his conflict with authority.

Florence and Italy, moreover, left him with a love of certain of their historic qualities which are important for our study. Fifty-six years after his birth, when he published his great *The Mystical Element of Religion*, which is generally detached from the problems of the Modernist controversy in which he was then engaged, he wrote:

> Born as I was in Italy, certain early impressions have never left me; a vivid consciousness has been with me, almost from the first, of the massively virile personalities, the spacious, trustful times of the early, as yet truly Christian, Renaissance there, from Dante on to the Florentine Platonists. And when, on growing up, I acquired strong and definite religious convictions, it was that *ampler pre-Protestant, as yet neither Protestant nor anti-Protestant, but deeply positive and Catholic world*, with its already characteristically modern outlook and its hopeful and spontaneous application of religion to the pressing problems of life and thought which helped to strengthen and sustain me, when depressed and hemmed in by types of devotion prevalent since then in Wester Christendom. For those early modern times presented me with *men of the same general instinct and outlook as my own*, but environed by the priceless boon and starting point of a still undivided Western Christendom; Protestantism, as such, continued to be felt as ever more or less unjust and sectarian; and the specifically *post-Tridentine type of Catholicism, with its regimental Seminarism, its predominantly controversial spirit*, its suspiciousness and timidity, however inevitable some of it may be, in its failure to win my love. Hence I had to continue the seeking and finding elsewhere, yet ever well within the great Roman Church, things more intrinsically lovable. The wish some day to portray one of these large-souled pre-Protestant, post-Medieval Catholics was thus early and has long been at work within me.[2] (emphasis added)

The italicized phrases give insight into the Baron's temper. Post-Tridentine Catholicism, a regimental spirit, a controversial bent, all are, to him, like a strong and distasteful dose of medicine. The hankering after a pre-Tridentine Catholicism is the sub-soil out of which so much of his thought will grow. In his later struggles with authority, the ideal which he thinks he can discern on some far distant horizon is the gradual emergence of such a pre-Tridentine type of Catholicism.

Baron von Hügel has generally, and with justice, been characterized as "Germanic." After all, his father, Baron Carl, was born in Ratisbon of a Rhineland family which had served Austria since 1790,[3] and served in the Austrian army. Friedrich was aware of his German origin. Seven-tenths of his reading was in German, and he bemoaned his Germanic-English style. Some Englishmen in 1914 thought he might be a German spy.

Yet von Hügel had a complex and predominantly Scottish strain in him. His mother, Elizabeth Farquharson, a convert from Presbyterianism when the Baron was three or four, was a Scot, although she was born, and lived at the time of her marriage, in India. She married the Baron Carl at the age of 19 when he was 57. To confuse the picture still more, Friedrich spent his first 15 years in Florence and Belgium, and all the rest of his life in England. Thus his origins were as complex and all inclusive as his later position. He himself, however, admitted that "the mental methods and habits natural to me, in matters of history, philosophy, and theology," were chiefly characteristic of the German tradition. Accordingly, when the Baron later turned to various German, non-Catholic exegetes, he was not merely looking across borders to discover the latest novelties (Rivière, the historian of Modernism, says that he had a "sens délibérément novateur"),[4] but he was rather turning towards his own hereditary tradition, and to what he considered the best scientific work being done.

The von Hügels and Diplomacy.   Friedrich's father, Carl, was an explorer for six consecutive years, a soldier for two, and a horticulturist of stature, but most of his public life was spent as a diplomat. The impression he left on his contemporaries is of more than mere bibliographical interest. In Anatole Hügel's collection of papers in memory of his father we learn:

> According to Reumont's judgment [Prussian minister at Brussels, and a German Catholic historian and supervisor of Friedrich's education when Carl von Hügel was Austrian minister there],

> Hügel's diplomatic career was throughout an honorable one, and his steady, conciliatory bearing won him respect even from those who opposed the policy which he had to represent . . . he carried through with ability and success the negotiations which preceded the restoration of the Central Italian Duchies. On the other hand, Reumont thinks he did not clearly foresee the political situation which was preparing itself in Italy at the end of the fifties.[5]

Reumont affirmed that "Hügel's bearing is always conciliatory, his behavior considerate, his judgment just." "Dependence upon religion is a characteristic of the Hügel family," and Carl had "dauntless determination when a noble cause or a law of humanity was in question."[6] Diplomacy had been one of the traditions of his family. Both Carl's father, Baron Aloys von Hügel, a Knight Grand Cross of the Order of St. Stephen, and his brother, Baron Clemens von Hügel, had rendered distinguished diplomatic service to the Austrian Empire.

Carl, himself a personal friend of Metternich, said that the reason he joined the Army during the revolution in 1848 was because:

> what was important was to raise a barrier against the dissolution of society, to prevent the break up of all that was great and noble, of all that had been shaped and hallowed in the course of centuries, that is to say, to serve justice and order—in one word, to serve the Emperor.[7]

Thus we get glimpses of a man of religious loyalty and scientific interest, who was familiar with the great, had a strong belief in tradition, and an outstanding ability at conciliation. It is impossible not to note how similar Friedrich's own character was.

Friedrich lived in this atmosphere of diplomacy for fifteen years. His father had first-hand experience of the maneuverings of Church and State, having been sent in 1849 on "a secret mission" to Pope Pius IX. The Grand Duke of Tuscany, to whom Carl was later accredited, was favorable to the Holy See, but was surrounded by opposition to Rome. A grudging concordat with Rome was signed in 1851, apparently while Carl was minister there. He lived in the midst of important personnages, and dealt with ecclesiastical officials. It is no wonder that Friedrich, growing up in this atmosphere, was influenced by it in his attitude towards life.

"Von Hügel's measures were diplomatic." This phrase runs like a refrain through Maude Petre's evaluation of the Baron.[8] Miss Petre, who was a friend of the Baron and of Tyrrell, was ill at ease with this facet of von Hügel's character. Loisy dissected von Hügel's character as "rather reactionary, temporizing, opportunist: it is not for nothing that he was the son of a diplomat."[9] In many of these evaluations, one feels the estrangement between those involved in theological debates and the world of diplomacy. The silent presupposition is that it is wrong to be a diplomat, or at least to be a diplomat and engage in Church controversy at the same time. This study will show, however, that a kind of "diplomacy" is an essential human ingredient in dealing with authority, because the limits of authority have not, and possibly cannot, be exactly defined. "The artful management in securing advantages without arousing hostility," which is Webster's definition of diplomacy, and which sounds so cynical at first glance, cannot be avoided in the fringe areas of liberty versus authority. Everyone admits that there is a tension between the two, and where there is tension there is give and take. The "advantages" one takes for oneself concern liberty, not a cynically selfish thing, and the "hostility" one avoids should be that towards a legitimate authority accepted on one's own principles. Diplomacy becomes obnoxious only when the diplomat acts either merely to please persons or out of fear to oppose what one does not really believe in.

During his entire life Friedrich lived familiarly with the hierarchy, and without awe of it. He knew Cardinal Manning; Cardinal Vaughan, whom he knew well as early as 1877, was the spiritual director of the Baron's mother-in-law, Lady Herbert of Lea; he met and corresponded with Cardinal Newman. He knew Bishop Hedley, Cardinal Bourne, F. Mercier (later Cardinal), Archbishop Mignot; he had a twenty-two minute interview with Leo XIII, walked frequently, during the winter of 1895–96, with the, then, Don Eugenio Pacelli whom he found favorable to modern Biblical approaches; he corresponded with, and knew well, Cardinal Gasquet, was early a personal friend of Cardinal Merry del Val, met the future Pius XI twice, spoke often in Rome with Cardinal Rampolla, then Secretary of State, and Cardinal Satolli, Prefect of Studies, and was personally acquainted with other members of the hierarchy, both great and small, in Rome, in England, and on the continent.

Thus von Hügel's reactions to authority will have none of the emotional overtones or undertones of a small boy addressing the clergy. Rather, he will tend to judge decisions by those with whom he was well acquainted, according to his evaluation of these persons; he will see these decisions as a psychological overflow of a certain attitude towards life rather than as absolutes. These decisions, as is evident, could not draw from him the same emotional response of awe that they would draw from the ordinary layman of his time. Yet he will always keep a respect for doctrinal decisions, except during the tumultuous period at the appearance of the Encyclical *Pascendi*. That is why he will try to interpret these decrees, unlike Loisy who considered such interpretation a deceptive maneuver. Von Hügel's interpretations will enable us to give body to the abstract principles which are often proposed for the development of a theory of authority in the Church.

B. EARLY TRAINING AND PSYCHOLOGICAL TEMPERAMENT

Friedrich never went to school. He was educated first by an Anglican governess (the Baron's parents told her to use the Roman Catechism in his religious instruction), then by a Lutheran layman at Brussels under the direction of von Reumont, then by William Pengelly, a self-taught Victorian geologist of some repute who, incidentally, was not anti-religious. In geology von Hügel developed a double consciousness, "of cumulative evidence as an *instrument* of knowledge, of successive stages of development as a *subject-matter* of knowledge."[10] This double consciousness will never leave him during his entire life: love of evidence and a sense of development.

By 1890 he had begun to study Julius Wellhausen, and, under a Jewish teacher named Spira, he began work in Hebrew. By 1895 he was able to speak of "my own experience of four years close study of the Hebrew Genesis, Exodus, and Leviticus." All of the Baron's scriptural work was done in his own study, for he attended no university. Perhaps to make up for this lack of personal contact, he developed a burning desire to meet personally the authors whose works he admired.

Classing Nations and Judging Character. At this point let us pause a moment, and consider the Baron's ability to evaluate the persons he met. Closely related to this is his attitude toward race and nationality. He spoke German, English, Italian, and French fluently, and he was acutely aware of the need to understand the racial background of a person in order to size up his ideas. For example, he liked, in his friend, Percy Gardner, his "Scotchness," which prevented him from pulling a discussion up short with the question "whether this is all English." He found that many English book reviews had a "strangely chilling, damping effect" on him because of their fear of enthusiasms; this reaction he attributed to his Scots-German blood. Since the English spiritual writer Frederick Faber had a love of point, paradox, and hyperbole, von Hügel observes that he was of French ancestry. He sees most of the Latins as "abstract-thinking races." He endows the Irishman with the "unforgiving, unforgetting, temperament of the true Celt," and contrasts this with the "far less remembering Anglo-Saxon," and finds a "slumbering hostility" in the Irish and French toward the English. He prefers meeting Scotsmen who, more spontaneously than the English, "rejoice in thought and contemplation" with their "ardent attempts to reach the root principles and the absolute laws in the life of things." Countless other such statements are found in his works.[11] This sampling is presented because some concrete evidence is needed to give the reader a feeling for the Baron's interest in national and cultural background in understanding causes and people.

There are many instances of von Hügel's interest in the analysis of character. For example, he describes a young man by the name of Piastrelli at the famous Modernist reunion of August, 1907: "A young, round, blue-eyed, strong-chinned, thin-lipped, crop-haired, very clean, neat, alert, composed man of 24, in lay dress." Bernard Holland remarks: "This is characteristic: he always attached importance to the outer appearance, and began thence inwards his observations of character." The Baron analyzed Van Ortroy, the Bollandist, at length, and ended with: "A bluff, utterly honest man is a delightful thing; but two quite straight-looking and noting eyes, with a third one at the back of them, taking notes for another, quite *a priori* purposes, is quite another situation." Numberless other examples of his effort at discernment might be cited. Towards the end of his life the Baron was even the spiritual director of the great English mystical writer, Evelyn Underhill. It would seem that all through his life he was a master of insight.

But we are suddenly brought up short when we turn to von Hügel's friends and acquaintances for their opinions. Wilfrid Ward, Maisie Ward, Bernard Holland, Maude Petre, Loisy himself, Edmund Bishop, all agree on his defective judgment of human nature.

Before presenting these various opinions, let us ask why this appraisal of the Baron's judgment is so important. Nédoncelle, who touches so perceptively on many of the core problems in the von Hügel story, suggests that there is a lacuna in critiques of von Hügel, and hence in the history of Modernism, because of an ignorance of the Baron's peculiarities in assessing others. With this judgment I totally agree. Therefore, the subject is important, and consequently it is interesting to hear Wilfrid Ward, for example, say:

> Indeed he was in certain respects so truly great that at first he overpowered me. I did not see defects in what was so big and so thorough. Yet as time went on, while my admiration for his powers

and for his character never diminished . . . there were, I think, serious defects of judgment due to his insufficient knowledge of human nature. . . . His enthusiasms varied. . . . Le Play was all in all to him when I first knew him. Later he wholly disappeared and I never heard his name from von Hügel. Then came Bickell, the Biblical critic; he too disappeared; then came Loisy. . . .[12]

The Baron, the spiritual giant to whom Wilfrid Ward turned frequently for consolation and spiritual inspiration, is assessed by Maisie, Wilfrid's daughter:

This friendship [between Tyrrell and von Hügel] my mother always maintained was his [Tyrrell's] undoing. The Baron had a unique power of opening windows onto almost infinite vistas, but he had no power whatsoever of gauging another man's mind. He had certain ideals of what needed doing for the Church, and he valued all his friends primarily for their utility to this end.[13]

Similarly, Maude Petre affirms that the Baron was wanting in his judgment of people. Moreover, Bernard Holland, who was close enough to the family to be chosen, after the Baron's death, to select correspondence for publication in his *Selected Letters*, says:

The Baron was not, I think, in full touch, notwithstanding their continuous correspondence and many meetings, with Tyrrell's mind and its rapid developments. Of all men he least adapted himself to the varying characters of his friends. He was always one with his true self, and exact statement of the subject on which he wrote was the one motive that guided his pen.[14]

Loisy spoke of von Hügel's illusion about his own position. He described the Baron's efforts to convince him that their positions were really solidary. Edmund Bishop, English convert, liturgical scholar, and correspondent with von Hügel, complained that the "union of ideas" between himself and von Hügel was "less complete than von Hügel thought."

It should be pointed out that there is danger of magnifying von Hügel's naiveté to the dimensions of a legend.[15] However, taking the evidence as we have it, we must admit that von Hügel, up until say 1915, was not as profound a psychologist as he believed.

The evidence points to three factors which clarify the Baron's peculiar appreciation of others. He had a warm, overpowering nature, and he was deaf. When he was eighteen, he became sick with typhoid fever. De la Bedoyère says that this left him "a nervous wreck for some years, and a person of extremely delicate constitution all his life." The frequent mention of his health in his letters confirms this condition,[16] but its most adverse result was that it made him fairly deaf. He remarks to Tyrrell, June 30, 1904, with regard to a possible social engagement: ". . . deafness means crippledness and a handsome crop of little humiliations during such social attempts." The defect, which he bore heroically, and with a conquered sensitivity, nevertheless affected his character. A. A. Lilley, a friend, said after his death: "Owing to his deafness his talks were mainly monologues. But what monologues!" His niece remarks, in a stirring and warm human picture of her uncle: "I was so used to listening and accepting, not explaining." The defect thus contributed to his tendency, at times, to dominate and to read character without the necessary passive-active dialogue.[17] A second factor, which must be considered in studying the Baron's judgment, is his conscious bent to see the best in everybody, and in their work. He had the rare virtue of intellectual sympathy. Hence, he usually tried to meet authors personally, for he knew the dangers of knowing them only through their writings. He had a strong sense of intellectual charity, and a deep loyalty to friends. All these qualities led him to be uncritical in detail when he felt he was in agreement with the general drift of ideas in a writer who was his friend. Perhaps most important of all was the Baron's idea of an intellectual reform in the Church. Since he was so keen on what his "crusade" entailed, he tended to read agreement with his plan into others, and thus did not see clearly their real direction. This will be discussed later.

Without the characterization of von Hügel just sketched, the Baron would emerge as a plotter, a hidden instigator, a shadowy, sinister character. Rivière falls into this distortion, although his *Le Modernisme dans l'Eglise* remains a notable scholarly achievement.

If we avoid such distortion, we may not excuse all of von Hügel's actions, but we will understand them.

C. PERSONAL CONTACTS AND INFLUENCES

During the depression that afflicted him during his typhoid attack, von Hügel was under the spiritual guidance of the Dutch Dominican, Fr. Raymond Hocking, who directed him, as he puts it, away from his "gravely bad habits and inclinations." When the Baron was 32, he met his second spiritual director, Abbé Henri Huvelin, who was the spiritual guide of, among many others, Charles de Foucauld. The Abbé had a profound effect upon Friedrich, developing in him a deep religious sense, and a love for the Church. He warned him against relying overly on ordinary apologetics and scholasticism, and trained him in great confidence and liberty of soul. It would be false, however, to think that Huvelin's advice radically changed von Hügel's intellectual tendencies. For example, Huvelin counseled him in 1886:

> The Scholastics, it seems, have a language for the initiated and those who have not passed through their studies have not at all the right to speak. As for myself, I have never passed through them. Also I have been let know that I have no right whatever to speak. But I hold on to realities, while they have their formulas. They do not understand that life, all life, escapes analysis. What they dissect is the dead body. Pass them gently with a very gentle smile.[18]

At this very time the Baron was already reading mostly non-scholastic works, as will be seen shortly. Again Huvelin told him:

> You take apologetics just as it is found in life, just as it presents itself to the spirit which is candid and alone in the face of reality. Ordinary apologetics is worth nothing. It is often ingenious, but quite fraudulent ['*fausse*']. It consists of geometric figures. These have great regularity but no reality.

The Baron was at this time already very much interested in Blondel's *L'Action*, which was, in no way, the "ordinary" apologetic.

Yet Huvelin was a real catalyst to the Baron's thought. He gave him great peace and spiritual unity, and many of his sayings are echoed, again and again, in the Baron's later life. Huvelin pointed out the frequent changes in theological opinion caused by scientific discoveries. He implied that the term, orthodoxy, is often overextended, and that one's prior concern should be for fidelity to one's conscience, and for the search for truth. He warned him of narrowness (a term which was later the Baron's favorite derogatory epithet), of over-simple positions, of over-emphasis on miracles, of seeing the Church merely as something anti-Protestant, anti-rationalist.

Von Hügel said of Huvelin, in 1920: "I owe more to this man than to any other man I have known in the flesh," and he frequently reflected the Abbé's "winged words and fiery darts,"[19] which seem to have assured him that his bent towards liberal critical positions was a movement toward genuine spirituality.

When he was seventeen and a half, Friedrich began reading Newman, probably after a visit to him. Later, in 1876, the Baron and his wife stayed a week with Newman, whose remarks were recorded in von Hügel's notebook.[20] They discussed the vicariousness of Our Lord's sufferings; the question of certainty, "besides my three general rules in the *Grammar of Assent* . . . we can but trust that a certainty which has borne the test of time is the true one, and that God does not choose us to know more"; scholastic philosophy:

> the syllogism ignores the more and the less yet in moral evidences this is often the most important consideration. . . . As to such scholastic terms as have come to be mixed up with definitions—such as that of Transubstantiation—they only, as it were, express a truth in a particular language and the truth can be expressed in another. Bellarmine uses the words cause and effects instead of substance and accidents. But I do not pretend to

be a metaphysician—quite the reverse; so much of metaphysics seems to me playing about with words; I cannot thoroughly get hold of it.

They also touched on infallibility:

As to the Popes' decisions in early times, they were not called infallible but irreformable and though of course they would not be the latter without being also the former, yet it is by no means clear that the Popes were more than merely conscious of being certain and in the right as to each individual decision as it came to be pronounced.

Newman's remarks remind us of Huvelin's advice on scholasticism. In a letter to Fr. Ryder (1890) on Newman's death, the Baron wrote:

It was at $17\frac{1}{2}$ that I first had any book of the Cardinal's in my hand; and *Loss and Gain* was the first book which, amidst abnormal circumstances within and without, made me realize the intellectual might and grandeur of the Catholic position. Ever since then—especially during the ten years after that—my debt to him has been steadily, during that period, rapidly on the increase; and if I am now less conscious of such growth than I was then, that is owing, I have no doubt, to my having assimilated so much of the five Lectures of Part II on *Anglican Difficulties;* of the *Parochial and Plain Sermons;* of the letters of Dr. Pusey, and the Duke of Norfolk; above all, of the *Grammar of Assent*—that I talk Newman even oftener than I know.[21]

De la Bedoyère mentions that the few references to Newman in the Baron's writings usually sound a critical note. Let us look at some of these. Von Hügel told Holland that Newman was "not easy to talk with, because he was so sensitive and easily pained, like a very refined, sensitive old lady." He wrote to Abbé Houtin, on May 27, 1903, that Newman had a temperament which was "very impressionable, easily preoccupied at the end with the bites which flies seem to give him, a temperament to which he had more or less succumbed." He even wrote to his niece, on December 8, 1920: "I thought of starting you on Newman's *Parochial and Plain Sermons*—certainly classics and

well known to me. But then these sermons are rigorist—how they
have depressed me. Just the opposite from Fenelon who always
braces me."[22] He said, in an address in 1921, that he used to
wonder "in my intercourse with John Henry Newman, how one
so good and who had made so many sacrifices to God, could be
so depressing." He blames this on his "deeply predestinarian,
Puritan, training" and contrasts him unfavorably with Huvelin.[23]
A clash of temperaments—the Baron's warm, sensitive nature
finding little resonance in Newman's—and a consequent finding
of rigorism in his doctrine, this seems to account for the antipathy.[24]

Nevertheless, the Baron's personal dislike of Newman
should not obscure his real debt to the Cardinal. Much of the
debt, as the Baron confessed, was not conscious, but we may say
with certainty that Newman's two great insights into the Church,
deeply and explicitly influenced von Hügel: an inner experience
of the Church, and the development of doctrine, both of which,
in turn, later influenced his own ecclesiological positions. Von
Hügel never studied religious facts under any other aspect than
that of development. It was he who introduced Loisy to Newman,
sending him, among other books, *The Essay on the Development
of Christian Doctrine*. Into his sporadically expressed "doctrine" on development, von Hügel injected his own theory of
purification and friction (*see* Chapter 6). He viewed science as
acting in healthy friction with religion, and thus helping to purify
false leads towards development.

Newman also influenced von Hügel on the question of the
attitude of the laity toward ecclesiastical authority. In 1912,
von Hügel wrote about "unresting absorption or elimination of all non-Papal, non-Curialist powers and activities by
Rome." He said that "Rome depends upon its subjects as truly
as its subjects depend upon Rome." "The Curialist presentation
of the situation, as a simple alternative between anarchy and
autocracy . . . will not forever terrify the freely docile children
of Jesus Christ and of His Vicar. : . . They will, on the contrary,
come to feel with Rosmini the holy, and with Newman the far-
sighted . . . that no fellow mortal . . . can ever come to be

beyond learning and receiving from men."[25] Again, speaking about the danger of emphasizing, in isolation, the institutional or any other element of religion, he cites only two men who balanced, in themselves, the three elements of religion (rational, institutional, and mystical); namely, Newman and Antonio Rosmini.[26] Here we see Newman as the symbol of the right attitude toward authority, as the symbol of the balanced institutional view of the Church.

Newman, of course, developed an ecclesiology in which the layman had an important role.[27] The Baron was well acquainted, for example, with Newman's famous articles which appeared in *The Rambler* (1859) on "Consulting the Faithful in Matters of Doctrine." He assisted Wilfrid Ward with his biography of Newman in which the *Rambler* controversy is discussed. Ward once even compared the Baron's position in regard to Rome to Newman's position when he was with the *Rambler*.[28] Both the Baron and Wilfrid Ward worked, like Newman, for permission from Rome for English Catholics to attend the national universities. Thus, the whole question of the layman's role was in the air within von Hügel's circle; he breathed it whenever he visited the Wards. How much in this question the Baron owed directly to Newman is impossible to say. But Newman certainly was the source of that fresh current of thought in England, and von Hügel was heir to this. One imagines that Newman never anticipated a lay disciple, with all the diplomatic talents of a von Hügel, putting his early theory into operation. (Cardinal Ledochowski called it an "impertinenza" on the part of a layman, when the Baron reached as far as Cardinal Rampolla to discuss Anglican Orders.)[29]

Von Hügel was influenced by Newman and his school, not so much to write a theology of the problem of the laity in the Church, as to embody that problem in himself. What he wrote on the subject is scattered, but there was a unity to his life which offered a tentative solution in action. Newman "opened windows" which let in a breeze whose force, apparently so often spent, has had no small effect on the various decrees on the laity at Vatican II. Von Hügel, too, was affected by it, even by that faint echo from the *Rambler* controversy: "It seems to me that a man who opposes legitimate authority is in a false position." [30]

A brief word is called for about von Hügel's first encounters with L. Duchesne, A. Loisy, G. Tyrrell, M. Blondel, and R. Eucken, and about his early reading. In 1884 the Baron met Mgr. Duchesne, the witty and scholarly Breton who was a professor at the recently established theological faculty of the Institut Catholique in Paris. Duchesne inspired von Hügel with a love of the historical method, and "the hatred of the insignificant book." In 1885–86 the Baron was writing brief reviews for the *Bulletin Critique*, founded in 1880 by Duchesne. Years later, he still had a deep appreciation of what Duchesne had given him, but he remarked a little querulously that Duchesne had taught his juniors critical method, but never showed them, when they got into trouble, how and where they had misapplied that method. [31]

On April 30, 1893, the Baron wrote his first letter to Loisy, who was then professor of Scripture at the Institut Catholique, and, in 1892, had founded as an organ for this thought *L'Enseignement biblique*, the same year that Lagrange founded *Revue Biblique*. On March 5, 1895, von Hügel wrote his first letter to Maurice Blondel, who had published his great *L'Action* in 1893. On September 20, 1897, the Baron first wrote to Fr. Tyrrell, who was publishing in *The Month* in London, and had just issued his first book, *Nova et Vetera*. In 1898 he speaks of his good friend, Professor Eucken of Jena, who was working on a philosophy of the development of personality. We will have occasion, later, to speak of these friends of the Baron; here we wish merely to situate the period of his acquaintance with each.

In view of our later treatment of von Hügel's thought on the Church, it is worth noting here how little he was influenced by two important nineteenth-century authors, Döllinger and Möhler. As early as 1877, the Baron was reading Döllinger, yet he rarely mentioned him, and when he did, his reaction was much more negative than Tyrrell's. The latter had some sympathy for Döllinger's ecclesiological position, as is clear, for example, from *Medievalism*. The Baron later summed up the reason for his coolness: "There was Döllinger, who had this precise feeling toward all philosophy; he handed on this feeling to Lord Acton, and Lord Acton handed it on to spiritual sons of his, well known to myself, and they again to their disciples. All these men had, and have, nothing but an impatient, amused, superior smile for that frothy, shifting, arrogant, over self-confident, overweening thing men will call philosophy."[32] Von Hügel's love of philosophy ultimately saved him from some of the excesses of the "cold objectivity" school with its hidden tendentiousness.

The writings of the great Tübingen Catholic ecclesiologist, J. Möhler, exerted very little influence on von Hügel. In 1913 he told Loisy that, not only had Newman and Tyrell probably never read Möhler, but that he himself had read only the "chapter on the Church" in *Symbolik*. This statement is somewhat important for our study. While we will show that the Baron found the contemporary treatment of the Church distastefully juridical, still he never quite achieved a picture of the Church that projected its full organic richness. His theory remained somewhat geometrical; the influence of Möhler might have helped here.

At any rate, von Hügel's early reading of Newman, and even of Döllinger, brought him into an atmosphere in which new stances were taken. This atmosphere, as Congar has pointed out, was one in which "the prophetic function of the theologian as doctrinal interpreter in relation to the magisterium" was the unsolved question at issue.

CHAPTER TWO

THE BROADER THEOLOGICAL
BACKGROUND

Von Hügel was the child of that vast confusion of inequalities in theology that marked the nineteenth century: the decadence of theology in general in the early part of the century; later, the great historical studies in Germany; Vatican Council I; the outburst of negative, rational apologetics mushrooming into a more positive personalist approach; the Church-State controversies. Von Hügel was concerned in all these areas, but for our purposes we shall consider his influence in only three fields: (1) the attitude to scholasticism, (2) the level of Biblical studies, (3) the ecclesiology of the period.

(1) *"The incompatibility between all sincere interpretation of the results of scientific criticism with scholastic epistemology."* [Such was von Hügel's reaction to the Encyclical *Pascendi* (Loisy's *Mémoires*, II, p. 569)]. Frequent derogatory allusions to scholasticism occur in the writings of von Hügel, Tyrrell, and Loisy. These men were not unique, although their reactions were, at times, exaggerated. For example, Father J. Hogan, an Irish Sulpician who taught from 1855 to 1884 at St. Sulpice in Paris, wrote in 1898:

> In the first half of the nineteenth century, scholasticism became passé. Its language was so little used, so little understood, that

in the general instructions given in 1832 to the Professors of
Philosophy in the Society of Jesus there may be found the
following recommendation which has the air of a concession: let
the students of Philosophy learn at least the sense of the scholastic terms that they will meet more in the study of Theology.

Scholasticism, he says, did survive in certain schools and
religious orders, but philosophy was mainly presented "under
the patronage of Descartes, Malebranche, Leibnitz, Balmes,
Rosmini. . . . It was a sort of eclecticism, neither profound, nor
systematic, nor powerful."[1] That the situation had not totally
changed when Fr. Hogan wrote in 1898 is evident from the tone
of the work.

This situation existed in much of Europe until Leo XIII's
Aeterni Patris in 1879. Thus the generation ahead of von Hügel
as a rule knew little of the genuine scholasticism of St. Thomas.
The word scholasticism had overtones for them that we must
be careful to catch.

With *Aeterni Patris* a new tide began to flow, but its full force
would not be felt for several generations. The danger also existed
that a neo-scholasticism might not be genuine scholasticism.
Léon Ollé-Laprune, writing in 1895, catches the atmosphere of
the period following the encyclical:

> The Encyclical wants re-done in this century what St. Thomas did
> in his. It does not want St. Thomas repeated purely and simply,
> or copied, abridged, or overloaded. Finally it does not want
> him reduced to little formulas which are easy to remember
> but dead. Else a thomistic verbalism will replace the other
> verbalism. What it wants is that he be studied in depth.
> Nourishment must be drawn from the marrow and his principles
> penetrated.[2]

The neo-scholasticism of those early years is generally
admitted to have been the child of someone other than St.
Thomas.[3] Too much then appeared in the manuals, labeled
"according to the mind of St. Thomas," but lacking the large
spirit of its presumed source. Wilfrid Ward, a sound critic,
who studied in a Roman seminary in 1866–78, found that memory
and authority constituted the two pillars of orthodoxy.

This picture of neo-scholasticism (greatly over-simplified here, and omitting mention of its real contributions) is the picture von Hügel perceived. If we sum up the experiences which went to shape his thought, a coherent picture of his position regarding scholasticism begins to emerge.

Wilfrid Ward, the Baron's close friend, had never had intimate contact with genuine scholasticism, and never really appreciated it. Abbé Huvelin's attitude toward scholasticism had been adverse, and the scientific and critical circles in which von Hügel moved, e.g. those of Duchesne and Loisy, regarded the scholastics with scorn. The Baron's interests had gravitated towards the non-scholastic Blondel even before he met him in 1895, and he was very much interested in the non-scholastic, non-Catholic philosophers, Troeltsch and Eucken, whom he met in 1898.

In 1898 von Hügel finds Cardinal Francesco Satolli, who had published five volumes on the *Summa*, "too scholastic to assimilate or (even) to guess at the meaning of historical method or many of its already certain results." In 1899 he speaks of "this rigorously unhistorically understood scholasticism." Later he begins to specify it more exactly as neo-scholasticism, and contrasts it with the spirit of St. Thomas. By "narrow scholasticism" von Hügel means that Aristotelian-Thomistic tradition which lacks both a sense of development and an appreciation of strict historical method.

As a consequence, when von Hügel faced ecclesiastical decrees, in addition to thinking of the persons behind them, he also envisioned the doctrinal aspect of the decrees as hidden behind, or squeezed into, a scholastic or neo-scholastic pattern. A great deal of later reading in St. Thomas (through the influence of the Lutheran Troeltsch) will be necessary before he adequately appreciates genuine scholasticism; but even then he will not totally change. His reaction to statements of the magisterium will never be wholly separated from his dislike of the "profoundly unhistorical" Aristotelian scholasticism.

(2) *"While on our side there is poverty"* (P. Durand, *Etudes*,

Nov. 1901, p. 456). At Vatican Council I, Cardinal Meignan had warned: "On all sides, people are demanding a fixed rule with regard to the relationship of Biblical revelation with science. The response of Catholic scholars is obscure and hesitant."[4]

But Meignan was the exception in his awareness of Biblical problems. Until the establishment of the Catholic Institutes in France, begun in 1875, there was little awareness among French Catholics of critical biblical problems. After their foundation, a clerical elite became aware of the dimensions of the problems, but the rest of the clergy and laity lagged far behind, even in awareness of the questions, not to mention attempts at solutions.

In Germany, the situation was somewhat better, especially in biblical archeology. Yet in exegesis the preeminent leaders (B. Weiss, J. Wellhausen, J. Weiss, H. Holtzmann, A. von Harnack) are all non-Catholic, and if they went to extremes, they did live in an atmosphere of scientific critical work. When one looks for Catholic exegetes, working around the year 1895, to contrast with these names, few are found. The Baron remarked in 1897:

> These fine, virile studies, inaugurated by Catholics of genius, like André Maes, Richard Simon, Jean Astruc, commence only little by little to take the place which they ought to have among us.

He believed that German Catholics had done great work in patristics, Church history, and religious philosophy, but in general he found their exegetical work very backward.

In England, the problem was particularly acute because of Catholic disabilities. Cardinal Nicholas Wiseman, at the Congress of Malines in 1863, gave statistics which show the growth of the English Church, but which also reveal the problem with regard to scholarly pursuits:

> In 1834 the number of priests in England was 434; in 1863 they numbered 1242...there were no religious houses of men or monasteries in 1830; in 1863 there were 55.... In London...the advance in the number of priests since 1826 was from 48 to 194.[5]

In such a climate scholarship obviously could not yet flourish. In 1890, just before his death, Cardinal Manning says that there are now "200,000 English Catholics with much of John Bull in them," but that there were one million English Catholics of Irish descent generally without opportunities for education.[6] Not until 1895, under Cardinal Vaughan, were Catholics positively permitted by Rome to attend the national universities, even though, previously, there had been no such Catholic centers.[7] Many of von Hügel's own friends had attended the national universities, and were aware of the vast lacunae in Catholic scholarship.

In France, in the meantime, an immense effort in biblical studies had begun between 1880 and 1900. In 1890, Lagrange founded the *Ecole biblique de Jerusalem*, and the conservative *Dictionnaire de la Bible* was begun under Vigouroux. From 1890 to 1893 Loisy was professor at the *Institut Catholique* in Paris. Other names began to appear: for the years 1890–1907 Hocedez, in his *Histoire de la Théologie au XIXe Siècle*, lists among the conservative exegetes, Kaulen and Cornely in Germany; Lamy and Corluy at Louvain; Meignan, Vigouroux, Fillion, and Brucker in France. Among the progressives he lists Hummelauer and Bickell in Germany; von Hügel and Father Robert Clarke in England; and in France, de Broglie, d'Hulst, Batiffol, Prat, Condamin, Durand, and Lagrange, among others.

Some of these figures, however, were scarcely on the horizon when von Hügel began to write. And as late as 1902 A. Houtin, the French priest who later left the Church, was able, gleefully, to quote Père Durand, from an article which the Baron had read:

> The equipment for oriental and biblico-critical studies comes almost entirely from the precincts of the heterodox and the unbeliever in Germany and England; polyglot texts, dictionaries, treatises on archeology, grammars for the two Testaments, concordances, up-to-date historical commentaries. The Protestants have all of these in profusion, while on our side there is poverty, and often enough penury. Not a single classical edition

of the original text of the Old Testament; the same has to be said for the critical text of the Septuagint and New Testament, Scholz being now outmoded. We have not even a critical revision of our Latin Vulgate which we have left to the enterprise of the Anglican Bishop Wordsworth.[8]

It is not surprising, therefore, that as von Hügel began his work he turned to the German critics like Wellhausen, Holtzmann, B. Weiss, and to British exegetes and Loisy for his assistance.

Before his death in 1890, Cardinal Manning wrote some notes on the obstacles to the expansion of the Catholic Church in England. Among them he placed: a lack of cultivation among the clergy; an exaggerated reaction against Protestantism which discredited bible reading among Catholics; the spirit of controversy; an officialism that ranked official powers higher than subjective perfection in work; an excessive *ex opere operato* sacramentalism; and an "excessive," no-salvation-outside-the-Church attitude toward Anglicans.[9] Von Hügel's diary records that he read Manning's work on Feb. 19, 1896, and though he disagreed with some of the Cardinal's ideas, these sound almost like an echo from his own spirit. From the foregoing discussion of the status of biblical studies at the time, it is easy to see why he was so eager to get into the fray. His high standards of criticism, his burning love of truth, and his uncommon awareness of the weaknesses in Catholic exegesis, drove him into unremitting efforts at correspondence, making contacts, and writing.

(3) *"Hierarchiologie"* (Congar, *L'Ecclesiologie au XIX siècle*, p. 113). The birth of ecclesiology as a particular branch of theology dates from about 1301–02, when Philip the Bel and Boniface VIII clashed on the relationship of civil and ecclesiastical power. With the Reformation, this struggle began to revolve around the idea of some of the Reformers that the external in religion is a non-essential element, even sinful in itself. In reaction to this, about the time of the Council of Trent, the ecclesiastical position

tended to be expressed in a polemic between the Church and the Reform.[10] Gradually, other movements arose which stimulated this tendency: Gallicanism, Jansenism, Febronianism, Josephinism, and added stimulus came from rationalism, the discrediting of the priesthood and the hierarchy. To counteract these movements, ecclesiology played up the visible, institutional, hierarchical side of the Church, and shifted the emphasis from discussion of the Church as a spiritual organism to consideration of the aspect of authority. The theological manuals picked this up and digested it into an exposé, largely dominated by an apologetical and polemical tone, and limited in vision to the constitutional structure of authority in the Church; under such treatment, theses on papal primacy began to come to the fore. This ecclesiology performed a valuable and necessary service in the face of contemporary movements, but it resulted in what Congar terms a "hierarchology." Although this term cannot have a simple, derogatory connotation in view of existing problems, it does highlight the distortion that crept into the image of the Church.[11]

Other important ecclesiological currents were at work in the nineteenth century. Newman, it is true, emphasized, in his doctrine on the Church, the need for authority, as well as the infallibility of the Church and the Pope, in the face of both doctrinal liberalism and Anglicanism; but his approach did not rely exclusively on the aspect of authority. He emphasized, also, the role of bishop and layman in the Church, and his work attained a balance between the institutional aspect and that of religious interiority. Von Hügel's attitude towards Newman's position on this precise point has been described in the previous chapter.

Another current, rather mystical and dogmatic, and placing less emphasis on the aspects of law and authority, was represented by such important figures as: Johann Möhler in his *Symbolik* (1832); the school of Roman theologians—whose antecedents went back to Petavius and Thomassin—men like Passaglia, Schrader, and Franzelin; and Scheeben, who did his great work at Cologne between 1860 and 1887. This current, while stressing hierarchical authority, also considered the Church within the dimensions of the mystery of salvation, and duly took account of its sacramental nature as rooted in the Incarnation. This aspect was sorely wanting in the manuals.

These currents, unfortunately, made only a slight impression on the definitions of Vatican Council I. With the invasion by the Italian armies, the Council was suspended, leaving the hierarchical aspect highlighted to the point of placing the other facets in the shadows.

Von Hügel was convinced that this excessive emphasis on infallibility, the hierarchy, and the juridical aspect of the Church, coupled with a meager treatment of the sacramental and spiritual life of the Church, made for a narrow view of the nature of the Church. The import of the decrees of Vatican II on the nature of the Church, the liturgy, revelation, ecumenism, and the laity, emerges more clearly from a study of the struggles of von Hügel and others at the beginning of this century.

CHAPTER THREE

EXEGESIS AND THE BIBLE
(1890–1900)

From 1893 to 1898 the Baron made his first contacts with Loisy, Blondel, and Tyrrell. On April 30, 1893 he dispatched his first letter to Loisy,[1] and it should be noted that it encouraged Loisy in the direction of his work. This is important, for it shows that von Hügel had already taken a similar direction even before Loisy began to influence him deeply. The Baron speaks also of the great English Biblicists, Robertson Smith, Montefiore, and Driver, as his personal acquaintances. Thus there was another world of biblical influences on von Hügel, a world scarcely perceived in reading Loisy's *Mémoires*. This is mentioned, not to depreciate Loisy's influence on the Baron, which was tremendous, but to prepare us for the fact that in some of von Hügel's later positions (as on the consciousness of Christ, for example), he was not a solitary English robin which had strayed into a French vineyard, and was hopelessly trying to warble the song of a bird he did not understand. (Loisy's nickname, which the Baron picked up, was "l'oiseau.") Such is the image of him held by some of his English Catholic friends.

A. THE PETRINE CLAIMS

In September, 1893 the Baron wrote *Some Notes on the Petrine Claims* to an anonymous High Anglican friend.[2] It is an ingenious and clear concatenation of texts, mainly from the German liberals, B. Weiss, H. Holtzmann and A. Meyer, and it develops into an intelligent, totally orthodox demonstration of the claims for the Papacy drawn from Scripture and the Fathers.

The book follows a dating of Scripture which was not common among Catholics at the time, namely, an Aramaic Matthew, followed by Mark, then by our Matthew, then by Luke. The Johannine Gospels he holds to be written between the years 90 to 100, either by John or by his immediate disciple editing his memoirs. The whole works into a crescendo in the following finale:

> ... that there is no serious *a priori* reason against the primacy, consistently with a visible-Church position; that the primacy is undeniable in the Gospels and requires to be, somehow or other, maintained through Acts and Epistles; and that Church history shows us that it was truly there from the first, but as truly grew and had to face as real difficulties as the other doctrines and institutions; and only through it do you get unsuspended Church doctrine and full docility and life.

Issy von Hügel, the wife of Friedrich's brother Anatole, when she was 91, on seeing *Some Notes on the Petrine Claims* published, summed up the general reaction around 1930:

> What a book!...I...would have thought of 1893 as a time of great worry to him...and I would have guessed that it must have been many and many a year yet, before he could have spoken with the peaceful insight, that he does here. Why, oh why, if he already then saw so well, did he say, and do so many strange things, so many seemingly unfilial things—or things at least not piercingly filial.

The Baron did shift from a few of the positions in this book; but the change was not with regard to his "filial" attitude to the Church, his attitude toward authority. Already in that book he was saying:

> ... interior assent to the pope's *ex cathedra* pronouncements is always due; obedience to the pope's governmental orders is

generally and presumptively due. Saints have at times privately disobeyed single orders or have remonstrated with the popes as to their neglect of duty.

Von Hügel's filial attitude always sought the theological level, and his later theory and practice are never inconsistent with the statement just adduced, although the theological position itself is certainly simplified. There is no middle ground here between what is *ex cathedra* and what is disciplinary. Later, that middle terrain will be respected by the Baron. If his filial attitude did not change after this first book, his exegetical conclusions did. For example, in *The Petrine Claims* he held that Mt 16.18, the "Thou art Peter" text, is an authentic saying of Our Lord. However, afterwards, and even as late as 1918, he made allowance for the independent critics' position as to the presence of later strata of interpretation in the Gospels. He will include the Petrine text under "apparently later constituents" of the Gospel.[3]

Much more important than this text, however, in fact, at the *root* of all his later evolution, is his attitude toward the consciousness of Christ. This will be the capital change of direction in von Hügel's thinking, and therefore it is instructive to see what he says in *The Petrine Claims* on this question. With regard to Mt 16.18 he says that we have to hold either that "it has no ascertainable meaning," or

> that it was intended to last but a lifetime, thirty years, and that Our Lord either shared the Apostles' first idea that the end of the world would come then, or that He deliberately kept back the short duration of the privilege and as deliberately used words of the most impressive—surely over-impressive and misleading import . . . ,

or that it means what Catholic tradition says it means. He rejects the first two positions as "an insult to Our Blessed Lord; as God he could and did foresee. . . . " Thus he rejects any dichotomy between Christ's divine and human knowledge of the Parousia.

Later, when the Baron radically changed his position on the consciousness of Christ, he will attribute the change, not primarily to Loisy, but to "Johannes Weiss," and he will say, in 1902, "I do not think any discovery cost me, emotionally, as much to finally accept as this one."

B. *PROVIDENTISSIMUS DEUS* AND THE BIBLE-CHURCH CONTROVERSY

Loisy's ideas on the interpretation of the Bible had already begun to stir up disturbance and displeasure. Bishop d'Hulst, his rector at the Institut Catholique in Paris, partially to win toleration for Loisy, wrote an article in 1893 in the *Correspondant*, in which he contrasted the stricter and the more liberal approach to the Bible. He showed himself sympathetic to the liberal approach which retained the dogma of inspiration, but would allow imperfections and inexactitudes in the human author, provided these did not touch the dogmatic and moral purpose of the book. The article compromised Loisy, and he was forced to cease teaching. A tempestuous debate arose.[4] Finally, on Nov. 18, 1893, Leo XIII published the encyclical *Providentissimus Deus*.

The encyclical re-affirmed the doctrines of *inspiration* and inerrancy. It denied that inspiration can be limited to certain parts of Scripture, or that it involves matters of faith and morals and nothing else (*res fidei morumque, nihil praeterea*). It insisted that the Bible can contain no error, since God is its author. It warned of a rationalistic bias in those who found errors in the Bible, and warned the Catholic scholars to follow the analogy of faith and patristic tradition. It accepted the idea that the Bible was not aimed at teaching scientific fact. Finally it encouraged a greater scholarly study of the Bible and especially of Oriental languages.

The encyclical reflected a duality of attitude which Maisie Ward plausibly traces to the fact that Leo had under his patronage Cardinal Mercier's Institut at Louvain which fostered scientific study, while Cardinal Mazzella's influence moved him toward ultra-scholasticism and conservatism.

Von Hügel was piqued by an article on the encyclical by Charles Gore, afterwards Archbishop of Birmingham. Gore said that "in the encyclical we witness an entire victory of the extreme theologians," especially in its attitude towards inerrancy. Roused to action, the Baron wrote a reply for *The Spectator* in which he defended the idea of inerrancy, and advocated the liberal aspects of the encyclical.[5] The liberals, like Loisy and himself, he remarks, are not in the serious position that Gore imagines.

If, the Baron contends, we avoid "anti-Christian presumptions," and bring down that *ballon d'essai* about *obiter dicta* not being inspired, we are left with the propositions that God is the author of the Bible, that inspiration enters into every part, no matter what the subject matter, and that all error is excluded. This is not to deny "relativities, imperfections, inaccuracies of composition . . . of mental method and of popular conception . . . of successive, slow, often halting growth of even elementary religious ideas," but nothing in the Bible violates "the literary ethics of their time and people." The statements on science, for example, nowhere express "formal convictions on the part of the sacred writers."

The Church, von Hügel states, will not give up the tradition of inerrancy. If Gore feels that this is a subtlety, why does he himself accept such a "subtlety" as regards *extra ecclesiam nulla salus*, by agreeing with Pius IX, who allowed for invincible ignorance; why does he accept that the Mass is a sacrifice which is followed by the "subtlety" that this is painless and bloodless; and the same is true for Original Sin, since it is sin in a "subtle" sense? The Baron concludes movingly, in a reference to the "Imperial Church" of which Gore spoke: "We have found her well worth even greater trials than those that you imagine."

In the same issue of *The Spectator* the Baron's ideas are criticized by an anonymous person: "This elasticity which the highest ecclesiastical authorities themselves attach to the meaning of words [here inerrancy] used in infallible definitions, makes the word 'infallibility' extremely difficult for ordinary men to construe." The critic asks: would it not have been easier to say that Pius IX, for example, admitted "literally speaking that the doctrine (*Nulla Salus*) is not true?"

But von Hügel never adopted such a position. His thought moved along the following lines: in the past there was little room, in a totally Christian Europe, for a sufficient and formal analysis of invincible ignorance (as in the *Nulla Salus* doctrine). It took time and history for this to evolve. So in our time, in the non-scientific scriptural world, there has been little thought given to the "invincible ignorance" of science and historical fact by scriptural writers whose purpose and formal convictions did not aim at such knowledge.[6] His consistent principle in interpreting the *Nulla Salus* doctrine and the doctrine of inerrancy is to find the "formal convictions" of the authors.

The Baron was not, of course, exegeting the encyclical so much as underlining the liberal allowances in it. Wilfrid Ward did this more simply, and perhaps more felicitously, by harking continuously to Augustine's phrase quoted therein: "The Holy Spirit did not want to teach men the intimate constitution of visible nature, things in no way advantageous to salvation."

Ward's approach underlined the fact that the encyclical accepted a solution which preserved inspiration in the face of the Bible's treatment of *natural* phenomena, but there still remained the problem of the relation of inspiration to the biblical presentation of *historical* data. The Baron was more aware of this. This latter problem lingered on for years after the encyclical, and was not settled authoritatively until *Divino Afflante Spiritu* in 1943. In that encyclical, what some called historical error was termed "nothing else than those customary modes of expression and narration peculiar to the ancients." This was precisely von Hügel's position in 1893. *Divino Afflante Spiritu* merely accepted, officially, the work of solid exegetes through the intervening years.

Providentissimus was interpreted in extremely conservative fashion by such men as S. M. Brandi, S.J., in Italy, and J. Brucker, S.J., in France. It looked as if the encyclical was to be captured by such interpreters, and von Hügel decided to act.

C. THE CHURCH AND THE BIBLE ARTICLES

The Baron stated, in a letter to Wilfrid Ward, June 14, 1894:

> I most certainly do not "utterly condemn" the encyclical;
> indeed, I do not condemn it at all. With all my heart I hold
> its central doctrine, and with all my heart I believe that its own
> commentary, if one works up one part with and into another,
> defends and leaves the doctrine thoroughly defendable [sic].
> I only thought and think that it is not a document so finished
> and guarded as not to lend itself, in a good many passages, to
> the attacks of malevolent outsiders, even if they are fairly
> honest.... I do not see that such a view is either disloyal (if
> kept private) nor distressing to one's faith or devotion to the
> Holy See; indeed, speaking merely for myself, I know full well
> that I could strain my faith by it, but only by pretending to
> see greater perfection in it than I do see.[7]

The Baron became thoroughly disturbed when he read an
anonymous critic in the *Spectator*, who said:

> nothing can ... [be] more embarrassing to genuine scholars like
> M. Loisy ... than to be told to go on studying Scripture with
> constantly increasing earnestness and devotion, but at the
> same time to suppress steadily the inferences at which they have
> arrived with more and more confidence ... and even to distrust
> their own conclusions and look out carefully for evidence ...
> of perfectly different and quite inconsistent conclusions.

Von Hügel accordingly felt obliged to treat the question of
exegesis and its relation to the Church.

From October 1894 to October 1895 the Baron wrote
three articles on "The Church and the Bible" for the *Dublin
Review*,[8] and later a paper to be delivered at the International
Scientific Congress of Catholics held at Fribourg in August,
1897 on historical method and the Heptateuch. The *Dublin
Review* articles are not so much a commentary on the encyclical
as a presentation of the latest scriptural thought, together with
a justification of this thought in the light of a liberal interpretation of the encyclical.

It is noteworthy that the articles took their departure from the incomprehensibility of God. "God is ... absolutely unfathomable and incomprehensible, and this even supernaturally and in the immediate vision of God." Within this perspective of the mystery of God, von Hügel moved into a developing, dynamic idea of revelation, in which much of what he said is startlingly modern, and accepted today. Much, however, was brilliantly suggested rather than clarified, as, for instance, when he wrote that revelation and the Church are practically identical,[9] whereas revelation and Scripture are not. Revelation must be sharply distinguished from Scripture which results from Divine inspiration to write. (Lagrange was on the same track at that time.) He dated the Gospels as we do today, and not as the manuals did fifteen years ago; he proposed the priority of Mark, and showed that the artificial grouping principle in the Gospels has apologetic value in avoiding old problems.

Further, von Hügel held for a developing revelation, and proposed the (then ticklish) theory of different layers in the Pentateuch; the Jahvist, Elohist, Priestly, and Deuteronomic documents, the non-Mosaic authorship of the final work, the attribution of books in the Old Testament, and of Hebrews and II Peter in the New Testament to writers of an earlier period; and the need to recognize a type of Rabbinic exegesis in the New Testament. He concluded that the apologetic value to be found in modern scriptural conclusions is extremely powerful for the theist, and in no way weakened by the encyclical *when it is interpreted liberally*.[10] Inerrancy, he insisted, is a technical term which must be understood as such, and later, in a letter to Tyrrell (Dec. 18, 1901), he explained his understanding of the term by saying: "Everywhere God communicated *as much of that kind* of His truth as could be assimilated by man at that time and place."

Von Hügel's later paper on the Hexateuch was actually delivered with a heavy Italian accent by his Barnabite friend, Fr. Semeria. At the same Congress, Lagrange presented an article on the Pentateuch in which he gave the reasons why

Catholics had not yet applied modern criticism to the Pentateuch; he found these reasons to be prejudices.[12] For this, Lagrange was attacked by the Jesuit Mechineau, among others, for concessionism, but, curiously, von Hügel was left publicly unscathed.

This was the first time, it seems, that the possibility of the non-Mosaic authorship of the Pentateuch was presented in public discussion by Catholics.[13] Some of the positions presented by the Baron were: the fact of different documents in the Pentateuch, i.e., the J, E, P, D sources; the facility thus afforded in answering the old rationalist objections about contradictions, since it can be seen that the different redactors were consistent with themselves; the non-Mosaic direct authorship of so much of the material; the more dramatic, interest and rich pathos of a developing view of the Bible; the great difference of the Oriental mind from ours, and God's adaptations to it. All these elements, though revised in detail, may be found in any modern Catholic handbook, but they were dangerous topics at the time.[14]

Principles of exegesis. Two problems are of capital importance in the question of the nature of biblical exegesis. First, to what extent is this science subject to presuppositions, and second, what is the relation of the Catholic exegete to the doctrinal positions of his Church. In these early days von Hügel developed his position in a way that later influenced his role in the modernist crisis.

As to the first question, it must be recalled that, what we call modern personalist philosophy, had not yet developed full insight into the role of the writer in his handling of history. Contemporary historiography tended to draw a closer parallel between natural science and history than it does today, and von Hügel, with his background in natural science, could not but be influenced by this tendency. Under the impress of thinkers like Newman, Ollé-Laprune, and Blondel, however, he had become vividly aware of the personalist insight, and this emerged in his articles on the encyclical.

Reason, he said, begins with assumptions, and "both reason

and faith begin and end with moral dispositions and moral truths and acts." Neither philosophy nor history can totally avoid the question of grace and purity of heart. He wrote of the "pre- and trans-scientific convictions which are the very salt of all true life, of the life of science itself." He insisted on the truth of Newman's idea: "After all man is *not* a reasoning animal; he is a seeing, feeling, contemplating, acting animal. He is influenced by what is direct and precise." The Baron held that evidence appeals to one who already believes to be possible and desirable what this evidence proves to be actual. Revealing traces of Blondel and Eucken, he wrote:

> These studies [of the Old Testament] isolate me, because even now a good number of those who are capable of observing historical development see only that and they do not at all penetrate from these *phenomena* to the *noumena*, from these changing means and appearances to the identical author and transcendent end of all. And many of those who really penetrate to the cause and end of all things are resolved to use only metaphysics and to see only fixed points. Neither the movement as seen by all these sceptics and phenomenists, nor the fixity of so many dogmatists are possible in isolation. Could one not unite them in a concept in the represented truth as this is found in the subject in us, as in a germ or leaven ..., as life, as something *dynamic* rather than something *static*; the *individual* painfully fashioning himself into a *personality*, the soul ascending and God condescending—all in movement but with a fixity of orientation: a powerful attraction for the poor modern soul which is benumbed and lost outside the Church, but which so much fears to be stopped short and smothered within the Church.[15]

While stressing the role of moral dispositions, von Hügel insisted that, otherwise, only two demands were made on the exegete in the course of his work. First, he must have "theistic assumptions": this would seem to mean either a reasoned acceptance of God or a belief in a personal God as in Newman's *Grammar of Assent* (Ch. X). Second, he must have spiritual sympathy, since "no one can understand the Bible thoroughly without it." The Baron, of course, did not think of the

Catholic exegete as totally prescinding from his faith; but he wanted to set up a large area where Catholic and non-Catholic exegetes could discuss on a commonly accepted terrain, as was demanded by the theistic Synthetic Society of which he was a member.[16]

This, however, was merely to obscure the fact that the exegete was working all along within the belief of his church in trying to clarify its scriptural record. Von Hügel did admit, after all, that for the Catholic exegete the Church entered in indirectly as a negative norm when his work was complete. The reader may feel that this presentation places the Church in a non-vital and too extrinsic relation to the exegete, but the question is by no means solved today. Karl Rahner, for example, admits that the exegete should be able to prescind from the inspiration and inerrancy of Scripture. Otherwise he would suffer loss in moving from fundamental theology to dogmatics. Yet Rahner reprimands the exegetes for handing over conclusions to the theologians without giving them any hint as to how these can be reconciled with Catholic doctrine.[17] Von Hügel felt that a final judgment about such reconciliation was, in the last resort, up to the Church. Any other approach, he felt, would be dangerous, since one might too easily read back into Scripture what was not there, and perhaps support as faith what was really only theological opinion. Citing the English exegete, Robertson Smith, he wrote:

> But our spiritual sympathies are generally bound in with theological prejudices which have no real basis in Holy Scripture. It is easier for us to correct the errors of a rationalism for which we have no sympathy than to rid ourselves of prejudices deeply tied in with true convictions. It is always in the interest of truth to discuss historical questions according to purely historical methods, without permitting theological questions to come in till the historical analysis is complete. This indeed is the chief reason why scholars indifferent to the religious values of the Bible have often done good service by their philological and historical studies.

This is an extremely delicate question, and it can perhaps

be best evaluated only after a discussion of how the principle was applied during the modernist crisis.

What, then, is the relation of the exegete to the doctrinal positions of his Church, in von Hügel's view? Provided, he said, that "scholarship starts from, and everywhere applies theistic assumptions, and does not deny the possibility of a subsequent supernatural teacher of subsequent supernatural truths about and from the Bible," then in the region of "research into the historico-literary phenomena of Scripture, there it is in possession." (The phrasing here is at least misleading, since the Church is not a "subsequent" teacher—the Bible is her teaching, and she existed before it.) But, von Hügel continued, the Church has a jurisdiction over the exegete which is ordinarily indirect, and predominantly disciplinary. This was later rejected by Loisy.[18] Presumably the jurisdiction is indirect because it is seen as more over the faith of the one who works with this material than over the method itself.

Thus von Hügel consistently maintained that systematic, formal theology must not enter exegisis *in via*, but only *in termino*, and that the Church *in termino* has jurisdictional rights indirectly over exegesis. He is not unaware that the Bible is the Church's book, "the Divine library given to the believing churchman," but it also is a "human document," whose greater clarification by genuine scientific method makes more intelligible the content of the faith.

CHAPTER FOUR

WILFRID WARD AND AUTHORITY

Wilfrid Ward was one of the best informed men on the ecclesiastical history of the nineteenth century. He authored *The Life of John Henry Cardinal Newman* (1912), *William George Ward and the Catholic Revival* (1893), *The Life and Times of Cardinal Wiseman* (1898), among other works, and was the editor of the *Dublin Review* (privately, though unjustly, attacked during the Modernist crisis) from 1906 until his death in 1916. Despite some coolness and difference of opinion, the Baron and Wilfrid were friends until the end. The coolness resulted from a conflict of opinion on the rights of authority and the rights of liberty.[1] As one reads Wilfrid's comments, it becomes evident that one is in touch with a very moderate and sound critic. He could stand as a symbol of the intellectual and moderately-liberal Catholicism of the period: his critiques of von Hügel are therefore of value.

Up to the period we are now discussing, from 1890 until just after 1900, the problem of authority in the Church seems to have not been a major problem for the Baron. On the other hand, Ward, although moderate in his opinions, and respectful of authority, was not entirely at ease with the contemporary situation. In August, 1894 he wrote an article on the recent encyclical for the *Nineteenth Century*, in which he distinguished between the actual teaching of the encyclical, which he found

compatible with the new criticism, and the oratorical form
that tended to discourage that criticism. Another example of
Ward's discomfort is found in the epilogue to his life of Wiseman
which was published in 1898. In this he pleads for a patient,
gradual, assimilation of the facts established by the modern
world:

> The critics and theologians in the Church have been modifying
> their practical explanation of what she enforces in general
> language, in the narratives in her hagiologies, in her statements
> that Scripture does not err. But this must be a matter of time.
> The critics and men of science must gradually eliminate incidental
> error and superstition [p. 547]. The Church treats the urgency
> of her formulae as due to their truth in *sensu Ecclesiae*—to their
> being symbols, confessedly inadequate, whereby she expresses
> the truth she professes to hold. . . . The immediate appeal, then, of
> each definition is to the obedience of Catholics rather than to a
> reasoned acceptance of it [pp. 555–556].

The Secretary of the Holy Office asked Wilfrid, in 1910, to
withdraw the chapter. All this should forestall the suspicion that
the complaints Ward levels against von Hügel's position on
authority are merely the objections of a static conservative.
On the contrary, Ward had a deep sympathy with Newman's
position on development.[2]

Ward criticized von Hügel out of a climate of appreciation.
The Baron, he knew, had a basic respect for Church authority,
and even Loisy pointed this out often in his *Mémoires:* "He used
to receive the Roman decisions with a sense of religion and he
made it his duty not to *tourner* [interpret or get around] them
except with the greatest respect" (I, 426). Loisy's irony in no way
touches von Hügel's respect for authority. Respect was not the
point at issue in these early discussions. What was at issue was
the matter of prudential judgment, timing, and political
activity. No doubt, closely allied to this prudential problem,
was the speculative problem of intellectual freedom. Ward said
that von Hügel's general position was that "provided you have
the spirit of the saints, intellectual freedom is as safe for a

Christian as it is desirable."[3] Ward, without denying this spiritual criterion, took his stand rather on the level of the prudential:

> That liberty of expression, even of saying what is useful and good, should be practically possible must depend on toleration not being abused by *reckless* discussion which has all the dangers of inflammatory mob oratory.[4]

Nevertheless, Ward was alive to the difficulties of the contemporary situation. In the same letter he says:

> Even were our rulers alive to the real difficulties of the situation (I quite agree with you that they are not), the best way of dealing with such abuse of freedom would be a difficult problem to solve.

Ward envisioned the Church within the framework of Newman's development of doctrine. The Reformation reduced the Church to a "state of siege," a condition that was actually an adaptation to the needs of the times. He compares that state to the conditions of war:

> Intellectual exercises became primarily controversial. The truths were safely sheathed in the definite *formulae*, and the *formulae* were defended by polemic. . . . Tyranny is among the greatest dangers in time of peace; [but] debate and dispute, the very life of civil constitutions, the normal means of giving citizens a share in public affairs and in determining the fortunes of the country, the safeguard against injustice, and against the sense of injustice, are fatal in time of war. At such a time . . . authority is rightly appealed to constantly. There is need for a dictator.[5]

But, he said, the state of siege is now over. The battle in which everything was at stake was no longer between Rome and the rebels, but between religion and anarchy or unbelief. Against that, the best defense was not polemic, but an intensification of the Church's life, both sacramental and intellectual. The question now, he observed, is what is the normal—not the wartime—relation between rulers and thinkers.

The problem, of course, lay in the fact that the state of siege was *not* over. New forces could, and did, cause the Church to retreat into another citadel, but Ward was actually pleading against continuing this state of siege against the new enemies:

> There are two classes of enemies to the true conservatism which would preserve for present use an ancient building—those who would pull it down, and those who would leave it untouched . . . surreptitiously fearing that to alter it *in any respect* is to violate what is venerable and sacred.

The question arises, at this point, as to how such a liberal-minded man could have come into conflict with von Hügel. A solution might be drawn from one of Ward's favorite sayings: Men are always liberal ("wide") on their own subjects. Wilfrid knew little of biblical criticism, and in that he believed in deliberation and slowness. His friend, Fr. Cuthbert, the Capuchin historian, said that what concerned Ward most with regard to the human mind was that it should go forward in orderly activity. He described Ward as belonging to that class of thinkers which, in the best sense of the word, we might call "politicians of the world intellectual."

Ward, who was liberal in his political philosophy of the Church, and liberal also *in principle* with regard to freedom for biblical criticism, was fearful of the details of critical conclusion as proposed by the Baron during this period. (Actually, he was later influenced by the Baron against his own better judgment to support indulgence for the exegetes in much more delicate areas.) Thus, in the face of exegesis, Ward did not feel the same pressure to take new positions that he felt in philosophy, theology in general, and in ecumenism.

In an article in the *Nineteenth Century* of June, 1900, Ward mentions the hostility of some English Catholics against everything—the Roman Curia, the Index, scholasticism—as if all were part of a corrupt system. The only obvious solution, he affirmed, is that the "corrupt system—which is hard to distinguish from the existing Catholic Church—should be abolished; and one wonders why those who so think

belong to it at all." The Baron sent him a piquant letter, part of
which is worth quoting:

> The progress of all science and philosophy necessarily springs
> from earnestness and enthusiasm, from some keen sense of the
> defectiveness of an existing position . . . ; without heat and passion,
> no more will be achieved than without light and self-repression;
> without drama, conflict, tragedy, life will be correct only to be
> barren.
> And so I would want a theory on the whole to sympathize with
> friction, up to the point where it would no more favor healthy
> motion, but would clog it.

Later we will describe more fully this principle of friction. Von
Hügel continues:

> The taking upon ourselves of all these complications and
> conflicts will be impossible or at least oppressive, unless they
> are all met and interpreted and used as instruments by the
> soul in her inner life. More and more I feel and see that here is
> the very heart of the matter; and though your paper elsewhere
> allows for it, it is so little prominent that the real reason or
> motive why, I think, all this evolutionary modification of dogma
> is accepted by us, not only as possibly compatible with its
> substantial truth, but as part and parcel of our very life—is
> thereby obscured and remains insufficient. Nothing but a very
> deep and constantly pressing reason can suffice for such an
> acceptation, and this *pressingness* I do not feel in your pages
> to the extent to which I should like to feel it there.

The Baron, then, felt a pressure that Ward did not feel. This
is the point of their divergence. It was a pressure exerted by
biblical science to move into territory whose outposts were
occupied by authority. On Dec. 18, 1901 he wrote to Tyrrell that
he had explained this sense of pressure in Rome to Father
Lepidi, the Master of the Sacred Palace:

> I wanted to put on record, with as much respect and temper,
> but also of wholehearted conviction and finality as possible, my
> slowly acquired certainty that we were face to face, not with a
> question of individuals, and their possible and real eccentric-
> ities; or of specific theological doctrines, true or false; but

with that of a new science with its own immanent methods, laws, and practically irresistible force.

The sense of pressure the Baron felt was generally valid, and most of the broad critical conclusions which he supported *at that time* have become part of Catholic exegesis. On one occasion the Baron carried over this sense of "pressingness" to the case of St. George Mivart, a Catholic scientist who, late in life, began to attack the Church (perhaps through mental illness), and died outside its communion. Ward wrote to von Hügel:

> As to Mivart, do you remember how utterly wrong-headed I thought his letter to the *Times* which you thought serviceable though exaggerated? I do not say this as merely an "I told you so," but because I am quite sure that, in the difficult time I see coming on us, we must look very sharp to distinguish friend or foe if we are to hold our own.[6]

Ward warns that an abuse of freedom of speech will cause the authorities to lump together all forms of liberalism and to meet the situation with sheer intolerance:

> The only solution I can see is that, if wise liberals are very careful not to shock, wise rulers should be brought to see that, in a most difficult time of transition, they are our only hope for the future. But self-restraint on the one side is the only possible means of securing a tolerant attitude on the other. I mean of course by "wise liberals" the cautious and thorough specialists in biblical research. . . .

Ward promised a forthcoming article on "Liberalism and Intransigence," but von Hügel responded that he was "a little fearful of finding that you have treated the questions *under the aspect of their orthodoxy and the limits of the latter*." This question of orthodoxy he wished to leave to God and Church authorities. Since the time of Huvelin's spiritual maxims on orthodoxy, the word lay like a live coal on the Baron's mind, and he probably heard the word in a different sense than Ward intended. The letter hurt Ward, and in amends, the Baron wrote that he had read the article, and agreed with Ward's exposition. He then traced the development of medieval ideals in the Church and

commented that many had outlived their utility. The real
cause of intransigence-on-the-right he found in that group's
desire to save the honor of the Church as regards this medieval
system, but, he observed, "it is not necessarily revolutionary
or in any way disloyal, to feel and suffer under even the ghost
of a modified medievalism." Ward answered that he did not
think there was much difference between them as to their *ideal*.
"Where I think we differ is in our *diagnosis* of individuals,
and a little as to the wisest method." With regard to attacks
on the Church, "I think *you* are ready to believe in a *maximum*
of intelligent disapproval and a *minimum* of sheer 'cussedness'
and I should reverse the proportions." Furthermore, "a certain
patience with the inevitable, a certain moderation of aim,
are not, surely, inconsistent with wanting much more than you
can get, or than it would be wise to ask for" (June 24, 1900). A
few days later Ward wrote: "I think much the greatest practical
difference between us is that you more or less *welcome anything*
on the left side though you yourself may not agree with it, while
I feel that there is a species of agitation so indiscriminate and
unintelligent that it simply injures the cause of progress and
justifies the reactionaries" (June 28, 1900).

But there is one lacuna in Ward's judgment, his lack of
real acquaintance with exegesis. If Lagrange had written
these letters, they would be more easily conclusive. Ward lacked
the sense of urgency brought on by scriptural work. On June
8, 1900, von Hügel wrote to Loisy complaining that Ward
"always tends to trace limits, to settle areas of going too far,
but this only imprisons us in the old cage."[7] Ward would not
feel, to the extent that von Hügel did, the decision of the Holy
Office of Jan. 13, 1897 about the Johannine Comma.[8] This spoke
of 1 Jn. 5.7: "For there are three that bear witness in heaven:
the Father, the Word, and the Holy Spirit; and these three are
one. And there are three that bear witness on earth." The
decision stated that it was not possible safely to deny or throw
doubts on the authenticity of this text. Even moderate Catholic
critics, for a quarter of a century, had rejected the text with
episcopal approbation. Von Hügel found the decision, not a

matter of *pace*, but of *direction of movement*, a distinct and serious retrogression. To Tyrrell he quoted Duchesne's reaction: "There are three persons that are doing most useful work in Rome since last winter: *Pater et Filius et Spiritus Sanctus*." The Baron, however, did not take it so gaily; to Ward he wrote: "I could not and would not attempt one word in defence of this condemnation; the thing could only be done at the cost of a transparent special pleading which would discount beforehand such future defences of other matters which may want defence. . . ."

This was one of those decisions in which the Baron sought out a personality behind it, this time Cardinal Mazzella.[9] The decree was equivalently rescinded by the Holy Office on June 2, 1927.[10]

The Baron, then, felt the "pressure" much more than Ward. He opposed what he called "paper demonstrations" against a Wellhausen or a Darwin, and demanded a positive encouragement of exegetes. To Ward he wrote that Wilfrid's father had been wrong: "He would speak at times as though" critical scientists "were people who undertook this kind of thing at their own risk and peril, and who could be tolerated only if they reported themselves periodically to the ecclesiastical police."[11]

The Baron's sense of "pressingness" was rooted in spiritual vision. He felt that he was responsible for the image of the Church in the mind of others. On Dec. 4, 1899 he wrote to Tyrrell: ". . . Our Lord has not guaranteed more than that the Church would continue to *exist* to the end of the world, but in what state and degree of attractiveness would depend on ourselves." He felt that he was being used by God in the making of history.[12] The generating force behind his sense of urgency was not yet a temperamental love of risk. There was not, at this period at any rate, what Ward would later call delight in being in the van of discovery, in being "on the crest of a wave," nor what Rivière would call the temperament of the "deliberate innovator."

At this period the Baron was beginning to see the Curia and

the traditionalists as a sort of police force interested only in external religion.[13] With regard to this, Ward said, years later, that the Baron spoke of the Curia as if it were corrupt, which it was not, and that he transferred the problem of making delicate decisions about balancing intellectual and other decisions to the area of moral corruption. The Baron felt that there was a type of objective corruption in refusing to face intellectual problems squarely, and that it was rooted deeply in the spiritual life, and in one's concept of religion. His attitude reminds us of Congar's statement that our age, while still scandalized at corruption, is even more scandalized at narrowness, backwardness, and intellectual insincerity.[14] The Baron already sensed this spirit in his contacts in England and on the Continent.

Ward himself was not unaware of this danger. He remarked: "The thoughtful young man suffers far greater danger to faith from an impression that the Church cannot candidly face modern research, than from hearing speculations at variance with hitherto received theological views."[15] He limited the danger to specifically intellectual groups, and felt that the Church had other interests that it must watch out for. Von Hügel, on the other hand, while he admitted that there was danger for unprepared minds in the new criticism, felt that this was a secondary danger.[16]

What was the reason for this difference in evaluation? It would seem that it lay in the difference between the two minds in their view of religious reality. Ward believed in clarity, but the Baron was wary of clarity and believed in vividness and richness of thought. Ward's dislike of "dim, half-expressed intuitions of deep truths," as typified by German philosophy, caused Ward to define theology in much clearer terms than von Hügel did. It was easier to fall away from such "orthodoxy" than from the Baron's more vital one. Thus, Ward was more apprehensive for the faith of the unprepared than was von Hügel, who feared most for the faith of the intellectual:

> ... minds belong, roughly speaking, to two classes which may be called the mystical and the positive, and the scholastic and theoretical. The first of these would see all truth as a center of

intense light losing itself gradually in utter darkness; this center would gradually extend, but the borders would ever remain fringes, they could never become clear-cut lines. Such a mind, when weary of border work, would sink back upon its center, its home of peace and light, and thence it would gain fresh conviction and courage to again face the twilight and the dark. Force it to commit itself absolutely to any border distinction, or force it to shift its home or to restrain its roamings, and you have done your best to endanger its faith and to ruin its happiness.[17]

The use of the symbol of an intense light and the reaction against all geometric metaphors was characteristic of the Baron. If one envisioned theological approach in the Baron's way, there was less danger for the minds that were unprepared for the modern criticism; but there was danger that the mind of high quality might be forced "to leave the sun entirely" by the contemporary neo-scholastic approach to criticism, and he was afraid that the image of the Church would be tarnished. Von Hügel seems, for the moment, to have convinced Ward, for we find Ward, in 1901, in Rome pleading for tolerance for Loisy.

The period between 1890 and 1900 is the time of the Baron's work on the Old Testament (the Pentateuch, Genesis, Inspiration), an area where he was advanced, but not ultra-progressive. The next period which we will discuss, was devoted chiefly to von Hügel's debate on the New Testament, and here the Baron considers more serious problems.

CHAPTER FIVE

LOISY AND THE NATURE OF THE CHURCH

A. VON HÜGEL'S ATTITUDE UP TO THE APPEARANCE OF *L'EVANGILE ET L'EGLISE* IN 1902

We will not endeavor here to give a full and penetrating analysis of Loisy. Rather we will confine our study to the relationship of von Hügel with this keen but puzzling personality.

Loisy, noting that, from 1901 until mid 1902, the Baron's letters grew progressively scarcer, said that von Hügel was asleep, although, as Loisy knew, he had plunged into work on his great book, *The Mystical Element of Religion*. It is rather astonishing to find him at such a task at the moment when the waters of scriptural controversy were beginning to boil. Throughout the whole controversy, however, the Baron was anchored in calm depths; a sense of prayer pervaded his life. Loisy spoke of him as the good Baron "who saw God face-to-face in his prayer."[1]

Von Hügel was actually far from asleep. He was extremely active in Rome, where he was pleading for tolerance for the new scriptural movement, and especially for Loisy; having read most of Loisy, he was in substantial agreement. During these two of his "nine winters at Rome," he organized a circle of intellectuals interested in biblical criticism, and made many contacts with Italian scholars.[2] He discussed with Mignot, Archbishop of Albi and a supporter of Loisy, and with Gismondi, afterwards to lose his scriptural chair owing to Loisyian sympathy, means of working for greater toleration of biblical criticism. He had an audience with Leo XIII on the same subject, and brought it up with Cardinal Mariano Rampolla, the Secretary of State, and with Father Alberto Lepidi, master of the Sacred Palace. He felt that just as the Church had changed in its condemnations of Aristotelianism and Copernicanism, so it would change in its attitude toward scriptural criticism. He actually favored the Church over-reaching itself in some decision which would cause a favorable counter reaction.

Meanwhile, he went on pleading for Loisy. He even wrote a letter to the review *Studi religiosi* praising Loisy as the Catholic leader in historico-critical method. In it he admits that Loisy may be defective on some particular points, but asserts that he is right to study the Bible first as a contingent and historical book before it is studied as dogmatic and inspired.[3]

The Baron's efforts were not totally in vain. One result, no doubt indirect, was the formation of what was to be known as the Biblical Commission. In a letter to Tyrrell (Dec. 18, 1901) the Baron writes that Loisy's case "has been withdrawn from both Inquisition and Index, and has been transformed into a *special commission on the Biblical question*." The twelve members of the Commission would not be asked to move to Rome. From one-quarter to one-half of the members (including the Englishman, Father Fleming, and the Italian, Father Gismondi) were favorable to the Baron's campaigns for biblical science. The Baron looked on the Commission as a "breakwater" or as a "safety-valve." It would alleviate the need for constant appeal to the Congregations, and would allow Rome to shunt the conflict off to a "side-line of traffic."[4] Shortly afterwards, however, the Commission would be more conservatively staffed, and the Baron would see his hopes totally reversed when Pius X raised the decisions of the Commission to the same value as those of the Congregations.

At this period Father Lepidi offered the Baron a position on the Commission, but the Baron refused, saying he did not want to compromise his friend, Loisy, now under suspicion. Lepidi did not take the refusal as final, but at last drew this response from the Baron on December 7, 1901:

> ... not even the Church and our respect ever and in all things for her rights and inalienable duties can dictate to us the necessary conditions of our activity: without sufficient air, we would not be able to breathe even if one commanded us. I should respect the Church at all cost and consequently preserve a strong loyalty in my attitude towards her. But by my action I would be able only to further her belief that we were content and sure of the present and the immediate future. Therefore I must wait and see what will happen, I and my friends, before we can act with justification.[5]

This document reveals the Baron's spirit at this time: he refused to join the Commission not only because of his attitude towards authority, but because of his loyalty to a friend. Nevertheless, he saw the Commission as a body of lesser authority, as a merciful curtain between the new researches and the Holy Office:

> That here is a body to which they can refer, in all times, possible anxieties as to the tenableness of this or that, the orthodoxy of this or that person; or (much better) as to how to meet and what to think as to such and such apparent facts and difficulties; and that, since the Pope himself has appointed it, although possessed already of the ordinary congregations, *we shall be following his initiative and the evident trend of his action, if we henceforth treat the commission as the presumptive and primary authority and tribunal for the slow threshing out of these questions which have thus been declared to require very special and slow study.*[6]

This remarkably suggestive idea was to wither away when the Church came to feel that this Commission could not alone handle the growing crisis.

B. L'EVANGILE ET L'EGLISE

On Nov. 10, 1902, the first of Loisy's "little red books," *L'Evangile et L'Eglise*, was published. Superficially it was Loisy's attempt to combat liberal Protestantism in the form of Harnack's *Das Wesen der Christentums*, but it was also a channel for his whole system of ideas. The contents of the book are well known and we confine ourselves to a brief resume of its ideas.[7]

The Kingdom. Both Harnack and Loisy agree on the preaching of the Kingdom as the concept that dominates the teaching of Jesus, but they differ on the content of this concept. Harnack sees eschatology, the glorious coming of Christ, as a Jewish framework, a coloring to be eliminated, since it has no import for the true interior kingdom. This kingdom essentially consists in faith in the fatherly goodness of God offered by Jesus. Loisy, however, claims that this approach does not grasp Jesus' thought on his mission, but only our idea of what is valuable for today. For Loisy, Jesus' teaching has a clearly eschatological character. The teaching on the kingdom concerns the proximate establishment of a new order. This order is an objective, exterior, visible, world which is not confined to the soul of the believer, as Harnack held. Yet the very proximity of the kingdom allows the believer to feel that he has already anticipated it in germ, in accepting the Gospel. But the preaching of this eschatological kingdom of heaven and its proximity (pp. 5, 7, 25–26) is the essence of the Gospel. At other times Loisy said that the *hope* of this proximate kingdom is the essence of the Gospel (pp. 7, 25).

The Son of God. Harnack holds that Jesus was Son of God, and believed himself to be Messiah. The concept of Messiah is later to be discarded, but it was a necessary term to bring Jews who had eschatological hopes into the interior kingdom. Jesus is Son of God, but only in the sense of "revealer of the Father." The Father alone belongs to the Gospel. Loisy holds that Harnack's whole system rests on a poor interpretation of Mt. 11.25–30 ("No one knows the Father except the Son," etc., which Loisy held to be simply an imitation of *Ecclesiasticus*.) But Jesus' teaching shows that He essentially considered Himself as Messiah, the master and king of the Jerusalem to come. The title, Son of God, is to be interpreted by the notion of Messiahship, and the Messiahship assures the person of Christ a *necessary* place in His teaching. Therefore Harnack's "God and the soul, the soul and its God" is untenable as the content of the Gospel.

The death and resurrection of Jesus assure him an incomparable place in the Christian conscience, though the developed theory on the relationship between the death and resurrection goes back to Paul from where it reacted on the final form of the Gospels. The risen Christ no longer belonged to the order of sensible experience.

The Church.   Harnack's interior kingdom is an imposition of Protestant ideas on an earlier age. Thus he sees the development of authority and of definitions as a perversion of the Gospel, but Loisy sees the Gospel as already containing a circumscribed group, hierarchized and centralized, and involved in the exterior. So true is this, that Loisy finds the episcopacy and the papacy (abstracting from divine dispositions as becomes an historian) as the legitimate outcome of the Gospel. This development no more changes the Gospel than the change from infancy to manhood changes human nature.

Christian Dogma.   Harnack sees doctrinal development as something dangerous, while Loisy sees the development, when influenced by the Greek mind, for example, as in no way changing the basis of Christianity, but as going back to the germ of apostolic teaching. The development is merely an arrival at a more perfect consciousness of the nature of the teaching and its consequences. The Church demands faith in her formulas only as the least imperfect expression that is morally possible.

Cult.   The Church has adapted the purified rites from Jewish and oriental sources, it is true, but it has not changed its original direction. These rites, not numbered with exactitude, have their source in the thought and intention of Jesus, interpreted by the Apostles and their successors under the pressure of circumstances. They begin as living realities not as expressly defined institutions.

Jesus announced the Kingdom—It is the Church which came. The definitive coming of the Kingdom is deferred, but the purpose of the Gospel remains the purpose of the Church. The Gospel eschatology was, at bottom, an expressive symbol of indescribable realities. The eschatology of the Church would be also a symbol, always perfectible. The traditional theologian consequently may continue to place the essence of the Gospel where Jesus placed it.

Loisy's little book still reads as a remarkable document: so much is well said; so much anticipated later Catholic insights. The social nature of the Church is emphasized as against the old individualistic positions of the Reform. Yet this book, and the subsequent *Autour d'un petit livre* were the two most influential works in what later was called the modernist movement. Loisy opposed the liberal Protestant view of Jesus as the preacher of an invisible kingdom of the heart with an eschatological position. Central to Jesus' message was the preaching of a visible eschatological kingdom which was imminent. This kingdom involved, not just man's inner life, but society in its physical and exterior conditions, a reversal of world order (p. 8).

The message of this first book was ambiguous. At times Loisy said that Jesus' preaching of this imminent kingdom was a "hope." This would preserve Jesus' inerrancy, since no formal judgment would be involved, but the suspicion generated by reading the entire work (pp. 24, 36, 66, 111) is confirmed by the positions presented the following year in *Autour d'un petit livre*. What Loisy meant by a "hope" was a central conviction and judgment which turned out to be in error. Between the Jesus of the Synoptics and the later Church, Loisy's thesis cut a great chasm. For Loisy, Jesus' *whole* spirituality, the Kingdom, poverty, love, disregard of social solutions, is based on an unfulfilled, *proximate* event understood in a narrow sense. The

Jesus of history erred. The Jesus of faith transforms this error. The historical Jesus is corrected by the spiritual risen Lord. The arbitrary use of texts out of which this conflict arises has been exposed by subsequent criticism. We will return to the question later.

What was von Hügel's reaction to this disconcerting book? When he had read 140 of the 234 pages in the book, he wrote Loisy:

> I have read your anti-Harnack up to page 140. It is quite simply superb. Never have you done anything stronger, more beautiful, more suitable for beginning . . . the modification of the manner of presenting and conceiving Catholicism by *the official Church herself*. This modification seems so far from being even surmised by her (*Mém*. II, 159).

To Tyrrell he wrote, Nov. 17, 1902:

> *L'Evangile et L'Eglise* . . . I have just finished with great pleasure, though as a polemic against Harnack it is less pleasing than his more disinterested studies.

One trace of hesitation we find, shortly afterwards, when the Baron discussed the book with the liberal Bishop Bonomelli of Cremona. The bishop disliked the statement on page 203: "The time when the Church defined (in fixing it at seven) the number of the sacraments was only a particular point of this development and marks neither the commencement nor the term." The Bishop was afraid that this meant that one day there could be more than seven sacraments. Von Hügel suggested an explanation in the second edition (*Mém*. II, 174). This request to Loisy shows that the Baron was not conscious of any lack of Christian faith by Loisy at this time, a fact only revealed in 1913 in *Choses Passées*.

Early in 1903, when the second edition was being prepared, we find another hesitation on the Baron's part. While praising the book as filling a need for the next fifty years, he suggests some precisions, such as adding a note about the existence of an historical nucleus in Mark, which represent the "memoirs of

Peter" and of the existence of "notes written by Matthew" in the first Gospel. Loisy said that he did not believe in such a nucleus, but that the Baron needed this for his faith (*Mém.* II, 223). The Baron's suggestions were drawn from reading the German liberal, H. J. Holtzmann, a friend of his.

Why was the Baron so free from larger anxiety with regard to the book? Why did he linger on minute points, and not question a theory which held that Our Lord erred on the nature of the Parousia? To answer this question, it is not enough to point out that many other intelligent people at the time, like Ward and Mignot, were enthusiastic about the book.[8]

The fact is that while the capital difficulty of the book dawned only gradually on many people, the Baron had actually accepted that difficulty even before reading *L'Evangile et L'Eglise*. We have seen that he had already, at emotional cost, accepted Johannes Weiss' similar idea.[9] Loisy himself had written to the Baron on Aug. 8, 1897 that the Parousia-Messiah idea and the Apocalyptic conception of the Kingdom were an indispensable relativity (*relativité indispensable*) which the Gospel had to have in order to find roots on earth. This "indispensable relativity" (presumably this means that it was indispensable at the time, but dispensable later) does not prejudice the fundamental value of the Gospel.[10] However, that there really is a danger of prejudicing the Gospel through what the theory does to the image of Jesus is evident from what Loisy goes on to say:

> But the question is extremely delicate in so far as it touches upon the personal dignity of the Savior and upon the manner of understanding the Gospel in such a way that it would not be an enthusiastic illusion whose first victim would have been the one himself who preached it. There, it seems to me, is the real difficulty. The theological definition of the divinity of Christ is a thing insignificant in itself. It should not delay the critic, but this question of fact is very grave and fundamental. . . . It is this difficulty that all those people slip on who are led out of positive faith by criticism. It is for want of looking this problem in the face that our apologetic is fundamentally invalid.

The Baron himself had sent Loisy an article by the English Hegelian E. Caird, "Christianity and the Historical Christ," which faced the same problem, and which was one of the two works cited at length in *L'Evangile et L'Eglise*.[11]

Von Hügel was not taken unaware by the capital problem of Loisy's book. He had already accepted a miscalculation on the part of Christ with regard to the Parousia, but to push the question a step further back, why did this position not cause him insuperable problems with his faith? I believe the answer to this question, which we shall treat in the next chapter, lies partly in his principle of friction carried to a dangerous extreme.

At any rate, the Baron initiated considerable publicity in favor of the book: he recommended it to friends, had reviews prepared, and wrote at least twenty letters in support of it.

C. AUTOUR D'UN PETIT LIVRE

Von Hügel, Tyrrell, and Archbishop Mignot expressed to Loisy their desire for a brochure which would be, not a retraction, but a calm explanation of the difficulties raised by the first book. They got more than they hoped for: in early October, 1903, another little red book, *Autour d'un petit livre*, appeared. Here, an excerpt of the high points will suffice. The book is presented in the form of letters to various people.

> *Phenomenal exegesis.* History can seize only phenomena with their successions and mutual connections; it does not reach the base of things. Religious facts it sees in their limitation under sense form, not in their profound cause (pp. 9–11). Tradition does not answer many questions on the Bible because it never envisioned many of the problems now raised by critics (p. 36). The work of the theologian, and that of the critic are two different things. The Church, of course, is right in not allowing theologians to set up dogmas other than Catholic dogmas (p. 50). But the facts with which the critic (as distinct from the pastoral exegete) deals cannot be in contradiction with any dogma precisely because

they are facts, while dogmas are the ideas which represent the faith, the object of which is the incomprehensibility of God (p. 51). Exegesis cannot set up its conclusions as today's dogmas, yet it must follow the rules it uses for profane history (p. 57).

The Conscience of Christ. The truth of the phenomenal description of Christ cannot be incompatible with the profound truth of faith (p. 116). If the Messiahship conceals something greater, it is not for the historian to say (p. 115). Jesus spoke according to his human conscience (p. 116), and the theologian cannot set up compartments for when Christ is speaking as the absolute or the relative (p. 144). The historian does not perceive the absolute in the Gospel (p. 144).

The divinity of Christ is a dogma which grew in the Christian conscience; in the Gospel He appears only as the Messiah, the Son of God (p. 133). The intimate form of the conscience of Jesus largely escapes the historian. Christ's sentiment of union with God is above all definition (p. 138).

The unlimited knowledge of Christ is not a datum of history (p. 138). In the Synoptics, Mt. 11.27 is probably the fruit of later speculation, and John's ideas are mystical interpretations (p. 13!). For the historian, such a knowledge would be disconcerting, for he sees Christ abandon his followers to ignorance on many things which he could have revealed without inconvenience. The theologian can hold unlimited knowledge if he thinks it indispensable (p. 139), but the intelligence of Christ is a finite human intelligence. To say that the person of Christ had infinite knowledge seems a philosophical artificiality (p. 140). At the same time Christ is God for the faith (p. 155).

Kingdom and Church. The end of the Apocalypse announces the proximate return of Christ. The theologian, in some way, should interpret it as a symbol (p. 54). Catholic doctrine is the intellectual expression of a living development, not the simple explanation of some old text (p. 65).

The preaching of a proximate coming is found in the Apostolic generation. Either Jesus preached this same idea, or the major part of this teaching in the Synoptics loses its value (p. 68). His death was caused by that preaching.

The establishment of the Church has introduced a corrective in the Parousia idea, but the Gospel idea, and the Church symbol are not contradictories (p. 160). The Church is not founded by Him

so much as on Him, or on Him as risen (pp. 161–162). She belongs
to the will of the immortal Christ, and this was not manifested
before the Passion (p. 163).

What is the risen Christ? The risen Christ is the glorious Christ,
the Christ spirit, the Word returned to the glory of eternity (p.
100). Not a trait of the resurrection narrative is conceived in view
of a simply historical representation (p. 103). The Eucharistic
Christ, for example, is rooted chiefly in visions where Jesus
appears to break bread (p. 240). Paul himself sees two Christs,
one of Faith who was from all eternity in divine form, and one
of history who appeared in human form. This is the distinction at
the basis of the previous book (pp. 111–112).

Church authority. The principle of authority does not rest on
texts, but on the faith of the Church (p. 176), but the Church was
not only an inevitable, but also a legitimate consequence of the
Gospel. The purpose of the previous book was not to demonstrate
the divine truth of the Church, since history alone does not
furnish this proof (xxvii). The authority of Church rites rests, not
on the Christ of history, but of faith (p. 233).

While Loisy continues to say that history alone does not
prove the faith, the question arises as to whether this reading
of history would not demolish an incarnational faith. (Apparently
Loisy's own real life position at this time grew out of just
such a conviction.) Loisy's references to the earliest Resurrection
traditions, supposedly studied as phenomena, leave one with the
sense that the disciples believed that Christ was in eternity.
The omitted explanation implies that they had no conviction that
He had left the tomb, or that they had dealt viably with him
after the Resurrection. Further, although softened in this book,
the disruptive element between what Christ taught and what
the Church believes is still present. The *motive-base of all* of
Christ's teaching and existence, as Loisy sees it, namely, the
visible proximate coming of the Parousia, was later withdrawn,
and yet the result is still claimed to be a legitimate development
of what is no longer its cause. Ultimately, Loisy's whole position
rests on a selective and partial study of the tradition of Christ's
expressed consciousness. We will return to the eschatological
question in the following chapters.

I have not intended to give a scholarly critique of Loisy,[12] but only to point to what was disconcerting in this book, and even when we now look at von Hügel's attitude, we must be wary of judging him against this hind-sight view developed during fifty years of analysis of the book.

With access to the Loisy-von Hügel correspondence only as it is embedded in the *Mémoires*, we do not perceive the niceties of the Baron's judgment. Just before the second book appeared, he had written to Percy Gardner that "some discriminating principle is badly wanted in Loisy's scheme— some kind of test for distinguishing between truly superstitious or otherwise oppressive growths and genuine spiritual developments"; but when the book appeared, he wrote to Loisy congratulating him on his tenacity and serenity. On four points he found the tone irritating as regards personalities, but apparently he had no difficulty with the substance.

The question arises: was the Baron reacting more as a diplomat than as a scholar? We might better ask: is the Baron at this time more interested in the exact results of exegesis (the New Testament was not his special field), or with the question of liberty for the exegete (his role as diplomat)? We cannot make a choice. The Baron never lost his concern for scientific integrity, but the second aspect had begun to reveal its importance more clearly to him. He circulated copies of the book among his friends and wrote to Cardinals Merry del Val and Rampolla. To Rampolla he said that Loisy's case raised, not merely the question of orthodoxy, but of the legitimate liberty of historical science. Von Hügel had keenly sensed certan illegitimate encroachments by authority in the past. He loved to cite the condemnation of Aristotelianism, the Galileo case, the Johannine Comma decision, and, later, the decisions on Genesis and the Pentateuch. Unless one admits that the dangers of the misuse of authority are at least as great as the dangers of the misuse of the individual conscience, von Hügel's actions become inexplicable. But then, so do the actions of others at the time who shared the aspirations of von Hügel, and who remained Catholics; such men as Bishop Lacroix of Tarentaise, Archbishop Mignot of Albi, Gismondi, an Italian Jesuit on the first Biblical Commission, and Genocchi, an Italian and assistant general of the Congregation of the Sacred Heart.[14]

D.   CONDEMNATION AND AFTERMATH

L'Evangile et L'Eglise was condemned by Cardinal Richard of Paris on Jan. 17, 1903, because it had been published without the *imprimatur* (Loisy and von Hügel held that such a book does not need the *imprimatur*), and gravely disturbed the faith of Catholics. On Feb. 3, 1903 Loisy bowed to the episcopal authority and repudiated the errors that one might deduce from the book "in interpreting it from a different point of view than that in which he had written it."

On Dec. 16, 1902 the Holy Office put five of Loisy's books on the Index, the two books just discussed, as well as *Etudes Evangeliques, Le Quatrième Evangile*, and *La Religion d'Israel.* Pius X approved the decree on December 17, and Cardinal Merry del Val sent the decision, with a covering letter, to Paris on December 19.

The Baron's pen now grew hot over a spate of articles and letters.[15] The following is the substance of these articles:

> I never thought all of Loisy's opinions were true but "this little peasant's son" is a real man. The covering letter for the decree which mentions specific errors (on primitive revelation, authenticity of facts and teaching in the gospel, the divinity and knowledge of Christ, the Resurrection, the divine institution of Church and sacraments) is of less weight than the decree of the Holy Office which is vaguer. This is *doctrinal* in its drift but since it does not mention specifics it does not incriminate the whole. We specialists therefore must use the works with caution, since it contains hypotheses which if pressed from the Scholastic viewpoint we cannot reconcile with faith.
>
> But there have been other doctrinal decrees which have been reversed, as the decrees against Aristotelianism and Copernicanism. Here the Church had disciplinary rights. But in these philosophical and historico-critical matters when the authorities became absolute and doctrinal, grave perils for *all* arose. Today

theologians appeal to texts as phenomenal and yet will not allow phenomenal methods.

Loisy has submitted to Cardinal Richard and no doubt will now submit to Rome. So do I. These are acts of sincere deference. But it will not be a renunciation of his entire critico-historical conscience. There will necessarily be reservation in the matter of his historian's conscience and method.

As to the Resurrection, this is an "actual reality." The question was whether the *purely historical* evidence is cogent. We *believe* in "the fact of Christ's living for ever more." As to the consciousness of Christ, Loisy has not affirmed that Jesus' humanity had no consciousness of being God and consubstantial with the Father. But the historian has no constraining motive for affirming this.

Our historico-critical "facts" and methods may demand emendation. But this must come from the subject's intrinsic laws. Our *synthesis* of history and the intellectual presentation of the faith may be wrong. Here the Church has its rights. But it must not make us reject our method. Without "some such limited autonomy" we cannot be sincere.

Loisy never said that the final and entire truth could be discordant with what the Church teaches. The antinomy is apparent and temporary. We find it in all life, as in the problem of evil. We can't hold truths which are contradictory. But the unity is the ideal end of science and can't be imposed. We must distrust any view of life which does not include friction, conflict, mystery, pain.

The Church has the right to conserve and interpret the ultimate sense of facts and dogmas. But she must permit her sons to unite a science of religious phenomena, which is sincere and hence always renewable, with a faith which is indestructible in its ultimate spiritual meaning.

As we can see, the Baron is calling for a total autonomy and liberty in the study of religious phenomena within their domain. The limitation in this autonomy enters at the point where a *synthesis* with the faith is attempted. He admits this attempted synthesis in Loisy's books, but on historical method and facts the Holy Office had no competence. Before the Baron had written these articles, the subject had come up in correspondence with Loisy. An equivocation is present there.

The Baron's letter, cited by Loisy (*Mém.* II, 296), speaks of admitting possible error in making a synthesis between faith and facts. In his answer Loisy denies the Holy Office's competence in the synthesis. Yet the Baron went ahead and used this "synthesis" terminology as if he were interpreting Loisy's mind. This, plus the fact that von Hügel softened Loisy's letter to *The Times* without asking Loisy (*Mém.* II, 311), shows that the Baron had a clearer idea of how he wanted to go about getting "them" out of their predicament than he did of either Loisy's exact position or wishes.

Meanwhile, Loisy was trying to save his conscience with ambiguous retractions. The Baron was against total submission by Loisy. He suggested a memoir to the Pope containing a credo in the divinity of Christ and all the dogmas of the Church. Loisy later said that this would not be as easy as the Baron imagined, and wondered whether, in fact, it would be so easy for the Baron, himself, to accept all dogmas. No doubt, he observed, the Baron would be able to *tourner* (either interpret or get around) that problem too.

Next, von Hügel suggests four sacrifices to Loisy: an absolute retraction, withdrawal of the three apologetic books (the third being *La Religion d'Israel*), suspension of publication, and renouncement of his present teaching post at l'Ecole des Hautes Etudes for one year. All of this, however, was to be bracketed within certain reserves. Loisy considered this as mystical advice, where the reservation meant nothing. Finally, after two unacceptable drafts of submission, Loisy wrote to Cardinal Richard: "I declare to your Eminence that in the spirit of obedience toward the Holy See, I condemn the errors which the Congregation of the Holy Office has condemned in my writings." He told the Cardinal verbally, however, that people had attributed a sense to his words that he had not intended, and had worked from conclusions that he had not formulated. His retraction, which was accepted, rankled his conscience for life. This was written on March 12, 1904. On March 2, von Hügel opposed absolute submission (*Mém.* II, 354). By April 30, von Hügel was stating in *The Times* that for Loisy this was "not a renunciation of his entire historico-critical conscience." The Baron sees his mission as the quest of scientific autonomy, and not precisely the defense of Loisy's conclusions. This became especially true as he gradually discerned in Loisy a movement towards immanentism which he had begun to suspect in 1902. Years later, after the avowal by Loisy in *Choses passées* (1913) of the real state of his soul at this earlier time, the Baron complained of the pain for his friends caused by Loisy's dissimulation.

E. VON HÜGEL'S POSITIONS

The Baron's doctrine on the relation of exegesis to the Church is consistent with what he propounded in the Church and the Bible articles. Exegesis, he said, is autonomous *a principio* (provided it begins with theism), right to the *terminus*. There, the Church's jurisdiction takes over as doctrinal and disciplinary, but the process of exegesis itself is autonomous provided it does not deny "subsequent supernatural truths," and "the possibility of a subsequent supernatural teacher of subsequent supernatural truths." It is obvious that an exegete, while stating that he does not deny "subsequent" (logically, that is) supernatural truths, may form a synthesis which virtually denies them. Evidently, this is what the Church believed had happened in Loisy's case. Thus, the Baron was consistent in admitting the Church's right to enter with disciplinary or doctrinal jurisdiction into the second state. Here a synthesis may be made that contradicts the message of revelation conveyed by the Church.

The Baron was afraid of the Church's magisterium meddling with the first area, or what he called "phenomena," that is, the exegesis of individual texts. No doubt, even here, it would be a superficial view to rule out, *a priori*, the Church's right, at least in theory, to intervene, since what seems to be the exegesis of a specific text often enough involves an entire synthesis of suppositions which could be contrary to the Church's presentation of revelation. The real problem, however, lies, not in the area of the distinction between "phenomena" and "synthesis," which von Hügel, under the influence of nineteenth-century historiography, made too much of. Rather, as von Hügel saw clearly also, it lies in the danger of precipitous and imprudent condemnation by Church authority (in matters where the Church does not commit herself with absolute finality), before it has been sufficiently ascertained that the position condemned is truly in conflict with her saving message. As the model for this, von Hügel often cited the Galileo case.

As will be seen, one of the theses of our study is that precisely with regard to Loisy's eschatological theory, the Church's position was a prudent one. However, the condemnation was extremely vague and global, and not very specific on exactly what was erroneous. Global condemnations of this nature, sometimes made to protect what Newman called *pomeria* of the faith, are usually quite dangerous because of the possibility that they may bring the good down with the bad.

It is frequently thought that the Baron was now becoming incoherent in his attitude toward authority. For example, two months after Loisy's books were condemned, he wrote to Tyrrell, on Feb. 5, 1904, complaining of the impossibility of the disciplinary repression of critico-historical work, and of being obliged "to interior assent... towards acts not even claiming to be inerrant."[16] Is this a change in his thinking? It is not. In one of his earliest writings, *The Petrine Claims* (1898), he had said:

> Interior assent to the Pope's *ex cathedra* pronouncements is always due; obedience to the Pope's governmental orders is *generally* and presumptively due. Saints have at times privately disobeyed single orders or have remonstrated with the popes as to their neglect of duty (p. 49).

In his Church and Bible articles (1895), he wrote that in the "strict" Scheeben's opinion, with regard to the Fifth General Council's condemnation of Origen, interior assent to the condemnation is required, provided there are no reasonable grounds for assuming that the condemned expressions are not

Origen's. Joining these two statements, we can see that he is basically holding what is generally accepted by theologians. That is, that a doctrinal decree, which is not infallible, either from the Pope, or from universal Church teaching, demands from the Catholic an assent based on moral certitude. This moral certitude is not the absolute certitude given to infallible doctrine. In the rare case where there are overwhelming reasons for doubting such a teaching, the Catholic may then *believe* other than the doctrine proposed, but he should, at the time maintain, a respectful silence on the matter.

When the Baron says that there can be no disciplinary suppression of critico-historical work, he evidently means suppression of the *historical method*. Historical method might need revision, he admitted, but only according to its own insights.

Von Hügel agreed with Loisy on the limitation in Christ's human knowledge. Furthermore, he held that Our Lord's attitude toward the Parousia was actually error, the error of His time. He had seen the proofs for three articles that held this theory, and found them "admirable."[17] In 1904 he propounded the theory himself. This was to affect directly his idea of the nature of the Church. He held that "in all but its very rudimentary form ... Church organization and officialism is not the direct and deliberate creation of Our Blessed Lord Himself."[18]

Ultimately, this theory reverts to the question of authority. In 1904 he wrote: "There is something wrong somewhere with the working of the Church machinery—indeed with the conception of the Church's authority."[19] It is impossible that theologians on Church authority, generally, should have an inerrancy higher, or more extensive, than Our Lord Himself.[20] This is where his theory led him, but it is not his final word on the subject. Later, he accepted an inerrancy for infallible Church dogma. His break with Loisy was growing, not on these points, but on the question of immanentism. How could he have held these positions, fervent, praying Catholic that he was, without rebelling against them, and looking for other solutions? The reason we will now propose.

CHAPTER SIX

THE PHILOSOPHY OF FRICTION, TENSION, CONFLICT

Exposition of the idea. Von Hügel's mind was not only empirical; it was intuitive. He had a horror of reducing everything to "clever logic." Thus, what was a problem for the mind fashioned by scholastic logic was not a problem, to the same degree, for the Baron.

As early as 1896, in reviewing a book by Eucken, he spoke of the conflict with the outer world as a purification for the inner one.[1] We have seen him toying with this idea in 1897 as a suggested means of meeting the impasse between noumena and phenomena, i.e., divine faith and exegesis. Gradually, von Hügel evolved a theory of friction; this became one of his seminal ideas and pervades all his thought. There are three stages in his development of the theory: he applies it, first, to the general spiritual and personal life of man; later, to the problems of exegesis and especially to Christology; concomitantly and finally, to religion in general, institutional and mystical. The movement coincides with his own development from a moderately good exegete to a religious philosopher of major importance.

The grandfather of the theory, as the Baron admits, is Hegel,[2] but von Hügel so adapted it that it can scarcely be said to belong to Hegel's family. The two who fathered the theory in von Hügel were Abbé Huvelin and Professor Eucken (1846–1926) of Jena, Germany. The Baron uses the spirituality of Huvelin, and modifies the philosophy of Eucken.

The base of the theory is the foundation of all of the Baron's thinking, the incomprehensibility of God.

> God, our own souls, all the supreme realities and truths . . . are both *incomprehensible* and *indefinitely apprehensible.* . . . Actual ever increasing apprehension comes more through the purification of the heart than through the exercise of the reason, and without some experience (following no doubt upon some light) the reason has no adequate material for effective conclusions.[3]

Even in heaven, as the Lateran and Vatican Councils teach, God is incomprehensible. Our highest knowledge of God in heaven, intuitive knowledge, is inexpressible to others, and probably, as Scheeben holds, it cannot be given even internal expression.[4]

In this life, therefore, the more we advance in the knowledge of God, the more *our love* makes us see that we do not know anything that is worthy of Him. Our pretensions make us forget this, and we lose the sense of mystery in religion unless we are brought back to it, and are purified by a sense of friction and tension in our thought, personality, and life.

Apply this to our general spiritual life. Man is burdened with a sense of deep dissatisfaction, which demands that a more "substantial being" must lie hid in man. Man feels alternately a tension (a pulling apart), and a friction (a painful overlapping), between himself as a mere *individual*-coordinating-himself-with-the-world, and himself as potential *person*-made-pro-foundly-dissatisfied by an encounter with an interior Infinite which is infinitely more Person than he is himself. There is, thus, a conflict with the "outer world" which is needed for the purification of the "inner world."[5] Abolish this tension and friction, and one abolishes the possibility of a spiritual life, and of a spiritual personality. Ignore the inner drive for the Infinite with its consequent dissatisfaction and one becomes a materialist. Abolish the claims of the finite and the outer world, and one becomes a quietist, and loses the sense of the need for reform in this world.

Around the turn of the century, and gradually thereafter, von Hügel begins to apply this doctrine to Christology. He sees a certain tension between Christ in history and Christ in the soul. He speaks of the presence of the "inward Christ pushing us upwards and outwards, with a view to joining hands with the outward Christ Who is pressing inwards."[6] But we must not wear blinkers to avoid science and we must not construct careful apologetics to lessen or ignore the friction. There is always a friction, a "non-fit," of the absolute with the finite. A drama with three elements is always in progress. In the foreground are ourselves, units capable of making ourselves persons. In the middle is "the phenomenal curtain, a resisting, but spiritually not irresistible, medium of . . . physical, mechanical, determinist fact, law, and science." (Only in 1905 did the Baron begin to distinguish carefully between physical science and history [see *Mém.* II, 448; *EA* II, p. 32; *ME* II, p. 382]). In the background is noumenal reality, God. This drama finds an absolute unity in the mind of God, but in the human mind there is always a certain friction. In fact, we must not only admit, but, as Eucken shows, *we must carefully retain this friction*. Thus the Cross is planted in the intellectual life.[7] The solution comes through "the supremacy of love over knowledge and of action over speculation."[8]

Fr. Bremond, in 1904, at the very moment of the debate over the consciousness of Christ, is puzzled by the Baron's doctrine "of slowly acquired harmony in and by the resistance and friction of every kind of recalcitrant, apparently *disparate* material."[9] But the Baron replies, "what is all life but that!"

At that time the Baron was working on *The Mystical Element of Religion*, and the "friction" principle permeated the entire work. For the rest of his life the principle was in flood tide, and inundated every nook and cranny of his thought. He applied it to every facet of the conflict of science and faith, to religion in general, and especially to mysticism. Friction is not just to be tolerated; religion drives one to *find* obstacles, and it thrives on them.[10] Von Hügel's three great religious difficulties,

God and the presence of evil, Christ and His idea on the Parousia, and the Church with a tendency to excess in institutionalism, all involve friction and are solved, not by knowledge, but by purification in love.[11] We are brought to the conclusion that what we really seek is not clarity, but richness; not cleverness, but fruitfulness. The richer any reality, the higher on the scale of being, the more in part obscure and inexhaustible it is.[12]

If, where von Hügel uses the term "God" or "personal God," we insert the term "Thou," where he uses the term, "individual soul," we insert the term, "I," and where he uses the terms, "nature, science, determinism, phenomena, fact," we insert the term, "it," this new framework greatly clarifies the Baron's ideas and phrases without distorting his basic thought. (While von Hügel has similarities to Martin Buber, we do not here use the terminology exactly in Buber's sense.)

The encounter of the "I" (with its "ontological hunger" for the Infinite), and the "it" produces a twofold relationship: a) stimulation; b) opposition. a) The "I" is *stimulated* by the "it." It feeds its ontological hunger on the "it" in forming its notion of God. Without the stimulation of the "it" the "I" cannot find Infinite Being. The Infinite Being is seen to be a "Thou" in the interior encounter of the "I" with its infinite hunger. Its object must be personal. b) But there is also *opposition* to the encounter. The "it" often becomes recalcitrant. This is good. The "I" has a tendency to fall back into an encounter with a *non-mysterious* "Thou" without this opposition. Without the opposition, the "I" encounters a *too* anthropomorphic "Thou." The resistance of the "it" causes my encounter with God to take on aspects of an "I-it" encounter. The Baron speaks of the provisory value of a Pantheistic view (*ME* II, 329 ff.) But this in no way effaces the basic personalness of the "I-Thou" encounter. (Pantheism is always surmounted in the faith-encounter.) Thus my anthropomorphic idea of person is expanded, and my "I-Thou" relationship with God is pushed to unknown depths of truth. Without friction and opposition, there is very little growth in the "I-Thou"

relationship with God. Thus, the "I-it" relationship must
be respected within its own domain. The "it" of science, law
determinism, fact, must be given its full force and full liberty
of action.

There is no doubt that here is one of the richest veins of
von Hügel's thought. In these passages he is at his best, and
he moves on in a way that borders on poetry. One can see, too,
why the Baron, because of this doctrine, was less upset than
many by Loisy's ideas. We have no intention of making any
sweeping criticism with regard to the general theory, but a few
points are in order, especially with regard to Christology.

Loisy found this theory one of the most delicate, but not
most lucid, points of the "Hügelian philosophy" (*Mém.* II, 448).
He levels the criticism of logic against the system, saying that
it is impossible to define personality, and that the leap from
personality to God is illogical. In another quarter, two who
were certainly not logicians, Bremond and Tyrrell, were also
confused by von Hügel's theory. Tyrrell wrote to the Baron
years later:

> In your just revolt against the fallacy of simplification, I
> sometimes wonder whether you are not driven to value complexity
> for its own sake. *Ceteris paribus*, simplicity is a good and
> complexity an evil. I ask myself whether *Modernism* is not, in
> many ways, a simplification—a riddance of useless com-
> plications.[13]

The Baron, himself, was not unaware of the general danger
of pressing his theory too hard. He admitted that there are
some useless frictions, such as those between churchmen
and laity. Late in life, consistent with his permanent outlook,
however, he reacted against the insoluble conflict between
head and heart which he found in Tertullian, Pascal, and
A. Sabatier.[14] Twice he quotes Hoeffding's critique of Kierkegaard:

> Conflict, tension, indeed, can be necessary for the truth and
> force of the spiritual life.... But tension, taken by itself,
> cannot furnish the true measure of life. For the general nature

of consciousness is a synthesis. . . . Life's decisive element cannot
reside in tension alone.[15]

But von Hügel never expressly applied this last critique to
his own position on eschatology. Simply because the doctrine is
so rich, it must be delicately applied; friction can never become
an end in itself, any more than seeking pain can become an
end in itself. It is an ever-recurring, last-resort measure.
Always, and first, there must be an effort to eliminate friction.
The Baron, himself, had eliminated friction between science
and the Church on the matter of inspiration, but in that case it
was theological theory that he modified, not the facts.

So in his Christology, von Hügel thought that *the facts*
pointed to the ignorance and the errancy of Christ. He was
abetted in this belief by the scarcity, at least until 1905, of a
critical approach to the subject by an able Catholic exegete.[16]
Again, he was overly confident in his position on the "facts"
because, while he admitted a metaphysic involved in historical
interpretation, he did not clearly distinguish between the
results of the physical sciences and of history until about
1905.[17] Taking these last two factors into consideration, it is not
surprising that he makes use of his very rich theory of friction
and tension to release him from any rankling anxiety on the
problems raised by his position on the consciousness of Christ.
There is a paradox here. The doctrine of friction itself can
lead to an excessive simplicity. Theories which are "fruitful"
obstacles may be too readily accepted as facts. It took von
Hügel many years to admit that the facts themselves, on the
consciousness of Christ, were somewhat mysterious. Our
evidence suggests that his friction doctrine was probably a
contributing factor to the delay in his being recognized. If so,
it was merely being excessively applied, and the admission would
in no way touch the heart, truth, and richness of his vital,
healthy, and profound philosophy.

The Baron, in 1899, was struggling to see the good in
people, and "not to judge, not to criticize the rest."[18] He was
also under the spell of the powerfully logical, keen mind of
Loisy, a quality which he himself lacked. He saw exegesis,

partly because of his own scientific training, partly because of Loisy's influence, as leading to very restricted conclusions. In his theory of friction, he considered knowledge important, but secondary to love, for which it is a *means* of stimulation. All these factors led him to accept, as established, the proposition that Christ erred as to the date of the Parousia. The consequence is a weakening in his conception of the authority of the Church. Meanwhile, however, he commenced to drift away from Loisy because of an immanentism which he began to suspect in him.

CHAPTER SEVEN

BLONDEL: THE LIMITS
OF EXEGESIS

Von Hügel had often been depicted as following blindly in Loisy's wake, with the resultant charge of being "naive." The evidence we have seen suggests that he was principally involved in a crusade for greater autonomy for exegesis in general.

The literature we have cited merely nods to the German influence on the Baron, and usually omits the English influence. It is impossible to judge exactly, the directness of these influences, but it is a fact that, before he met Loisy, the Baron was reading the Germans, B. Weiss and Wellhausen; that before he read *L'Evangile et L'Eglise*, he had accepted Johannes Weiss' position on Our Lord's idea of the Parousia; and that, in the period of controversy which followed Loisy's two controversial books, he was pushing Loisy to admit Holtzmann's idea of a real, historical witnessing at the core of the Gospels.[1] Von Hügel's German leanings are evident also in the philosophical area. His first love was Eucken, Max Scheler's teacher, and he gradually retreated from the positions of Blondel and Laberthonnière to those of the German, Troeltsch.

In England, the question of "kenosis" and the consciousness of Christ was at its peak between 1890 and 1910. One of the main participants was Charles Gore, by 1895 a personal friend of the Baron. In his essay on inspiration, in the volume *Lux*

Mundi, which, according to his diary, the Baron read on
Sept. 20, 1890, Gore said that Our Lord "willed so to
restrain the beams of Deity as to observe the limits of the
science of His age, and He puts Himself in the same relation
to its historical knowledge." He speaks of Christ's "self-
emptying," as a "continual act of self-sacrifice." In an essay
on "The Consciousness of Our Lord" in *Dissertations* (1896)
the Anglican Gore reacted with horror to the idea of an infused
human knowledge of Christ that would be practically equivalent
to omniscience. He wanted to safeguard what he believed was
the Gospel picture of Christ's real humanity. Thus, he referred
to Christ as abandoning divine "prerogatives," and once wrote
of an abandonment of divine "attributes," but modified this
in his second edition. Whether this self-emptying was a *refusal*
to exercise the divine consciousness, or a *necessary* limitation
of the Incarnation, was a question Gore considered to be beyond
our knowledge. In a review of Gore's book, Fr. Lagrange
criticized the positions, but called for renewed research on
Christ's consciousness by theologians, and praised Gore's call
to study the interior Christ as revealed in Sacred Scripture.[2]

Another favorite book of the Baron's was Driver's
Introduction to the Literature of the Old Testament. In the
preface, Driver espoused Gore's views on the consciousness of
Christ. Only after this, according to the Baron's diary, did
he begin to read Loisy's first book, an orthodox study of the
canon of the Old Testament.

It may have seemed to Bremond, in 1904, that von Hügel
was more concerned with Loisy's personal position than with
his ideas.[3] Yet, when all the evidence has been assessed,
especially the correspondence with Tyrrell and Blondel, it
must be concluded that the Baron was crusading for a principle.

A.   BLONDEL'S "LETTRE"

During March, 1895 in Rome, von Hügel met Blondel for the
first time. By July 2 he records in his diary that he is reading

Blondel's *L'Action*. In 1896 he read Blondel's articles entitled "Lettre sur les exigences de la pensée contemporaine en matière d'apologétique" as they appeared in the *Annales de philosophie chrétienne*.[4] Blondel's thought struck a chord in von Hügel, partly because it moved along lines vaguely similar to the thought of Eucken. He found himself in great sympathy with the *Lettre*.[5]

Blondel's basic thesis is that none of the apologetics developed in recent times was truly philosophical. To be so, they would have to be grounded on what he calls the method of immanence (or as he more exactly terms it in *L'Action*, "a logic of action").[6] The apologetic of the manuals, especially, lacked this base. They set out to establish, first, the possibility of revelation, and then its reality. This method, it is true, is probative for the believer, but by no means such for the unbeliever. To prove the reality of revelation, such a method would have to demonstrate rigorously the reality of miracles, at least that of the Resurrection, but miracles are probative only for those who are interiorly ready to receive them. This method is defective because it does not show revelation's *necessity for us*, and the "us" would include the unbeliever. Thus, one would establish an objective, personal imputability for not accepting the revelation. It is not just credibility *in itself*, but *in us* that must also be established, otherwise the unbeliever is never faced with responsibility in rejecting revelation.

The method of immanence (the logic of action) reveals that there is in man a basic inadequacy between what he consciously thinks, wills, and does on the surface, and some deeper reality of thinking, willing, and doing. No matter how many obscure compensations one tries to find, one cannot make the equation. Man may not be conscious of this inadequacy, and hence it is the role of the method of immanence to reveal it.

It is thus shown that man is seeking, on the deepest level, something *uniquely necessary*, but at the same time *inaccessible* to his human action. This is the "pierre d'attente" which makes man responsible for an option between the "unique

necessary" and self. What is indispensable is at the same
time naturally inaccessable. Thus, at the first stage, man is
faced with the *absolute* necessity of some undetermined
supernatural. At the second stage, there is posited a
hypothesis, a *hypothetical necessary*, the Christian supernatural
order. Blondel, in *L'Action*, shows that man, in analyzing his
action, is brought successively to face an undetermined
supernatural, and then a hypothetically necessary Christianity.
The first step invites us to a kind of faith of reason which
is generosity of heart. The second step invites us to
Christian faith. In conclusion, then, apologetics should
not reassess arguments in order to offer an *object*, when it
is the *subject* which is not disposed.

Later, in 1904, the debate turned on the question of
history. Here, however, Blondel had already shown that it is
not enough to scrutinize "the great Christian fact" of revelation
in order that the reasoning philosopher be converted. The logic
of action shows that there is a movement within man whose
analysis should open him up, and bring him to the threshold
of revelation.

Von Hügel believed that he had understood the article
because he had already read *L'Action*, but later he expressed
perplexity over several points, and found the language quite
obscure. He shared, he said, Blondel's attitude toward scholasticism, and saw it as "a mountain of ice floating in the middle
of a southern sea." There is no real knowledge of the past stages
of human thought without the three elements of *relativity*,
development, and *interiority*. By this last word the Baron meant
something like Blondel's logic of action.

B. THE ERUPTION OF THE CONTROVERSY

Immediately after the appearance of Loisy's *L'Evangile et
L'Eglise* and *Autour d'un petit livre*, Blondel exchanged several
long and important letters with Loisy and von Hügel. These
formed the preamble to two important articles by Blondel.
The first, *Histoire et Dogme*: *Les lacunes philosophiques de*

l'exégèse moderne, is an exposé of the defects of "extrinsicism" and "historicism" as approaches to exegesis, followed by the presentation of a notion of tradition as a solution to the problem. The article is evidently and predominantly aimed at the approach of Loisy, but "historicism" is frequently painted with somewhat broad strokes so as to include the whole movement, and to avoid a public attack against Loisy. The very broadness of the picture led to a great deal of unnecessary quibbling, and perhaps clouded, a bit, for the readers the clarity of Blondel's insight. We will confine ourselves chiefly to the Blondel-von Hügel controversy.

Von Hügel replied in his article *Du Christ Eternel et nos Christologies successives*.[7] The prior exchange of correspondence between Blondel and von Hügel, and the two subsequent articles define a distinct area of discussion.

As the debate evolves, the observer feels that he is watching two contestants trying to come to grips through a glass partition. Each man is, to a degree, locked inside his own system. Yet despite this problem, genuine insights emerge, and the debate is important. Today, the question of history and tradition are often discussed along general lines. Here, however, a very exact and specific issue is at stake, the nature of exegesis as specified in its approach to the consciousness of Christ. Here, too, we have a genuine philosopher brilliantly analyzing the limited function of exegesis, yet at the same time he, himself, cannot resist totally the ever-recurrent temptation of donning the exegete's cap. On the other hand von Hügel united in himself, as Blondel said, both philosophy and scientific criticism.[8] The Baron's positions will lead him to a crisis with authority. Here we leave the area of a *general* discussion about exegesis and authority, and examine the question as focused in the *conscience* of a man who ran the risks of his position.

The discussion falls under four main headings: (1) the relation of history and exegesis to metaphysics; (2) Christ's consciousness of His Divinity, and of the date of the Parousia; (3) the notion of tradition; (4) incidental exegetical positions. Since the last is the least important, let us dispose of it first.

(1) *Incidental exegetical positions.* Von Hügel held that the Synoptics must occupy first place in any critical study of the Gospels. The fourth Gospel is not a history in the same sense, but focuses rather on the spiritual significance of Christ.[9] Blondel, however, maintained that both were history in the sense of "real history," and that alone was of total value. Historicism's study of "phenomena" is never adequate. By "real history" Blondel meant that it is the total revelation in Christ passed on to His disciples, not only in conceptual, but also in non-conceptual forms, and not only in Scripture, but in life.

With regard to the synoptic Gospels themselves, we have already seen that von Hügel held that there were secondary layers ("couches") in them. Blondel believed that one found these secondary layers in the Gospels mainly by *a priori* reasoning and imagination.[10] Yet it is interesting to note that Blondel prudently avoided such statements in his published articles. For years von Hügel had witnessed this type of thinking in the opposition to the existence of such layers in the Pentateuch. The experience made it hard for him to listen now.

(2) *The relation of history and exegesis to metaphysics.* The term, phenomena, covers a broad range of meanings. It may mean statements of a reality by witnesses, or it may signify the reality itself. This reality may be, in its turn, a phenomenon which is archeological, geographical, a time sequence, or an event; it may be something suggestive of a state of consciousness; it may be something suggestive of an invisible state of being.[11] Statements about phenomena could not cover readily all aspects of reality. They generally gravitate around the last two aspects.

On April 20, 1902 von Hügel had written to Maude Petre about Albert Ehrhard's book *Der Katholizismus und das zwanzigste Jahrhundert:*

> I think it is remarkable not only for its very fine and literary distinction, but even more because of the way in which he, an historian by profession, never for one moment forgets how that,

ultimately, the whole question is philosophical and depends upon what is elected as to the true and adequate affirmation and interpretation of life. It is here that he towers above the otherwise most capable and competent Mr. Edmund Bishop [a critical historian of liturgical origins] whom we have among our few English Catholic serious workers. It is quite curious to note how this latter can never have enough flings at *all* philosophy as so much *a priori* pretentiousness; and yet (of course) the good man is talking a philosophy of his own all the time.

Thus, the Baron is not unaware of the problem of presuppositions in history. In the present debate, Blondel warned him against accepting an empirical method that was oblivious of its metaphysic. The Baron agreed, and said that a man is always and inescapably "a metaphysical being." He pointed out that even Loisy, despite some disconcerting statements, admitted this in *L'Evangile et L'Eglise* (pp. 142–144). But the Baron insisted that one cannot substitute metaphysical decisions for historical ones. Blondel was convinced that the Baron was holding for a sort of extrinsic metaphysic which was only antecedent and subsequent to the exegete's work. He warned him that metaphysics comes, not just before, as a leader, nor after, as a follower. It exists before, during, and after, and is immanent to every work that touches humanity.[12]

Von Hügel replied that one could make sure to use "good metaphysical principles." Here he was evidently thinking of a bad metaphysics as one which is anti-theistic, anti-supernatural, but no more than this, for he says we cannot be allowed to adduce specifically Catholic-ecclesiastical "prolegomena" for critical work, for example, in establishing the character of the soul of "the Christ-Object."

Blondel, however, was speaking of a metaphysics as a type of "determinism" which limits what can be scientifically known to phenomena, understood in the narrowest scientific dimension. The four principles of this "historicism" would be: (1) It tends to judge historical phenomena, in the scientific critic's sense of this word, not, perhaps, expressly as if it were the reality itself, but at least as the measure of what one can know scientifically.

(2) It tends to take the exterior act, the portrait, the stereoscopic view of several witnesses as if it were the inner actor, the real action. (3) It tends to take the *explicitly conscious intellectual* effect which is produced in others as the whole initial act of the producer. (4) Thus it seeks the entire matter of history in an evolution of only consciously intellectualized ideas, a *logical* evolution, but it omits a study of *organic* development which would demand a recognition of other antecedent, concomitant, and final causes.[13]

It is evident that, on the base of scientifically determined phenomena alone, one cannot construct an integral apologetic for Christianity, for, as Blondel echoes over and over, history does not suffice for dogma, nor the facts for the faith. Facts do not automatically manifest the supernatural.

These last phrases, which occurred so often, annoyed von Hügel, and bifurcated the movement of Blondel's thought. Von Hügel was upset, since this very statement about the facts not sufficing for the faith, was continually recurring in his own writings and those of Loisy. He said that for Blondel to see, in the writers he was criticizing, an effort to make the faith arise automatically out of the facts was an "unbearable pretension,"[14] although he admitted that Loisy gave this impression at times.

Neither Blondel nor von Hügel is denying the right of the exegete to work within a *provisory* determinism. Blondel had admitted this privately to von Hügel, and had said it in his article, but Blondel's recurring phrase about the facts not sufficing for the faith seemed to make this the central point at issue. Von Hügel made it clear that he, himself, held that the facts were only occasions, the necessary condition, and the necessary matter for the faith.[15]

Blondel's frequently repeated phrase—"facts not sufficing for faith, nor history for dogma"—is ambiguous. The first meaning could be: the facts (in the narrow sense) do not automatically manifest the supernatural. This, of course, would be the heresy which says that natural facts can cause the supernatural, and this is the meaning which von Hügel disengaged, and was annoyed at, in its application to himself and Loisy.

The second meaning could be: the facts (in distinction to "real history") are not alone a *sufficient preparation* for the passage from facts to faith. They provide no sufficient base for a theoretical justification for such a passage; they provide no synthesis which manifests a type of solidarity between the facts and the faith; in contradistinction to "real history" they are not a satisfactory intermediary for the passage, either from the facts to the faith, or from the faith to the facts. Blondel's expressions give the impression that he vacillated between these two meanings, although without doubt he intended the second. His system of tradition, then, will "manifest the supernatural" and "suffice for the faith" in the sense that it prepares for a genuine, and not merely specious, passage between facts and faith. Blondel is merely extending the thought of his *Lettre* where, as we saw, it was not enough for the reasoning philosopher to scrutinize the Christian fact to be converted, but this second meaning is not the one von Hügel understood (*CE*, p. 305).

Von Hügel, on the other hand, since he saw no possibility of establishing the preambles apart from the fact-phenomena, cherished these with all his energy. His insistence that metaphysics cannot bypass facts leads us to his and Blondel's respective understanding of phenomena.

Phenomena. Von Hügel well said that the key to the whole misunderstanding was the meaning of "phenomena."[16] He asserted that Blondel did not sufficiently distinguish scriptural phenomena from their spiritual meaning. What he meant was that Blondel did not seem to face squarely enough the texts of the Gospels, especially on eschatology, before he tried to solve the question through his theory of tradition. The Baron claimed that one must first *traverse* the phenomena (the texts) before reaching the noumena, the spiritual significance, and his difficulty was precisely this: how can one discover the "real history" if the texts are not given their due consideration, for example, in studying the human knowledge of Christ? Von Hügel quested the historical character of many parts of the fourth Gospel which dealt with "the celestial Christ," while the Synoptics presented "the terrestrial Christ." He averred that in the

Synoptics Christ admitted a limited human knowledge, and
manifested intellectual growth, but not so in the Gospel of
St. John.

Blondel, therefore, wrote to him: "The heavenly Christ
cannot be what you say if the terrestrial Christ is not more
than you say." He meant that if Christ's human soul could
really grow in knowledge, there would be a growth in knowledge
of His Divinity, and, thus, the heavenly and the terrestrial
Christ would be theologically different.

Von Hügel did indeed distinguish exaggeratedly between
the synoptic Gospels and the fourth Gospel; this led him to
speak of the "Christ-object" and the "Christ-subject." The
Baron does not propose this distinction in an acceptable sense.
For him, the Christ-object becomes the terrestrial life of Christ,
and the Christ-subject becomes the celestial (post-Resurrec-
tional) life.[17] Thus, he does not, as he should, speak of both
Christ-subject and Christ-object as having had a terrestrial
existence. Such a separation logically leads to the Jesus-of-
history and the Christ-of-faith distinction that Loisy maintained.
Von Hügel bases his distinction on Rom 9.5 and II Cor 5.16.
This latter reads: "So that henceforth we know no one according
to the flesh. And even though we have known Christ according
to the flesh [a better reading is "we have known according to
the flesh Christ"] yet now we know him so no longer. "[18] Paul
is distinguishing between knowledge in the spirit and worldly
knowledge, but he does not here distinguish between Christ in
his glorified state *only*, and in his terrestrial state. Thus, von
Hügel's distinction between Christ-object and Christ-subject
should be operative even for the pre-Resurrection life of Christ
Himself. The distinction, however, should really be between
the Christ-phenomenon and the Christ-Person, or between
the phenomenological Christ and the Person of Christ.[19] This
would put the distinction, from the start, in the temporal order,
and allow for a mutual openness between "phenomena" and
"noumena," or history and faith.

(3) *Christ's consciousness of His Divinity.* We must recall

that, in his two little books, Loisy held that Christ believed and taught His own proximate return, the Parousia. This Loisy tries to establish by treating those parts of the Synoptics that clash with this idea as secondary layers. He further asked why Christ would have abandoned His disciples to ignorance on details about the Church when He could have revealed them without difficulty.

In what follows we must remember that we are speaking of the *human*, not the divine, consciousness of Christ. In the debate between Blondel and von Hügel, an ambiguity obscured the points being made. Blondel, from the beginning, rejected any denial of Christ's *consciousness of His Divinity*. Von Hügel, on the other hand, speaks about the consciousness of Christ *with regard to knowledge of future events*. These two positions are not quite the same, though they are related. Von Hügel begins *a posteriori* on the level of exegesis where, it seemed to him, that a *limited* knowledge was admitted. Blondel was on an *a priori* philosophical or theological level. He presupposes that to admit limitation in knowledge is to deny a state of being, a consciousness of divinity. The distinction and relation between these two points was nowhere handled in the debate; Blondel approached the problem from the aspect of consciousness, von Hügel from the aspect of knowledge.

Thus, Blondel presumed that von Hügel denied Christ's human consciousness of His Divinity. What exactly was von Hügel's position? He did, it is true, suggest that Christ was not "always ... in full beatific light," but this would imply only lack of knowledge about future details and a *dimness* of some aspect of Christ's consciousness of His Divinity, not its denial. The Baron claimed that he was pleading for a consciousness that leaves room for something "implicit and instinctive," for a consciousness that is really *in statu viatoris*. Later, in his published article, the Baron reacts against the insistence that Christ had a human consciousness of His Divinity that was "without restriction, without interruption, without progress, but immediately explicit and complete."[20]

Thus, the Baron held that Christ possessed a progressive,

human consciousness of His Divinity. But what does the phrase, "without interruption" ("*sans arret*"), mean? It is linked, naturally, as a contrast with what follows: "without interruption, ... but immediately explicit and complete" knowledge. This interpretation is in accord with the Baron's idea of the Agony in the Garden where the "beatific light" was not complete. It also justifies the Baron's surprise (*CE*, p. 310) that Blondel defended a consciousness which is "*continuous*, direct, and explicit, of His *full* Divinity." (Von Hügel meant that, if Christ lacked some knowledge, His human soul did not have an explicit and comprehensive knowledge of all that was in God.) Another key to von Hügel's thought is found in the series of articles previously mentioned, *Lettres Romaines*. The Baron revised the proofs for these articles five or six months before his *Quinzaine* article, and in them the anonymous author opted for Christ's progressive human consciousness of His Divinity.[21] He claimed that some authors spoke of the infant Christ as if He were a mature man, and hence he implicitly questioned the dimensions of His consciousness when He was a baby, and while asleep. The Baron's statements, therefore, suggest a theory about the very early stages of Christ's consciousness, while, for the rest of Christ's life, he holds that the texts themselves suggest that there were moments when His human consciousness of divinity was instinctive, implicit, and darkened, and not always full and explicit. No other explanation will be in accord with his expressions. When the Baron is at his boldest, speaking of the Agony in the Garden and the "mysterious distress" on the Cross, he says, merely, that "the Divine light reaches Him only across dolorous obscurities."

In a later chapter we will attempt to clarify von Hügel's notion of consciousness. Here, we might recall that consciousness may be considered under two aspects. It may be looked at as an experience, or as a witness to this experience; as an empirical state, or as an intellectualized and rational state; as an awareness, or as an awareness of an awareness; as something spontaneous, and as something reflexive. It seems that von Hügel held that Christ was, at times, in only one or other of these states, while Blondel, until nearly the end of the discussion, maintained that Jesus was always in both states.

Further, Blondel asserted that the Baron totally denied Christ's human consciousness of His Divinity, and this explains a subsequent puzzling statement by Blondel. On Sept. 16, 1904 the Baron published a letter in *Quinzaine* in reply to an attack on his previous *Quinzaine* article by Abbé Wehrlé, Blondel's friend. Blondel said that this letter cleared up the Baron's "worst equivocations" by now giving them "a more clearly orthodox sense, and the last phrase I think expresses almost our own thought."[22] What was this last phrase?

The Baron had said he believed in "a human progressive consciousness of His Divinity which was there from the first." He ended the letter as follows:

> He who had consciousness and what He had in His human consciousness was God, yes. But this tells us nothing about the quality, the degree or the stability ("fixité") of this consciousness, especially at the beginning. Certainly our own personal human consciousness is given confusedly at the beginning and becomes explicit and reflexive afterwards ("en dernier lieu"). And [so also] the complete meaning of Christ's own personality, which as Divine was infinite, can never be exhausted by the human, that is limited, consciousness of Christ.

But this was exactly what the Baron had been saying all along. Even his previous strong word "interruption" is here implied in the statement that the "stability" of this consciousness is unknown to us. It is strange that Blondel now saw von Hügel veering toward his own position. Fr. Marlé compares von Hügel to Bultmann: Bultmann denied the Messianic consciousness of Christ; the Baron defended "the ignorance by Christ of His Divinity."[23] This blunt statement cannot stand. As we have shown previously with regard to the word "interruption," so here "stability," almost certainly, involves only the permanence of explicit awareness.

The Baron asserted that it is beyond the scope of historical method to show Christ as having "continuous, direct and explicit

consciousness of His full Divinity." The word "full" expresses
his position that the human knowledge of Christ was deliberately
limited in the Incarnation. This fact of this limitation, he held,
was a conclusion demanded by historical method, but the
method itself showed also that Christ was conscious of His
Messianic role. This Messianic consciousness, if "pressed,"
would reveal that the union between the Messiah and God was
so "purified, intimate and profound" that the Messiah was
truly God.[24] If an observer can "press" this data so that it
yields the idea of Divinity, then von Hügel is certainly not
holding that Christ Himself was without consciousness of His
Divinity. We must recall that von Hügel's continual point of
departure is the question of the limitation of Christ's human
knowledge on earth, and not the metaphysical question of
consciousness.[25] He contrasts the Synoptics with John. He
finds that John pictured as a totally actualized perfection in the
very beginning of Christ's earthly life what the Synoptics see as
an unfolding bud. He began to contrast John and the Synoptics
in their portrayal of the celestial and terrestrial Christ respectively. This sweeping dichotomy is unfortunate, for he had
already found indications of the "celestial" Christ in the Synoptic phenomena.

CHAPTER EIGHT

BLONDEL: THE PAROUSIA
AND TRADITION

Christ's knowledge. Blondel did not handle the problem of Jesus' human knowledge apart from the question of His human consciousness of His Divinity. Thus, he says that in this consciousness of His Divinity there can be an intensive, but not an extensive, growth.[1] Von Hügel points to Mk 13.32: "But of that day and hour no one knows, neither the angels in Heaven, nor the Son, but the Father only"; Blondel, however, is unwilling to admit that this implies real limited knowledge, for it would then imply also the possibility of an extensive growth.

What does this "intensive-extensive"growth mean? Blondel applies "extensive" to consciousness both of Divinity and knowledge. If Christ could truly grow in human knowledge about the future, for example, He would thus grow in human knowledge of the divine essence, i.e. extensively. This is exactly what the Baron had found in Mark, and what some of the Fathers had held. Blondel made no distinction between limited human knowledge and error, although some such distinction cried out for clarification all during the debate.[2] Both Blondel, working from philosophy, and von Hügel, working from exegesis, fuse the last two terms of the trilogy: unlimited conceptual knowledge, limited conceptual knowledge, mistaken judgment.

Later, after his article, Blondel wrote the Baron explaining the Kenosis of the Word in such a way as to allow growth *respectu*

conscientiae (with regard to consciousness). This would leave
Christ *in fieri*, inadequate to Himself in some way, submitted to
a genuine trial of obscurity."[3] Blondel admitted that this position
accounted for all the texts the Baron had adduced, but claimed
that it was different from the Baron's position. He slightly
distorted that position, charging that von Hügel held two Christs
who were not just two states of the one being; this the Baron
often denied. Ultimately, however, it seems that their thought
of Christ's human consciouness of His Divinity was more in
accord than appears at first sight.

We have to realize clearly that there were two separate
questions being handled simultaneously: (1) was Christ's human
knowledge limited? (2) did Christ fall into a mistake formally
connected with religion? It is interesting that the first question
was treated in the following year, 1905, by the Sulpician, Marius
Lepin.[4] According to him, Christ had two orders of human
knowledge, one inferior and experimental, the other superior and
supernatural, *independent of the human faculties* ("organes").
Under this distinction, aspects of the superior (infused) knowledge would not, by divine will, flow into the human faculties.
Thus, when Christ said that He did not know the date of the end
of the world, He was not feigning or implying that He did not
have a mission to reveal what He really knew in His human
knowledge. He did not have such knowledge in a human *conceptual* way, and thus could not reveal it since speech flows
from concept. Lepin's presentation found qualified favor among
many Catholics at the time, but von Hügel made no reference
to it and did not employ the theological notion of infused knowledge.

The second question, namely: did Christ fall into a mistake
formally connected with religion? brings us to the problem of
the Parousia.

Parousia.   The Baron maintained that Jesus' words about
not knowing "the day nor the hour" could not be accounted for
by a mental reservation. Likewise, when Jesus said, "Amen I
say to you, this generation will not pass away till all these things

have been accomplished," He meant His public and glorious return, not merely a spiritual one, and He was referring to the contemporary generation.[5] In the published article von Hügel suggested no way out of the dilemma. He leaned heavily, as we have seen, on the need for friction in life and religion. He maintained that the first witnesses have fixed forever the lines of Christian history, and that a metaphysic cannot bypass it. The Synoptics were not perfect portraits, but they were closer to the phenomenal truth than John who adds to the Synoptics the traits of "the eternal Christ." The Baron, however, offered no solution *but* friction, and confined himself to showing that Blondel had not accounted for the Synoptic statements about Christ's ignorance, and his expectation of a proximate Parousia. Thus, we see that he accepted Loisy's conception of Christ as not merely hoping for an imminent Parousia, but as actually basing his teaching on it. The Baron held that Christ so acted, not through ignorance, but in error.

Blondel, on the other hand, never explained Mk 13.32: "But of that day or hour no one knows, neither the angels in heaven, nor the Son, but the Father only"; he admitted that the sense escaped him. He suspected a contradiction in that the Baron simultaneously held Mk 13.32, and yet said that Our Lord was convinced that the Parousia would be soon. (At this period von Hügel probably agreed with Loisy that Our Lord admitted ignorance only about the *exact* day or hour within the generation.) Blondel continually bypassed Scripture in an effort to find the solution in tradition and real history, but tradition itself had not given a definitive explanation of this text.

Blondel claimed that if one took the Parousia "literally" (that is, in von Hügel's sense of finding Christ in error in this regard) one would submit Jesus to completely human illusions in violation of certain texts; one would rule out *a priori* other paths to a solution, and find, not development, but evolution without finality; one would deny the design of Providence in Christianity, and be led to hold that other doctrines, such as Christology and Christianity itself, are only phases, and perhaps even religion itself. (We might add here that other teachings of

Our Lord could also become phases, for example, the moral teaching of Our Lord in view of the Parousia, and the existence of Hell which the Baron clung to most tenaciously). The Baron could not logically answer these powerful objections.

The Baron took the position that, unless Our Lord were subject to this ignorance, He could not totally sympathize with us in our obscurities, but notice that, since the Baron includes error here, Our Lord would be in a worse state than ordinary men of intellectual integrity, for He would have been certain of the false. On the other hand, Blondel maintained that unless Our Lord humanly foresaw our human trials, He would not have had true sympathy *for us*. The Baron's thought, however, would envisage the human soul of Christ as having sympathy for mankind *in general*, while the knowledge of specific future individuals would be reserved to the Divine intellect.

Blondel's own explanation of the general picture of the Parousia is valuable:

> The expectation of the Parousia was only a first imaginative synthesis. For minds which were earthly and slow to believe, which had been prepared by all the Jewish Messianism, it was a point of insertion. It was the prolongation ... of all their political ambitions and sensual eagerness. It was a sketch about the metaphysical destiny of man within reach of the fishermen of Tiberias. It was the commencement of the transposition from the material sense to the spiritual sense, for the Parousia seemed to be simultaneously of the earth and not of it. Was it not also the providential means of communicating to simple souls the *élan*, the enthusiasm, the absolute detachment, the inebriation of martyrdom? Was it not especially the concrete realization of a truth which the annual feasts of the liturgy artificially express, that the world is incessantly close to ending for each one of us? The truth that the goodness which God promises to His children is not just some sort of a vague idealization or other, but a full and real satisfaction, the transformation, both material and spiritual together, of the entire man and of the universal order.[6]

This primitive, imaginative synthesis may have occasioned a temporary illusion; as the vehicle for transmitting the Divine force, it may have been a strategy of the Son, or a work of the will of the Father. But it was only the human and deciduous ('caduc') aspect of an originally divine truth. If you do not hold this, Blondel warns the Baron, beware of the abyss you are inclining towards.

Blondel goes on to say that Christians felt no deception because in the Good News there was something beyond the expectation of an Eldorado. There was an appeal to a doctrine of sin and of justification, to penance and interior life which was intimately attached to the person of the Savior. One loved Christ more than His glory, and the Gospel resulted in an invincible love for the adored person of the Master.[7]

Blondel's thesis is bound up with his remarkable theory of tradition.

The notion of Tradition.   Just as in his *Lettre* Blondel had criticized existing apologetic systems with an eye on the logic of action, and ended in crescendo with an explanation of that logic, so in his *Histoire et Dogme* he criticized historicism with his eye continually on the idea of tradition, and ended in crescendo with an explanation of the notion of tradition as related to the logic of action. This theory is important today, and has found support among first-rate theologians.[8] Therefore let us situate it within the present debate.

Blondel first pointed out inadequate views of tradition. It cannot be reduced to something that simply struggles against the forgetfulness often occasioned by the mere lapse of time. It is not a principally oral transmission of historical facts, truths received, teachings communicated. It is not merely something that reports things said explicitly, prescribed expressly, or done deliberately in the past by men whose considered ideas alone are sought for as they themselves formulated them. Rather:

> It is a preserving power [which is] at the same time conquering. It discovers and formulates truths which the past lived, without being able to articulate them or define them explicitly; it enriches the intellectual patrimony by minting little by little the total deposit and making it fructify.

Its power is preserving because it transmits from the past not so much the intellectual aspect as the vital reality. Without doubt, tradition bases itself on texts but above all it is founded on an ever-active experience that allows tradition to remain, in certain respects, the master of the texts instead of being strictly subject to them. It makes something pass from the implicitly live in the past to the explicitly formulated, and each of the faithful, including the exegete, contributes to this development, which makes use of all human and scientific resources. But tradition does not move by dialectics, or through erudite research; it speaks with an authority independent of all grounds of judgment. The earliest traditions engendered a consciousness that God assured their truth. But the magisterium that proposes tradition has only a negative concursus, and thus God wills that man use all the resources of science in determining a real tradition.

In *L'Action* Blondel asked, "has life a meaning?" The question is answered in action—*all* action, including thought. He now applies this to tradition. The justification of tradition must be able to reach the subconscious, the unreasoned, the provisory, to what is partially irreducible to explicit thought. The philosophy of action does this. It studies the multiple ways, regular and methodically determinable, by which clear and formulated knowledge arises from the profound realities on which it nourishes itself. Certain words we heard as children and did not thoroughly understand, take on profound meaning later, in the light of acquired experience and progress in reflexion. They have been preserved in an ever-working memory which is not exclusively intellectual.

So it is with tradition. Christ did not, from the beginning, commit to the Church a totally explicit, completely formulated truth: "You cannot bear them now" (Jn 16.12). More, He did not present His revealed truth under a completely intellectual form lest the narrowness of man's intelligence distort it. A truly supernatural truth must be presented as a seed capable of progressive growth. Christ promised the guidance of the Holy Spirit; the human dimension within which the Spirit would operate would simply be: "keep my commands." What a man cannot totally understand, he can fully do, and in the doing he keeps alive his consciousness of that still half-obscure reality. Thus the Church is a proof of herself. She carries in her centuries-old experience and in her constant practice the verification of what she believes and what she teaches. Something in the Church escapes scientific control, and it is she who, without ever neglecting the sphere of exegesis and history, controls them, since she has in the very tradition another means of knowing her Author, of participating in His life, of connecting the facts with the dogmas, and of correlating essentials and accretions of ecclesiastical teaching.

Although he works his notion of action into his theory of tradition, Blondel does not find that theory "an element properly scientific and absolutely reducible to intellectual justifications."[9] His own "facts do not suffice for dogma" except for the person who experiences this in the gift of faith. But Blondel exquisitely clarified the intermediary between dogma and facts.

What did Blondel establish by his theory of tradition? Christ's knowledge, and a possible error on His part, were two points at issue in the controversy. The first point is not really solved by the tradition argument. What does tradition tell us about Christ's human knowledge? Loisy pointed out that, on many points, tradition does not solve problems because it did not envisage *our* problem. As regards the human knowledge of Christ, this is not totally true because similar questions were broached in the Monothelite controversy in the seventh century, and in the scholastic speculations in the twelfth century, on the beatific vision in Christ's soul. But it is curious that only once in the debate was a text from the Magisterium adduced specifically on this point, and that text was inconclusive.[10] Pertinent magisterial decisions came only after the present debate, as we will see in the next chapter. The historical method had given rise to new problems.

Thus Blondel's argument from tradition does not touch one of the points at issue. Tradition, gathered into a bright center of self-consciousness in the Magisterium, and most fully conscious there, had not definitively affirmed that Christ was humanly aware of the date of the Parousia. In fact, we can say that the logic of action, as applied to tradition, showed that the question was *not* of faith.

Does Blondel's approach through the logic of action of the early Church help us in the problem of the probability of human *error* in Christ's teaching? Here his approach is more forceful and convincing. Even though he did not develop his argument from tradition in detail on this specific point, we have enough of his thought to spell out its general movement.

After our Lord's Resurrection, the Church made a primitive, imaginative synthesis of His words on the Parousia. After some time, elements in this first synthesis were re-arranged. This was occasioned not only by the delay of the Parousia, but also by the new insights they achieved into the significance of Christ's death and Resurrection, and of the organization, rooted in Christ's words, of hierarchical leaders. This very *act* of rethinking and resynthesizing (as in some of Luke, Acts, John, and 2 Peter), shows that they were beginning to admit a confusion as to what, exactly, was to have been imminent. Their life in Christ brought forth elements of the original revelation that had lain fallow. The first synthesis was not a deception, but a temporary delusion which their Christian living began to uncover. They came to see that the person of Christ was more central and more to be loved than their concepts of a Parousia.[11] This deep knowledge grew out of a way of living that had been communicated to them through discipleship and faith. Thus specific life-knowledge reached back to nothing but Christ. If they had recognized a grave error at the basis of His teaching, the result should have been a collapse in action. The enigmatic quality of His statements emerged clearly into Christian consciousness. The logic of action through the Spirit drew forth from deep in the group-personality an awareness of an obscurity in the tradition they had received, and a realization that they had not irrevocably understood the proximate event as Christ's imminent, visible Parousia.

It is clear that this situation in the early Church necessarily, and in the last resort, rests on providence. Providence could have permitted momentary illusion, but it could not have intended to further its designs by formal error on the part of its principal agent. Christ's teaching would have been a strange *felix culpa*, stirring up only false desires (p. 259). Thus the main thrust of the argument entails the action of providence, since the logic of action, if it is artificially isolated from providence, cannot alone protect itself totally from deviation.[12] This is not to say that providence, in Blondel's system, is an artificial element pasted on from the outside. It is interior to that system, beginning, in germ, with the demand that life have a meaning, and leading to the option before a hypothetical Judaeo-Christian providence. Unfortunately, Blondel also used the tradition idea to show that there had to be prevision and explicit foresight in detail in Christ's human mind. In handling two points at once, he weakened the force of his argument. Blondel had nevertheless aimed a forceful attack on Loisy's position that the central message of the Gospel was the imminence of a totally transformed earth in the Kingdom. The logic of action showed that the center of the message lay elsewhere.

Blondel did not aim at, and was incapable of making, the necessary thorough analysis of the eschatological texts themselves, and, without this, one is left with an impression of simple *a priori* reasoning. But Blondel had meditated long and deeply on the New Testament, and what he had to say deserves a hearing by the exegetes. Today the liberal Protestant tendency is to accept an error on the part of Jesus, and to consider this unimportant. Blondel made some powerful, and still valid, remarks about the dichotomy between a Jesus who erred and a subsequent Church. Von Hügel, too, despite his own theory, later indicated further difficulties in such a position. Von Hügel was disturbed at Blondel's passing over the exegetical field. The major difficulty, he thought, was to admit that Tradition could give phenomenal knowledge of a prior time.[13]

In 1905, Blondel published the article "De la valeur historique de dogme," in which he explained that some events, which are contested by historians, as in the infancy narratives, can be established legitimately by tradition; but this is done, not solely by historical title, but by faith.[14]

On March 25, 1905, von Hügel wrote a very revealing letter to Blondel in which he specified certain qualifications. In an important, but unpublished, section of this letter he said that two points must be distinguished:

> The one would be to say or imply that Christianity could be true without *any* of its doctrines being grounded on historical fact in the full and ordinary sense of this word. I have never believed that, and if tomorrow I were to find myself (impossible supposition) sure of the *non-factuality* of all these facts—I would certainly feel that I was obliged to stop proclaiming myself Christian and Catholic. Christianity is essentially the religion of Incarnation; it is really God incarnated in time and space. The other would be to believe that Christianity could be and remain true without *all* its doctrines, including some which are apparently historico-phenomenal, being directly grounded on such an historico-phenomenal factuality.
>
> Certainly if it is a matter of defined doctrines, never could they cease to be true for the believer in a very real sense of the word. But in the history of dogma we see modifications in the interpretation of the category to which such or such a doctrine belongs. This truly seems to lead to the conclusion that while it is impossible for *all* the 'facts' of Christianity not at all to be also facts of a full and ordinary historicity, *one or another*, may in time be discovered to be, *not less true than formerly but of another type of truth*. But this is precisely *because the full historicity of so many other parts remains* and this can benefit those doctrines whose full historical factuality occupies us.

This general statement by the Baron needs specific examples in order to be understood. Later we will analyze statements like this one, and find an extreme position contained therein. Apply it, for example, to the Virginal conception—the import in these generalities then becomes clear.

During the debate, von Hügel made a distinction between the terrestrial Christ and the celestial Christ—a most misleading distinction that Blondel understood as pertaining to the order of being, or of the Hypostatic Union, whereas von Hügel intended it as a distinction between states of knowledge.[15] The meaning of this distinction was one of the sources of confusion in the debate.

No one, at the time, more clearly saw the *larger issues* involved than Blondel. He demonstrated that historical and exegetical interpretation can never totally extricate itself from some prior synthesis, from a philosophy of life, from a "metaphysic." His very vision at times blurred the specific details of the question. Yet it is only just, to remind ourselves that he intervened in this debate as a man and as a Christian, even more than as a philosopher. He saw a real danger to faith and he went to its roots. Many French priests who lived through that period have said that no matter what one feels about the details of his approach, he was the only one whose vision provided light at a time when the lowering clouds were beginning to hide the very nature of the Church.

CHAPTER NINE

TYRRELL: DOGMA AND AUTHORITY

The spirit that lives in us ... has already passed sentence of death on Medievalism, which has been tried experimentally, weighed in the balance, and found wanting (George Tyrrell, *Medievalism*, 1908, p. 175).

Endless patience; the knowledge of when to yield and bend, when and where to hold out ... these things I feel I must practice ... at a constant cost (von Hügel to Tyrrell, 1904).

A. GEORGE TYRRELL

George Tyrrell's life reminds one of a comet that raced across the sky, burned out in the atmosphere of friction, and disappeared.[1] To plot the position of that comet at any one moment is an extremely demanding task. Tyrrell's character was too rich and fluid for simplification. Maude Petre, who perhaps was closest to Tyrrell, said, at the Congress of the History of Christianity, after von Hügel's death: "Von Hügel was surely a saint but not very surely a martyr. Tyrrell on the contrary was not surely a saint, but he was surely a martyr."[2]

The long friendship between Tyrrell and von Hügel began on Sept. 20, 1897, when the Baron, then forty-five, wrote the Jesuit priest of thirty-eight in appreciation of his book *Nova et*

Vetera. Their friendship ripened to such an extent that by Nov. 30, 1899 Tyrrell wrote:

> I cannot tell you ... the strong developing influence your friendship has exerted upon my mind; in how many cases it has determined me at points of bifurcation to choose this road rather than that ... making my mind more of a Jerusalem, i.e. a city at unity with itself.

A slight estrangement arose later, but they remained loyal friends to the end.

Perhaps no three friends were less alike than Miss Petre, Tyrrell, and von Hügel. Maude Petre says that Tyrrell was as complex as she was simple and direct.[3] Von Hügel observed that his own temperament was so different from Tyrrell's that he rarely saw him at play.[4] The Baron told him that he had "a German brain, an Irish heart,"[5] and he later warned him of his "very hot, vehement, and sarcastic personal tone" in controversy.[6]

Tyrrell's intellectal powers were of a high order. When he first became known in the Catholic world he was thought, by many, to be a successor to Newman. Yet unlike Loisy, whose mind operated in cold arctic regions (as he himself put it, "I cannot love and ... yet I am capable of it ... and I have need of it"),[7] Tyrrell was a person of warmth and impulse, wit, and boyishness. His ideas take body in a smooth and easy style; rarely does one meet a writer who employs illustration and metaphor so naturally; but both his character and his style of thought laid the ground for disaster. One feels that he could have learned from his own adage, "If you squeeze a metaphor hard enough, it yields poison."[8] He more readily saw the poison in the metaphors of others than in his own. Tyrrell was certainly not a "safe" man; no one could be, who said: "Like Moses, I had rather be damned with the mass of humanity than saved alone or even with a minority."[9]

Tyrrell's thought. It is impossible to understand von Hügel's position without a somewhat extended treatment of

Tyrrell's thought, and for that we must recall the major events of his life (1861–1909). Born in Dublin and brought up as a Protestant, he was converted, entered the Society of Jesus in 1879, and was ordained in 1891. His first book, *Nova et Vetera* (1897), was a series of conferences. Among other writings, he published *Hard Sayings, External Religion, The Faith of the Millions* (1897–1901). *Oil and Wine* (1901–02) did not get through censorship and *Lex Orandi* (1903) barely passed scrutiny. He privately circulated *The Church and the Future* (1902–03), and *A Letter to a Friend, A Professor of Anthropology* (1903). In 1905 he wrote *Lex Credendi*, but it was not published until later. In 1906 he was dismissed from the Society for refusing to retract his ideas in *Letter to a Friend*, and the same year he defended himself in *A Much Abused Letter*. After the publication of *Lamentabili* (July 3–4, 1907), and *Pascendi* (Sept. 8, 1907), he was deprived of the sacraments for his criticisms on Oct. 22, 1907. In May of 1907 he signed the preface to his *Through Scylla and Charybdis*, but the work did not appear until the following summer.

This last book is a road-map, so to speak, of his total thought. It links early articles that had been approved by the censors with his latest thought of 1907. It straddles *Lamentabili* and *Pascendi*, being written before, but appearing afterwards, and is less biased by the controversy that bulks so large in *A Much Abused Letter* and *Medievalism* (1908), a reply to Cardinal Mercier's Pastoral of that year which criticized him. *Christianity at the Crossroads* (1909) was published posthumously by Maude Petre.

Tyrrell had been a strict Thomist during his professorship at Stoneyhurst (1894–96). He was introduced to Scriptural exegesis only in 1898 when von Hügel gave him his article on the Documents of the Hexateuch.[10] Under the Baron's encouragement he learned German, read J. Weiss and Loisy, and by the time of his death he had completely gone over to the eschatological school of Weiss and Schweitzer.[11]

Tyrrell summed up his view of the genesis of the contemporary problem with a summary of A. White's *A History of the*

Warfare of Science with Theology (New York, 1903):

> [There was conflict] as regards the matter, time and date of cre-
> ation, its sundry details; as regards the form, the delineation, and
> the size of the earth, the possibility and existence of the antipodes,
> the geocentric theory ... as regards natural signs and wonders,
> comets ...; as regards geology, the deluge, the antiquity of
> man ..., the theory of man's decadence; in the matter ... of
> causes and remedies of diseases ... ; in the explanation of excep-
> tional psychical phenomena ...; in the matter of philology
> and the origin of languages; finally as regards the origin of
> religion, of Christianity, of the Church and her institutions and
> of the Sacred Scriptures. ...[12]

White had said that the conflict was not between science and
religion, but between science and theology. Tyrrell went a step
farther, and said that the conflict was between science and a
pseudo-science we call dogmatic theology, or theologism. This
theologism intellectualizes revelation. It treats prophetic
enigmas and mysteries as principles of exactly determinable
intellectual value. Then, as a sort of revealed philosophy, it
pretends to impose these exact deductions as binding in faith.
This is the "Dogmatic Fallacy." Theologism has attacked
science

> often violently and injuriously, as being blasphemous and heret-
> ical ... as contrary to the Sacred Scriptures, to the consensus of
> the Fathers, to the very substance of Christian revelation; ...
> in each instance, science, beaten back again and again, has at last
> come out victorious, while the theologians have been reduced,
> first, to disingenuous compromises, and finally to discreet silence,
> ... and what was defended as the very essence and substance of
> revealed doctrine has been quietly let drop into the class of non-
> essentials and accidentals, and the whole episode buried in
> edifying oblivion.[13]

The solution, then, lies in separating religion or revelation and
theology ("theologism"), and thus exonerating religion from the
burden of guilt we should lay wholly on the shoulders of theology.

Revelation and prophetic truth. Revelation is the self-manifestation of the divine in our inward life.[14] It embodies religious experiences, both individual and collective, and is given in, and *with*, these experiences; it is not statement but experience, and "represents" the hidden cause of the total experience. Tyrrell conceives that revelation consists in the *total* religious experience, and not simply in the mental element of that experience.[15] He nevertheless admits mental elements in the experience, despite some slipshod statements.

Within the term "revelation" Tyrrell distinguishes three notions: (1) revelation as the action of God—a use of the word he does not often resort to; (2) revelation as received experientially by humans; (3) revelation as then communicated to, or recorded for, others—"prophetic truth."[16] Tyrrell's ideas can be schematized as follows:

I. *Revelation:*
    a) as experienced by the Biblical personages and the Apostles.
    b) as experienced by later individuals and collectivities.

II. *Prophetic Truth:*
    a) as communicated biblically, or by the primitive Church with its symbols and categories. This is *normative.*
    b) As communicated thereafter by councils, by the collectivity, and even by individuals. This is to be tested by the former.

(a) *First level of prophetic truth.* Those who made prophetic utterances would have refused to be tied to exact statements of their speculative value, but would have insisted rather on their *pragmatical, provisional*, and *approximative* truth as far as the "fact-world" is concerned, and on the necessarily indefinable nature of the "ought-world" and its eternal realities.[17] Prophetic truth is not the divine realities (or facts) themselves, but it is the imaginative, prophetic "presentment" of them which is their moving, living shadow. It is as real and concrete as the divine realities, but by no means conceptual or intellectual. Theology has forgotten this fact.

(b) *Second level: Councils.* Tyrrell says that later Church symbols are prophetic truth; he uses, as an example, the statement of the Athanasian Creed: "The Son is generated, the Spirit proceeds but is not generated." He claims that when the theologian finishes analyzing the notion "the Spirit proceeds," he arrives at "Spirit," a metaphor, and "proceeds," also a metaphor, since the Spirit does not proceed exactly as a work of its maker, nor as breath from a man, nor can spirit beget or expire other spirits. The theologian is left with the content "X equals X," but he should know the meaning of the equation since he says his salvation depends on it. It is an impossible situation. Thus, we are reduced to the position that these propositions do not have metaphysical, but only protective (devotional and practical) value. They dimly shadow forth a truth which defies definition, yet which excludes Unitarianism, Arianism, Sabellianism, and any other impertinence of intellectual curiosity. Revelation is under divine "guaranty, whereas the latter [theology and dogma] is fallible with the fallibility of the human mind."[18] Dogmatic decisions of the Church add nothing to, but only assert, the Apostolic revelation. Their sole faith-content is that part of it of which they are protective. It is a fundamental principle that Councils may not introduce new doctrines. Their function is to check innovation.[19]

In *Medievalism* Tyrrell was especially vehement against Vatican Council I. Originally, he says, a bishop was the highest ecclesiastical official answerable to no other official, but only to the universal Church of which he was the organ. But the new theology has concentrated the universal Church in the person of the Pope, and we have a double episcopate in each diocese. There is not a trace of this system in the first six centuries of Church history, but while the Bishop is the first official, what the Church really bows to is a *divine tradition of which the entire Church*, and not merely the episcopate, is the organ and depository. What is tradition in Tyrrell's thinking?

"Tradition" may be used for the process of passing on, or for that which is passed on, but not for the persons who pass it on.

> Even if the episcopate be the sole depository of tradition and
> the sole organ of its transmission, we cannot say that the episco-
> pate or the Pope is tradition ... tradition is to the episcopate or
> to the Pope what the law is to the judge. It is a rule set above
> them by higher authority; a rule which they must apply and
> interpret, but which they did not make and may not alter. Tradi-
> tion is the *faith that lives in the whole Church down from generation
> to generation*, of which the entire body, and not a mere handful
> of officials, is *the depository and organ of transmission*. Of this
> rule and law, the Holy Spirit diffused in the hearts of all the faith-
> ful is the author; the episcopate is merely the servant, the witness,
> the interpreter.[20]

To be truly a part of tradition a council must be confirmed
subsequently by the faithful. Tradition has the same inerrancy
as Scripture, but the mechanical view of inerrancy in Scripture
has yielded to a looser, and more dynamic, notion of inspiration.
So the inerrancy of the Councils must be interpreted with a
similar latitude. The utterances of authority must be given a
greater latitude than formerly.[21]

B. VON HÜGEL'S AFFINITIES

Von Hügel's reaction to Tyrrell's thought throws into relief the
significance of the Baron's own ideas; he wrote, for instance,
that Tyrrell had been

> chivalrously anxious to save me from any responsibility for his
> more polemical writings and the more adventurous of his practical
> steps; and hence in such cases he would not show me the final
> drafts—indeed, often he would not tell me what he was meditat-
> ing—till after he had irrevocably committed himself.
> ... to me he owed his initiation into German biblical criticism
> and a good deal of the psychology and philosophy of religion.
> Thus I am not indeed responsible for this most independent mind's
> conclusions, but I cannot well let him bear all the blame,
> where I did so much to stimulate his thought and conclusions.[22]

The extent of von Hügel's influence on Tyrrell (and of the rarely mentioned influence of Tyrrell on von Hügel) is a complicated question, but for us the more important question is: what positions espoused by Tyrrell did the Baron also hold?

The answer to this is threefold: (1) prudentially; the Baron began to reject the tone and attitude of Tyrrell's response to authority in 1907 after *Pascendi*;[23] (2) doctrinally, he more and more became apprehensive and reserved in view of the immanentism he thought he discerned in Tyrrell;[24] (3) and also doctrinally, he approved a great many of Tyrrell's positions on the nature of the Church. Since this last point has never been clearly brought out, it is worth dwelling upon here.

Von Hügel and Tyrrell's ecclesiology. On June 30, 1904 the Baron asked for copies of *Letter to a Friend* and *The Church and the Future*, in order to circulate them. Both contain Tyrrell's newly formulated, though not yet fully developed theory on the Church. The Baron hesitated about publication of *The Church and the Future,* which had been privately circulated:

> *The Church and the Future* is a grand piece of thinking and writing, but is, of course, a very big mouthful for almost everyone. And I should grieve if something so intrinsically great were to be given a "succès de scandale."[25]

In 1904 the Baron told Tyrrell he had read his *Letter to a Friend*, and greatly appreciated it. The *Letter* presents some of Tyrrell's ideas as to faith not being an assent to concepts. In the Church he distinguishes between the

> collective subconsciousness of the "People of God" and the consciously formulated mind and will of the governing section of the Church. May not our faith in the latter be at times weak or nil, and yet our faith in the former strong and invincible? (*A Much Abused Letter*, p. 55).

When *Scylla and Charybdis* appeared in 1907, the Baron was preoccupied with the authority crisis, and with the final preparation of his own *Mystical Element*, but he did record his reaction to one of the book's most important essays, "From Heaven or

From Men?" Tyrrell asserted that his whole conception of the Church

> stands or falls with its [the essay's] main contention. The authority of the collective over the individual mind as being the adequate organ through which truth, whether natural or supernatural, progressively reveals itself, has always been the fundamental assumption of Catholicism—*Securus judicat orbis terrarum.* Any interpretation of papal infallibility which finds the organ of Catholic truth in the miraculously guided brain of one man; which renders futile the collective experience and reflection of the whole Church, destroys the very essence of Catholicism in favour of a military dictatorship which is the apotheosis of individualism. To interpret the Church's collective mind is the office of bishops, councils, and popes. ... They are the witnesses to, not the creators of, the Church's faith and practice. They speak *ex cathedra* so far as they say what she says (p. 355).

Tyrrell went on to say that the representation of the Pope as God's vicegerent standing outside and above the community is mere symbolism. "As a pictorial and imaginative explanation of the source and meaning of authority, all this may be quite harmless, useful, and even necessary ... but squeeze any metaphor hard enough and it will yield poison" (p. 364). What we have cited seems to be the main contention of the chapter. In Tyrrell's essay the Baron found "the nucleus of his teachings, the nucleus that will abide." He found "its great main contention—so strong, so true, so pathetically winning."[26] Still, he was perplexed. He found that Tyrrell's emphasis on immanence allowed a more facile criticism of absolutist authority than would the necessary dualism of immanence *and* transcendence. Although the Baron admitted "You are so right in your general conclusions," he did not go as far as Tyrrell in his explanation of papal infallibility.

With regard to *Medievalism* the Baron wrote, on Dec. 7, 1908:

> You know how deeply I cared for and care for your *Medievalism*, and how glad I was for the line you took there, as to the interpretableness of the [Vatican] Decrees in the sense we wish.[27]

In the essay on the Vatican Council (pp. 78–87) Tyrrell asserted that the Council was not free, representative, or unanimous, but this was not what von Hügel praised; he never referred to this idea, and, after all, he felt himself obliged to hold, as we will see, some doctrine of papal infallibility. Tyrrell's interpretation of the Vatican decree was, however, similar to a suggestion von Hügel had made a few months before *Medievalism* appeared:[28]

> Now, though it was the deepest desire of the absolutist majority to merge the episcopate into the papacy, to eliminate every vestige of power that might in any way act as a check on Rome's claim to the monopoly of ecclesiastical power, ... yet for very shame they dared not define boldly what they desired. They were forced to speak of the bishops as of co-judges and co-definers; to give them an infallibility when "in union with the Pope." ... this qualification of the utter nonentity of the episcopate is meaningless and merely verbal. Still, it acknowledges tacitly that the Council has no power to abolish the episcopate; that so far as it seems to do so, it may be ignored (p. 85).

This interpretation of the Council is what von Hügel had in mind in his praise of *Medievalism*, but it is difficult to say how much he approved of other ideas in the book. It must be recalled, however, that von Hügel insisted that one consider the literary form in all writing. (Once he said that parts of Paul must be taken with "a grain of salt.") He definitely classed *Medievalism* as belonging to the literary form of polemics;[29] it would therefore be unjust to hold him to all Tyrrell's positions, and his later thought shows that he was not in total accord. *Christianity at the Crossroads* (1909), which contains a great deal on the eschatological conception of the Kingdom, was admired by the Baron, but as a book "only for the troubled few."[30]

In the light of what we have just seen, the judgment of the Baron's younger friend, Bernard Holland, in 1926, after von Hügel's death, is pertinent:

> The Baron was not, I think, in full touch, notwithstanding their continuous correspondence and many meetings, with Tyrrell's

mind and its rapid developments. Of all men he least adapted himself to the varying character of his friends.[31]

It is true that the Baron was not in full touch with Tyrrell's mind, for he was unaware of the extent of Tyrrell's contact with the Old Catholics, but he was in closer touch than this statement of Holland implies. As to the lack of adaptation to his friends, Holland's judgment, as from one who knew the Baron, demands respect. However, it should be noted how difficult it must have been during such turbulent times, when so much was at stake, for von Hügel to reconcile his own plan for reform and the details of his crusade for scientific freedom with all the attitudes of his friends. And certainly von Hügel was very sensitive to his friends' subsequent reactions.[32] He rarely reacted in detail to Tyrrell's work. Always positive more than negative in his criticisms, he knew he was dealing with "a sensitive, very sensitive man, a Celt of poor health, and profound depressibleness."[33] He also said that Tyrrell's:

> fundamental physical ruin—Bright's disease—largely accounts for the violence which sometimes somewhat marred the force of his work, and for the extraordinary recklessness which marked much of his correspondence....[34]

On May 30, 1913, the Baron wrote to Miss Petre that he did not approve of Tyrrell's last phase but:

> I loved him to the end, with deep feeling for his troubles, with warm sympathy as to all—much the most—of his ideas and affinities which we had in common from the first, or which we slowly achieved, together so largely. And I gladly accept all that accentuates this in the projected biography.

The Baron opposed Tyrrell on his tone and on what he believed was a one-sided stress on the immanence of God. Neither, it should be recalled, questioned the Divinity of Christ.[35] He agreed with Tyrrell on his distinction between revelation and theology, but he linked these two elements, whereas Tyrrell at times spoke as if revelation were so sequestered that it could never be drawn forth into infallible expression, but only into approximate orientation in action. He agreed with the large lines of Tyrrell's ecclesiology.

There are, however, important differences. For example, von Hügel never said that conciliar statements are only protective. They were, he admitted, chiefly protective, but with a "nucleus of truth which we . . . discover to be of priceless value." Second, he always upheld the definition of papal infallibility, although in 1913 he spoke about the definition needing "reasonable supplementation and interpretation."[36] This undoubtedly refers to his claim that the power of the bishops, as nondelegated and apostolic, should also be emphasized.

He never held (as Tyrrell did) that infallibility is valid only in so far as it is subsequently approved by the whole Church. In a private paper of 1904, published after his death, he spoke of Church "inerrancy" as primarily a spiritual instinct for moral and religious direction. This was to be "tested by the deepest spiritual intuitions, experiences, and actions of the most saintly of her children across the ages," but only with a view to "adaptation to the successive requirements of all that is good and great in God's wide world outside."[37] This idea is subject to orthodox interpretation, and nowhere does he make the "valid only if subsequently approved" claim. He approaches the question from a different angle.

In that same essay of 1904, von Hügel maintained that the subject matter of infallibility will need considerable remolding; he accordingly does not question the infallibility of pope or council, but rather the precise meaning of its object in certain dogmatic statements. At the end of the next chapter, where we treat his article in *Rinnovamento*, we will explain his idea of "purification" of dogma. There, Church and papal infallibility is "remolded" by restricting the really defined dogma. He proposed that in some dogmas the factual element is not part of the infallible definition, but only the spiritual element. The Baron's thinking in this area first appeared in the 1904 essay, in which he understood infallibility as a definition primarily (the word is important) "of spiritual instinct and affinity." When he says "primarily," he does not rule out *all* facts as coming under dogma; nor does he exclude the intellectual element of truth. This element, however, is only a "more or less inadequate mental scaffolding partly shaping, partly shaped by these immanent experiences of transcendent realities." Even then, nevertheless, von Hügel was no immanentist. He held strongly for external revelation, but later in life, as he moved more and more to emphasize transcendence, he never would have expressed himself in this manner.

In this early essay he wrote: "It is truly impossible that theologians, or indeed Church authority generally, should have an inerrancy, higher or more extensive in degree and kind, than Our Lord's; or rather that He should be less infallible than they."[38] The infallibility of the magisterium cannot be higher than that of Our Lord. Thus we see how closely linked are the questions of the teaching of Christ on the Parousia and the nature of authority. Later on, the Baron presented a shaded and interesting suggestion on the framework within which Christ developed His teaching on the Parousia. He compared His presentation to the prophetic eschatological pronouncements. The factual time element in that teaching was subordinated to the overwhelming vision of the transcendence of God's power over the world. Since the teaching on the Parousia and the nature of authority are intimately connected, von Hügel automatically proposed that the authority of the Church's pronouncements is chiefly concerned with transcendent realities rather than with historical facts, just, as he said, Christ was concerned with spiritual realities rather than with time. Dogmatic assertions demand the interior assent of faith only for those historical facts without which Christianity could not be. One of these was the actual appearance of the risen Christ to His disciples. Tyrrell's position was almost identical. Von Hügel saw the reality he and Tyrrell were trying to describe, not as a geometric figure, but as an intensely luminous center shading off to darkness; thus his ambiguity and obscurity derives from his idea of reality, but his movement was that of a slow but pressing continuity. Tyrrell's movement was more one of disruption, that of the "prime sauteur," as von Hügel put it.

CHAPTER TEN

THE DECREES OF THE MAGISTERIUM

A. THE MAGISTERIUM

As we pointed out in Chapter I, von Hügel was closely acquainted with many high Church officials; he had even been offered a position on the Biblical Commission. In 1898 he wrote to Loisy that the Jesuits were trying to hide Cardinal Mazzella's ideas under the mantle of Leo XIII's authority. Two years later he wrote to Tyrrell about his frequent visits to "Merry del Val's drawing room." (He disliked the Cardinal's being proposed "as the only sincere Catholic-type."[1])

To this familiarity with curial activities, we must add an episode the Baron witnessed at close range around 1898. After the decision in favor of the authenticity of the Johannine Comma (I Jn 5.7), Cardinal Vaughan was upset because of its effect on Catholic prestige among the Anglicans. He went to Rome, and obtained a judgment from "an excellent source ... that the Holy Office's decision had nothing to do with the critical aspect of the verse in question, but only with its theological value." Thus, a different meaning was given to the words "authentic text" than the Holy Office's statement seemed to demand.[2] Such incidents could not but influence the Baron's judgment.

On Jan. 11, 1906 Pius X wrote a letter, later published in *Revue Biblique:*

> Just as one ought to condemn the temerity of those who are much more preoccupied in following the taste of novelty than the teaching of the Church and do not hesitate to have recourse to excessively novel critical procedures, so it is fitting to disapprove of the attitude of those who dare not, in any way, break with the scriptural exegesis prevalent until now, even when the faith remains unhurt and the wise progress of research calls one in this direction.[3]

Did this presage a new outlook?

Moses and the Pentateuch.   On June 27, 1906, the Biblical Commission published its decree on the Mosaic authorship of the Pentateuch. It said that it could not be held "that these books have not Moses for their author but have been compiled from sources for the most part posterior to the time of Moses."[4] It admitted that some later modification, explanations, and glosses were possible.

As we consider the Baron's published reply to this decision, we must recall that he was closely connected with the founding of the Biblical Commission around 1901. He considered it as a sort of middle area between higher ecclesiastical congregations and critical work:

> ... since the Pope himself has appointed it, although possessed already of the ordinary congregations, we shall be following his initiative and the evident trend of his action, *if we henceforth treat the commission as the presumptive and primary authority and tribunal for the slow threshing out of these questions which have thus been declared to require very special and slow study.*[5]

In 1906 *The Papal Commission and the Pentateuch* was published.[6] It is composed of two long letters, one by the Baron, the other by Rev. Charles A. Briggs, a Presbyterian minister from Union Theological in New York, who had suffered in his own community for his Pentateuchal views. The Baron's letter is moderate and moving. It suggests to Briggs that the Church's future action will take care of the words of the decree. As to its authority, he says:

> ... I cannot but note that though the Commission's answer *has* received the Papal sanction, and hence that its proposals should be criticized only under the pressure of serious necessity and only by men thoroughly conversant with the complex critical problems directly concerned, it is not put forward as a dogmatic decision, but, apparently, as a simple direction and appeal from scholars to scholars. The endorsement of the opinion by working scholars, simply on the ground of scholarship, would evidently be welcomed by the issuing authority; and hence the contrary expressions—of difficulty or of sheer inability to apply the proposed solutions to the concrete problems of the case—can hardly be taxed as necessarily impertinent (p. 35).

The Baron goes on to say that although to speak now may be painful, it is the duty of those who love the Church; it will help to forestall something that may profoundly damage Rome in the future.

The Baron asserts that Moses existed about 1300 B.C., that the "D" document appears to have been the book of the Law found in 628 B.C., and that "P" cannot well have been complete before 400 B.C.[7] He protests that it is thoroughly illogical to say that statements are unhistorical, and to refuse to submit them to historical investigation. He always presented his opponents' objections with force and honesty, and he ponders such an objection:

> The Roman Catholic Church is indeed the mother of West-European civilization; but can a man enter a second time into his mother's womb? ... This decision of the Biblical Commission is surely but one link in a chain of official attempts at the suppression or emasculation of science and scholarship, beginning indeed with Erasmus and culminating with Richard Simon and Alfred Loisy.... When and where has Rome quite finally abandoned any position, however informal and late its occupation, and however demonstrated its untenableness? (pp. 53–54).

Von Hügel says that Rome alone can refute such a charge, and not by words, but by deeds, but at the same time he finds that "a logic immanental to the presuppositions and final positions of Catholicism" will solve the problem. Institutions, he observes, are always at their worst in their relations with science and scholarship because they are fighting inch by inch against the dissolution of man into a mere shifting phenomenalism. The "immanent logic" of the Church will do, with regard to the authorship of the Pentateuch, what it has already done with respect to the pseudo-Denis authorship, and the authenticity of the Johannine Comma (p. 61). (The Church later effectively rescinded the position of the Biblical Commission.[8])

The Baron's work was chiefly an assessment of the authority of the Commission's statements, and an evaluation of the motives for a future change in the Church's position, and he incurred no censure for publishing it. The Apostolic Letter of Leo XIII, which established the Commission (Sept. 27, 1902), left its exact authority somewhat vague.[9] The Baron's chief rashness lay in the fact that he joined Briggs in criticizing the competence of Vigoroux and Janssen, members of the Commission.[10]

In 1907 von Hügel, together with Tyrrell and their Italian associates Murri and Fogazzaro, found themselves severely criticized by Cardinal Steinhuber, Prefect of the Index, in a letter sent to Cardinal Ferrari of Milan.[11] The four are mentioned as "speaking," in *Rinnovamento*, with dangerous independence of the Church magisterium, and for forming themselves into a school which was preparing an anti-Catholic spiritual renewal.

Ironically, this is the only time that von Hügel was ever mentioned by name in a public Church document. The Baron had not yet written anything for *Rinnovamento*, though his name had cropped up in the review.[12] He kept silent. On July 3, 1906 he had written to Miss Petre that he was "very decided not to break with the Authorities, short of my most elementary conscience requiring it."

Lamentabili.   For some time the sky had been growing dark for all who were involved in the new thought. Pius X, after long hesitation, saw that the situation was getting out of hand. (We must remember that quite a number of articles, critical of received positions on historical and philosophical grounds, had already appeared. In addition to Loisy and Tyrrell, Abbé Houtin, who later became an agnostic, published documented attacks on the Church's position on Biblical criticism and Le Roy had taken a pragmatic stance toward dogma. Italian and German Modernists were active and the Protestant Paul Sabatier was winning Catholic support). The Vatican reacted in the decree of the Holy Office approved by the Pope, *Lamentabili* (July 3, 1907), and the encyclical, *Pascendi dominici gregis* (Sept. 8, 1907).

Lamentabili contained a series of sixty-five condemned propositions.[13] The decree's authority is doctrinal, but of intermediate value: that is, it was an act of the Holy Office, approved by the Pope *in forma communi*, and not *in forma specifica*.[14] The errors were condemned globally; some of the propositions were considered heretical, but they are not specified; and no names are mentioned. The original source of the decree was a series of propositions extracted from Loisy's works in 1903 by Paris theologians, and presented to Archbishop Richard to be submitted to the Holy Office.

We are fortunate that von Hügel's letter to Tyrrell on the decree, with some pertinent and previously unpublished parts, has been preserved. It is presented here with commentary.

> I have been much impressed with the way in which you bring out that much the more important point about the document is the way in which it, practically throughout, implies the Church officials', indeed the scholastic theologians' direct, and absolute, as it were, metaphysical (i.e., not *pure* disciplinary or indirect) jurisdiction and determining power and privilege in purely or at least primarily historical matters. This thus now more or less consciously and systematically asserted claim, now for the first time affirmed against historical method, become at last fully aware of its own laws and autonomy, is, as you say, a new claim, and would make as short work of the traditional apologetic, indeed of everything but a demonstrably circular reasoning, as it would of all historical science worthy of the name.

These typical Hügelian sentences show us that the Baron's chief fear was for the destruction of the rights of historical method. The Baron then told Tyrrell that he had found his analysis, which criticized parts of the Syllabus as caricature, very helpful. He said that he, himself, had gone over the Syllabus four times. The following points struck him:

> (1) the document is a *Feria quarta*—Wednesday—thing. Now David Fleming taught Duchesne and me, ten years ago, how ignorant we had been not to know the mighty truth that the Holy Office has two *very* distinct classes and sessions and Decrees. The *Feria Quarta* decrees are, even tho' sanctioned by the Pope (on a Feria Quarta or not, matters nothing), secondary, less solemn decrees; they can even go into the waste-paper basket, said David Fleming. The *Feria Quinta* sessions are always presided by the Pope in person or by a representative especially sent by him; and the decrees of such sessions are alone the most solemn and least mutable of the H.O.'s doing.[15]

Then he found two diametrically opposed notions in the "Syllabus." The first contained caricature: "these are, I am confident, the work, as they here stand, of David Fleming or some other secret friend of ours." These caricatures, he said, we could all sign, for no mortal could hold such things. But further, there was another set extracted by

> some deliberately hostile theologian (Billot?), and here subscription, even apart from the all important implied principle so well unmasked by you, would be, I think, all but impossible for us, at least I feel so at present as regards my own self.

A paraphrase of the condemned errors which "at present" von Hügel thought impossible to sign were:

> *12.* That an exegete should put aside all preconceived opinion about the supernatural origin of Scripture and treat it as a human document.
> *13.* (underlined by the Baron). The reason why Our Lord's preaching bore little fruit with the Jews was because the parables were artificially elaborated by the Christians of the second and third generations.

16–18. That John's Gospel is not history, but mystical contemplation, exaggerating miracles, and really giving the life of Christ for the end of the first century.

27–20. Christ's divinity is not proved from the Gospels, but is a dogma which the Christian conscience deduced from the notion of Messias. The Christ of history is greatly ("multo") inferior to the Christ of faith.[16]

30. (underlined). In all the Gospel texts "Son of God" is equivalent to "Messias," and not "true and natural Son of God."

32–34. The natural sense of the texts cannot be reconciled with the teaching of theologians on the conscience and infallible knowledge of Christ. Either Jesus taught error about the proximate messianic advent or the greater part of his Synoptic doctrine lacks authenticity. Unlimited knowledge is based on a hypothesis, historically inconceivable and repugnant to the moral sense, that Christ, as man, possessed the knowledge (*scientiam*) of God, and yet refused to communicate this knowledge.[17]

Propositions 32–34 undoubtedly coincide with von Hügel's private thought (see *EA* II, p. 19), and almost certainly with his published expression at this time (see *CE*, p. 302).

36–37. The Resurrection is not properly a fact of the historical order, but a non-demonstrable fact of the supernatural order which the Christian conscience gradually derived from other sources ("aliis"). Originally, the faith was not so much in the fact of the Resurrection as in the immortal life of Christ with God.

The Baron's inclusion of this sentence (no. 37) makes it probable that his letter to the *Times* defending Loisy (see Chapter V) implied such a belief, but he later insisted on the necessary reality of the objective appearances by the Lord.

38. The doctrine of the expiatory death of Christ is not evangelical but Pauline.

Later the Baron would disagree with Loisy on this idea. The remaining numbers cited by von Hügel (*39*, 40, *45*, 48, 52, 59–61) have to do either with the idea that Christ did not intend to found a church of long duration, or with the consequent idea that sacraments were not formally instituted by Him. The Baron concludes: "I continue disinclined to write anything on the subject—at least anything signed—unless and until we are morally certain that we are to be required to sign," and he calls Mgr. Benigni's *Corrispondenza Romana* the "organ of the dominant Vatican set."[18]

This letter, of course, must not be treated like a published manuscript, but all we know of the Baron's way of writing suggests that it reflects his mind at the time. He was not like Tyrrell who said: "I have never or rarely written anything which afterthought would not have mended in some respects." Even in his letters von Hügel trips over himself to qualify his meaning, and it is interesting that he omits reference to those propositions that refer to faith, revelation, dogma, and practical life. This was Tyrrell's terrain, and the Baron had, as yet, not focused his attention for long on this aspect.

Aftermath.   His wife's health and the arrangements of his daughter Gertrude's marriage in Italy provided von Hügel with the occasion to meet with the Italian group connected with the review *Rinnovamento*. Fogazzaro, Scotti, Murri, and Buonaiuti were all there. They discussed what to do if the review were condemned, and if submission to *Lamentabili* were demanded of the priests. The Baron agreed to write a paper on the New Testament, the critical methods, and general results of the "less disturbing cases." He proposed as the thesis of their deliberation that no authority exercised by men could be unlimited in principle and in right. The limits of authority were indeed difficult to define, but some things are beyond its limits, e.g. the suppression of *Rinnovamento*, the prohibition that he and Tyrrell publish, without the imprimatur (*Lamentabili*, n. 1). They discussed the Resurrection, the Virgin Birth, and the Parousia.[19] Their conclusions on these last points are not known, but later we will see what they probably were. The Baron, who never gave up his life of intense prayer, encouraged all to pray and struggle, to preserve unity despite their divergent ideas. He said their strength was in their weakness, in the absence of all plot, all organization, all a priorism.

Pascendi. This encyclical appeared in *L'Osservatore Romano* on September 16. Its first part presents one of the most comprehensive pictures of a condemned system. It situates the basis of Modernism in agnosticism, and on the theory that it is impossible for human reason to go beyond the limits of phenomena. Its positive foundation is vital immanence, i.e. the origin of religion in the needs of the human heart, and of the subconscious. Modernism denies external revelation, and makes revelation and consciousness synonymous. It says that the person of Christ is then transfigured to suit this consciousness. The meaning of dogmas is understood as the relation existing between the formulas and the religious sense. The relation is inadequate, and this inadequacy is termed symbol or instrument for the believer. These formulas, in order to be really religious and not merely intellectual speculations, have to be vitally assimilated by the religious sense, and thus there emerges an intrinsic evolution of dogma. The Modernist believer passes beyond the phenomenal determinism of the philosopher only by means of the personal religious experience in the heart. Tradition is a communication to others of an original experience, passed on often in intellectual formulas that are representative and suggestive stimulants to recover the original experience.

As an historian and critic, the Modernist says that faith occupies itself with something that science declares to be unknowable. Thus, while agnostic science answers negatively to the true resurrection and ascension of Christ, faith answers affirmatively, but there is no conflict between them. Therefore, faith is subject to science in all except divine reality and the experience of it in the believer.

As theologian, the Modernist says that since the principle of faith is immanent, so God is immanent in man. Thus the representations of the divine reality are purely symbolical, and we have theological symbolism. The formula should not be stressed, but rather its purpose, namely: to unite the believer with the absolute truth which it reveals and conceals. The Modernists differ in their idea of immanence.

The Church has its birth in a double need, the need of the

collective conscience to communicate its faith, and the need for a society. Authority, therefore, has its origin only in the religious conscience, and is subject to it. Autocracy is obsolete, and the present day idea of liberty cannot recede. Authority can impose the formula in the community, but the believer may follow his own judgment. In living religion everything is subject to change. In this evolution the conservative element comes from tradition, the progressive element from individual conscience. Thus emerges the pernicious doctrine which would make the laity elements of progress in the Church.

The critics thus speak of the Christ of history and the Christ of faith, the Church of history and of faith. Their position is based on a concealed philosophical a priorism. In the Pentateuch and the first three Gospels, they hold a primitive, brief narration, developed by additions, interpolations, theological or allegorical interpretations. Thus, there is a vital evolution in the Bible springing from the evolution of faith. Basing their thinking on an *a priori* assumption from evolutionist and agnostic philosophy, they say that Christ announced the proximate second coming. Thus, the Catholic religion is merely the immanent development of a germ which Christ planted. We must not be surprised that Christ erred on the time of the coming of the Kingdom, for He was subject to the laws of life, but with St. Augustine we reply that in an authority so high, admit but one efficacious lie, and there will remain not a single passage of those which are difficult to believe or practice that may not be explained as a lie to serve a purpose.

The Encyclical answered the attacks by referring to the Fathers and the Councils, and by the reduction of the system to Pantheism and immanent agnosticism. There followed a brief analysis of these errors. It found the causes of Modernism in curiosity and pride, and in the lack of knowledge of scholasticism. It admitted a true use of immanence in apologetics, but warned about speaking of a true and rigorous need of the supernatural.

The long conclusion is devoted to practical measures against this "synthesis of all heresies." Scholastic philosophy must be made the basis of the sacred sciences, while positive theology must be more appreciated than in the past. Anyone tainted with Modernism is to be excluded from teaching and government. The same policy is to be followed for those who strive after the new views (*nova student*) in history, archeology and biblical exegesis. The clergy must be free from the love of the new ideas (*novitatum*). Clerics must not attend secular universities when there are similar courses in a Catholic Institute or University. Bishops must prevent whatever savors of Modernism from being read, even if written by Catholics who are not ill-disposed, but who are poorly instructed in theology, and imbued with the new philosophy. Bishops may condemn books which have the *imprimatur* from another diocese, for the needs there may be different. A Council of Vigilance will be set up in each diocese that will inform the Bishop of errors which they detect. An Institute of Learning will be set up for the promotion of all knowledge under the guidance of the Church.[20]

Von Hügel. Probably no encyclical in modern times has caused such confusion and fear.[21] Wilfrid Ward wrongly thought that it had condemned Newman,[22] and Blondel feared for his own position, which, as it turned out, was untouched. Loisy, whose original condemnation in Paris formed the basis of the decree, ridiculed it in another book.[23] It was read from some pulpits in England. Many loyal priests were anxious about their positions. Von Hügel also thought that Newman was condemned, and even said he would point out to Loisy two allusions to Ward in *Pascendi* "to let it be seen how universal the range of the Encyclical's notions" were.[24] Tyrrell, finally excommunicated for his criticisms of the encyclical, apocalyptically wrote to the Baron, on May 23, 1908: "The wood is not green but dry. We must expect a destructive conflagration before men will hear of reconstruction."

Many, even among the moderates, were startled by some of the wording of the encyclical. The Modernists were described as "full of deceit," "lost to all sense of modesty," "most pernicious" with "sacrilegious audacity" and "domineering overbearance," "proud and obstinate," "arrogant," "puffed up with the proud name of science." The encyclical's reading of motives especially hurt the sensitivities of the English. Encyclicals have their peculiar literary genre, and unfortunately many were not, and are not, trained to interpret them.[25] Maisie Ward's mother, however, considered such phrases as merely "the medieval habit of strong language," but these readings of motives probably rested also on a theological basis. The Vatican Council had said that no one could have a just cause for doubting the faith, but this applies only to the objective order; in the subjective order, no one can give the reason why a person loses his faith. Some of the Modernists may never have possessed faith in the Church, and people like von Hügel, Le Roy, and the Italians, Semeria and Fogazzaro, never lost it. Von Hügel wrote to Tyrrell, Nov. 6, 1907: "Our motives, all our motives were held to be knowable and known as to be bad, and only bad,—so at least in Part II."

The basic difficulty with the encyclical was that it presented and attacked an abstract system that no single Modernist ever totally held. Loisy and Tyrrell were obviously targets, but it is likely, as Lagrange suggested, that Rome wished to avoid names in order to prevent a recurrence of the violent controversy that ensued when the Jansenists denied that Jansenius really held condemned propositions in the way they were understood by Rome. However that may be, this is an area wherein difficult prudential judgments must be made. Rome's accumulated experience is not an infallible norm for the most prudential detailed action in the present, and, while no one can doubt the need for some serious action at the time, it can hardly be denied that the approach of the encyclical left much to be desired.

On Nov. 6 and Dec. 27, 1907, orders were issued that anyone who wrote for, worked for in any way, or read Rinnovamento was excommunicated.[26] On November 16, the Baron sent a telegram to Rinnovamento: "Profonde sympathie vif désir ne pas changer résolutions Hügel."[27] Two days later, Pius X issued his Motu Proprio Praestantia Sacrae Scripturae, in which he said that

all are "obliged in conscience" to submit to the decisions of
the Pontifical Biblical Commission, and that those who contradicted *Pascendi* or *Lamentabili* were excommunicated.[28] The
Baron, in Milan, encouraged the editors to continue, and
promised an article, but he acted on the false opinion of Bishop
Bonomelli of Cremona, that no one is obliged to excommunicate
himself or to apply a general excommunication to himself.[29]
Working on this false idea, he proceeded to encourage the
editors, and to write an article for *Rinnovamento*. On Nov. 20,
1907 he had written to Tyrrell:

> We have to make a new mentality, a new *psychosis*; we cannot do
> so unless we hold out. And the risk of having to do without the
> Sacraments, for a while at least, would not prove disastrous . . .

As far back as 1893 he had written:

> Sixtus V excommunicated Elizabeth, and Pius IX excommunicated
> Victor Emmanuel: they both may have erred in so doing. Medieval
> popes have again and again laid the interdict upon whole
> countries: all Catholic Church-historians of the first rank
> admit that at least several times it was done wrongly, or at least
> excessively. . . . Interior assent to the Pope's *ex cathedra* pro-
> nouncements is *always* due; obedience to the Pope's governmental
> orders is *generally* and *presumptively* due. Saints have at times
> disobeyed single orders or have remonstrated with the Popes. . . .

He continues that there is no instance of a saint not trying
to reconcile himself, for he knows the Church is the true Church.
This may explain the Baron's idea of doing without the sacraments
for a while; he felt that his conscience had led him to this conclusion. While encouraging the *Rinnovamento* group to stand firm
(one of these at least, Fr. Murri, had a different conscience
and momentarily submitted), von Hügel wrote anonymously
for *Rinnovamento*, and was cautious lest an excommunication
hurt his *Mystical Element* which was about to appear.[30] He was
worried also about his family.

Even in this period of tension and confusion, an excommunication of von Hügel would have been solely an act of

"brinkmanship." In the last resort, as Loisy said, von Hügel believed in the Church more than in his own views. His phrase about doing without the sacraments "for a while at least," shows that he would never have carried his crusade so far as to incur permanent excommunication. "I still feel that the reform of the Roman Church is *the* point for us whom Providence has made, or allowed to be born, members of that Church; and that all secessions, individual or corporate from it ... but help further to narrow the Church which they have left."[31]

B. RINNOVAMENTO AND "DE-MYTHOLOGIZING"

Von Hügel's actions may seem to have an element of the quixotic about them if we are unaware of the lengths to which he was willing to go in demanding liberty for scriptural science, and thus, automatically, in the reform of the Church doctrine. De la Bedoyère seems unaware of the extent of the Baron's aims. Nédoncelle, alone, pointed this out as far back as 1935; his excellent treatment leaves, however, some questions which we hope to clear up.[32]

In 1908–09 the Baron published in *Rinnovamento* a four-part article of over 150 pages, in Italian, on Loisy's *Les Evangiles Synoptiques*.[33] A summary of the same was published in a little noticed review in the *Hibbert Journal* for July 1908. The Baron writes that he does not attempt to approach the book in a spirit hostile to the authority of the Church, as to decisions already made or to come. He recognizes occasional temerities in the 1800 page work, says that we ought not "swallow" all of Loisy's ideas, and finds him glacially discouraging for a devout soul.

This tedious commentary on Loisy is perhaps the Baron's most boring literary effort, but his most extended thought on the relation of revelation to dogma and theology is found in sections of this article.[34] The Baron holds fast to the idea that religion and revelation must be distinguished from theology and reflective reasoning. He distinguishes three elements, two on a profound level: "an obscure but rich apprehension" and "a devoted will," and a third on the level of clear reflexion and reasoning.

In reality it is only in the proportion in which men exchange the pure gold of their obscure and vivid apprehension and of their obscure but devoted will for the silver of their clear reflexion and reasoning that these profounder, richer, and truer components of their conquest become easily transmissible to the future generations in their simultaneous and successive variety. And because this more obscure apprehension and will are profoundly true when they are spiritually fecund, the other element, the clear conception, which is thus built on the previous two, is found necessary, for their transmission, at least, for a large extension in space and time. Each possesses a certain truth and a great importance.

Thus it is that the authority of the Church is the official regulator and formulator both of the obscure, profound experience and of the clear and more superficial conception of the body of believers, and this authority has reason to always move slowly and cautiously in the matter of theology.

Only with difficulty and after a long demonstration of the impossibility of conserving some particular system of theological interpretation, will authority be able to abandon or modify it.[35]

The theological interpretation which the Baron here speaks of abandoning or modifying, is, as we will see in a moment, not just scholastic theology, but at times the very explanation of the meaning of dogma.

The Baron's distinction is along the lines of Tyrrell's. However, where Tyrrell proposed three elements, a revelation experience, a prophetic truth, and theology, von Hügel posited two, a revelation experience which contains an obscure apprehension and a religious will, and clear theological (or conciliar) conceptions. Before we give concrete examples, let us remember that the profound experience is not, for the Baron, an immanental one. It initially comes from a transcendent God, and is rooted in Christ.

The Baron asserts that the distinction between theology and revelation allows for necessary and possible purifications of the true import and significance of revelation. For example, reinterpretation of the dogma of the descent into hell and of the Ascension leaves the faith-content the same as previously, but the spatial imagery has lost its absolute significance under the pressure of fact and of our progress in thought.

The Baron's conviction is that what has happened in these cases is based on a principle which allows for a similar re-interpretation of the Virginal conception and bodily Resurrection of Jesus. He thus moves from a cosmological de-mythologization to an historical one. The historico-phenomenal aspect in these is dependent on science, not faith. "My conviction as to the bare, strictly historico-phenomenal character of the Virginal conception and of the corporal Resurrection of Jesus would not be faith but science."[36]

It is crucial that we distinguish his position here from Loisy's. The introduction to Loisy's book did not fit the pattern of von Hügel's idea of the purification of dogma. The intro-duction had a "gleeful destructivity" about it which went beyond the Baron's own conception. Thus he erroneously thought that it did not express Loisy's real faith. In the introduction, Loisy left the impression that, after His Resurrection, "Christ did not mysteriously impress with His presence the mind of any disciple," but that His appearance was an illusion. The Baron suggests here, and explicitly states in his later thought, that without this minimum the dogma of the Resurrection was meaningless.

The Baron believed that the empty sepulchre narratives were to be judged by science and not by faith. These seem to be later additions, possibly a "projected shadow from the light of the faith and the fact of the Resurrection."[37] Since the Resurrection is supported by good reasons, he says there is little problem if the sepulchre accounts are not sustained by one. Von Hügel makes it clear, however, that he is not convinced by Loisy's rejection of these sepulchre narratives, but on historical grounds.

The Baron then explains his conception of the Resurrection. Life is possible without *sarx* (flesh), but not without *soma* (body). "A human life is conceivable without flesh but not without body. The body can exchange its material substratum, the heavy terrestrial *sarx* for the luminous ethereal *doxa* (glory) and still remain the same." *Sarx* and *psyche* die with man, but the *pneuma* at the resurrection awakes the sleeping *soma* (body), and transforms its old material substratum from *sarx* to glory. The Baron cites Holtzmann on this point. He suggests that the popular mind had *sarx* rise with *soma*, and thus we have, in Luke, Our Lord eating. Apparently the Baron is undecided as to the reality of the empty tomb. The sepulchre narratives (which are secondary) derive their importance from the Resurrection accounts.

The Baron holds that the infancy narratives are secondary; Paul seems to be unaware of them. Some may think that divinity and Virgin birth are essentially connected, but this is not objectively necessary. As with the descent into hell, so this doctrine may be re-interpreted in the future. Finally, infallibility is an inerrancy of spiritual orientation, an inerrancy of timely movement, and of the law of spiritual progress.[38]

Critique. Much of the literature on von Hügel seems unaware of the reaches of his thought. De la Bedoyère asserts that the Baron never reworked his earlier thought, point by point, when he began to realize the trend to immanence in Modernism, but the Baron was never a pure immanentist. We have no evidence that he rejected the *general* movement of his thought, and there is evidence that he retained much of his approach, as we will see.

The Baron certainly differed from Tyrrell in tone and prudential procedure, and in his emphasis on transcendence, but there is a great similarity on many of the views we have traced. However, there is a prime distinction of capital importance to be made between their two systems. In discussing the relationship between theology (really dogma) and revelation, Tyrrell spoke, at times, as if it were impossible for dogma or theology to express revelation, as, for example, in the dogma of the Trinity. He seemed to feel that the stained-glass windows of dogma are not vehicles of true light. Man is not staring at the sun with a naked eye. One could say that the basic problem lay in Tyrrell's conception of the analogy of being; his position was rooted in

philosophy and he should have a philosophical, as well as
a theological, response.[39]

Von Hügel's system is quite different. He never couched
his theories in polemical rhetoric; his judicious, and more precise,
expressions did not plunge him into these philosophical difficulties. In fact, he greatly disliked, and continually opposed,
Kant and his system. He never implied that there was a
contradiction between revelation and dogma. For him dogma
and theology are "necessary," they "protect" and express "a
certain truth."

Von Hügel (and Tyrrell, in his better moments) held an
approximative value in the type of dogma that included spiritual
reality but did not contain historical facts. The word "approximative" is Tyrell's, but it does not distort the Baron's views;
the expression may be vague, but it is legitimate.[40] The dogma
of the Trinity does not exhaust, even conceptually, the nature of
the Trinity, but this is not to make it a free-floating relativity;
it has its axis in the Absolute. *In* the representative and conceptual factors fixed by the Church, we simultaneously attain the
Absolute, the Trinity. Just as in the Gospels, *in* the phenomena
we can come into contact with the noumena, so here *in* the
conceptual representation we have an adequate approximative
grasp on the absolute reality of the Trinity.

Von Hügel held that *some* dogmas protected a nucleus of
historical fact necessary for Christianity, but whatever was
phenomenal in these, and therefore open to critical investigation,
belonged to history, and not to faith. "My true conviction of the
strictly historico-phenomenal character of the Virginal conception and of the bodily Resurrection would not be faith
but science." In 1914 he maintained substantially the same
position. He, himself, held on faith the real and non-subjectively
induced apparitions of Christ to His disciples. He considered
also the historical evidence for these to be most strong,
but he asserted that whatever was phenomenally verifiable
in them pertained to history, and not to faith. The harmony
between these, he was sure, would be protected by God in His
Providence.

Von Hügel suggested also (and let us remember that this was only a suggestion made, as he said, subject to the authority of the Church) that some dogmas that seemed to be protecting phenomenal facts were not really intended as such. Unfortunately, he held this with regard to the Virginal conception. The Divinity and the Virgin Birth, he asserted, were necessarily connected "for some times and for some people," but there is no necessary objective connection. The study of the texts, he observed, suggested a possible reinterpretation here, similar to the reinterpretation of the spatial imagery in the descent into hell, and in the ascent to heaven.

If we confront these suggestions with Church doctrine, it is evident that the Virginal conception has always been held as a belief obligatory in faith. This obligation was seen to come from the unanimous agreement of the Fathers, and from the creeds and Ecumenical Councils which included the belief in their definition of other dogmas. For example, the definition of Chalcedon against the Monophysites declares that the Son was generated in eternity from the Father, and in time "from the Virgin Mary the Mother of God according to the humanity."[41] This would rule out any interpretation like that suggested by von Hügel, or very clearly stated in private by Tyrrell.[42] The Church had already faced a similar problem in the early heresies of Celsus and Cerinthus on the virginity of Mary, but von Hügel here presents a challenge. As theology refines its notions of revelation and tradition, as the exegetes work with the tools of form criticism and redaction criticism, as conciliar history is exegeted, and ecumenical questions press on us, Catholics still await a handling of the dogma which will be both sensitive to the new data and of ecumenical signficance.

With regard to his liberal position on the empty tomb, von Hügel goes against general Church teaching. The exact nature of the Resurrection has never been defined, but the consensus of the Fathers and the consensus of the theologians have opposed the Baron's suggestion that it is a matter whose certitude depends on scientific evidence alone.[43]

The Baron's life was one of deep prayer, and his central,

intense devotion was to Christ in the Eucharist. His basic all-absorbing conviction was the continual presence and transcendence of God in his life. Yet he was already struggling in currents that later rose up in the great tide of literature on "de-mythologizing" the Gospels. Bultmann's dictum: "Cross and resurrection are one event related as event and meaning" is totally at odds with von Hügel's vision of life, history, and faith.[44] Still it had been shown that he pushed the rights of history far deeper into the domain of dogma than has been generally supposed. As late as April 25, 1919, the Baron wrote to Maude Petre about the publication of George Tyrrell's Letters (1920). He refers to the letter from Tyrrell which we have just cited (see note 42); his judgment on the letter has never been noted. He wrote: "A great letter, this, surely."[45] Von Hügel's thought did not undergo major changes as he grew older.

CHAPTER ELEVEN

THE NATURE OF THE CHURCH AND INSTITUTIONAL RELIGION

Von Hügel felt at ease in a pick-and-choose eclecticism. Much of his thought cries out against an "excessive tidying-up," a premature synthesis. He is often boldly groping rather than affirming with assurance, but he does confidently affirm that history has its rights, and that whoever violates these rights diminishes his own person and authority. Nevertheless, the Baron wrote in almost systematic fashion on two topics: man's experience of God and the nature of the Church as a religio-institutional structure.

Nédoncelle suggested that the Ariadne thread of von Hügel's thought lies in his ideas on the Incarnation. The Incarnation is undoubtedly a central idea for von Hügel, but his total thought seems to be composed of three strands. First, his thought is theocentric, but without heavy Trinitarian emphasis; second, it is incarnational, but with a stronger emphasis on Christ in glory than on the Incarnate in history; third, it is ecclesiological, but with more attention to the Church as a religious philosophy than as an organic mystery. No one of the three is a self-sufficient thread.[1] The study of the Incarnate in history is prevented "from falling into the dark precipice" by an overpowering, unescapable theocentrism. The interpretation of the meaning of Christ is also protected by the social, visible, and institutional nature of Christianity. The sense of the mystery of God, and the spirit of Christ, in turn, will soften the rigidities in the institutional, and make it more supple, but the institutional-social element, and the Incarnate Christ, in their turn, will clarify and vivify the mystery of God.

Only in this dialectic do we find the key to the unity of the Baron's thought. Consequently, it is impossible to treat his ideas of the Church without thoroughly involving the other two elements. Let us now briefly trace the roots of the Baron's thought on the Church as they wind around their feeding point in the idea of God.

Von Hügel published his great *Mystical Element of Religion* in 1908 and *Eternal Life* in 1912. After various essays and addresses, *The Reality of God and Religion and Agnosticism* appeared posthumously in 1931. We will include these works in the following interpretation.[2]

A. THE SENSE OF GOD

Von Hügel constructs no systematic presentation of faith or revelation. The sense of God is so powerful in his works that its sheer force leaves these other concepts as mere remnants of its movement.

From his earliest writing in *The Church and the Bible*, to his last work, *The Reality of God*, the incomprehensibility of God is stressed, and he loved to cite the Councils that condemned anyone who denied it. He held as a stable principle that the richer the object, the less clear is our knowledge of it.[3] Neither Our Lord Himself, in His teaching, nor the Church in hers, could ever begin to exhaust the richness of God. Our Lord's presence is God's presence, yet the Church, when she frames this presence in conciliar definitions, "pins it down" intellectually as "the skeleton pins down the flesh. What a hideous thing the skeleton, taken separately, is, isn't it? Yet even Cleopatra, when in the splendour of her youth, had such a very useful, very necessary, quite unavoidable skeleton inside her, had she not?"[4] At the same time, the Church must be careful that her authority does

not make these definitions a prison for the Christian. They are
necessary and valid, but they do not plumb the depths of God.
Authority has a characteristic solicitude for the past, and
this is legitimate and necessary, but in its pastoral care for
the majority and the average, it tends to neglect the soul's
aspiration to soar beyond the definition.[5] This might give an
observer the impression that "the infinite variety of the superbly
living Cleopatra is now being thrown, like so much mummy-
dust, into the wide-open, pleading eyes of living, light-seeking
souls."[6]

Von Hügel's thought circles and circles around the idea
of God, like an eagle. Loisy was so unsettled by this that he
closed his eyes to it as to a type of psychosis.[7] Von Hügel's
thinking moves from echoes of Blondel, Eucken, and Bergson,
in the early nineteen hundreds, to an echo of St. Thomas at
the end.

Time, he says, is a composite thing. Its two elements are
clock-time and duration. In duration man stands open to the
infinite. He tastes a quasi-simultaneity, and finds his appetite
whetted. Duration does not abolish succession, but it pushes
anxiety about succession out to a peripheral edge, and gives us
the flavor of something which is not in time. Man's personality
partakes of a quasi-eternity.[8] Strict eternity is not, and never
will be man's possession, but man cannot escape the impression
of being centered in a duration that the hands of a clock cannot
measure. This duration is vivid and deep, but not clear, whereas
clock-time is very clear, but shallow. It is a "joint product of
duration, which alone is truly experienced, and of space, which
alone is clearly picturable."

Against "the *totum simul* of this quasi-timeless Present,"
authority is anxious to protect the what-has-already been. Yet
it must be careful not to enthrone an external past only by
evicting man's deepest consciousness.[9]

In this consciousness the Baron finds a keen sense of
imprisonment in the contingent, a sense that leaves the most
sceptical mind unable to answer one argument: "If man did not
somehow have a real experience of objective reality and truth,

he ... could never, as man actually does in precise proportion to the nobility of his mind, suffer so much from the very suspicion of a complete imprisonment within purely human apprehensions and values."[10] This idea is a recurring theme in von Hügel's work. The thirst for religion is at bottom metaphysical. Man could not suffer from the very thought that he could be a purely rootless, transitory, contingent being unless he experienced this thirst. It is not just a craving for an idea, but a metaphysical thirst for a reality;[11] and a recurring experience which vitalizes what we learn from the formulas of our faith; a "hunger for God from God and God answers it with Christ."[12]

Von Hügel feared that the prevalent scholastic approaches in the early part of the century dulled this thirst. He remarked that the scholastically trained priest, when he met difficulties in faith, frequently fell into atheism or agnosticism because he lacked this sense.[13] The authority of the Church must accordingly foster it if it is to guide its children. He often observed that some Church officials were not spiritual; he did not mean that they did not lead good lives, but that they showed little awareness of this thirst.

During the last ten years of his life, as he assimilated St. Thomas More, and moved away from reaction against neo-scholasticism, he became less concerned about the danger. It was not that he had abandoned the approach to God through inner aspiration. Rather, he had learned how to combine this with what he believed was St. Thomas' more external approach.[14] He did not cease to speak about the thirst for God,[15] but he depicted it as being less restless and feverish, probably because he found in the mystery of the Church with its "givenness," its sacraments, calm satisfaction in the midst of mystery. This is the period when we more often catch glimpses of him on his knees before the Blessed Sacrament.

Von Hügel's powerful sense of God partly accounts for his assurance in presenting daring Scriptural interpretation for his attitude towards authority.[16] He held that there is a point where what is being protected by authority begins to lose its vitality because of that very protection. Few have pointed out more strongly than von Hügel that an increase in authority may occasion a lessening of the sense of God. On the other hand, he became keenly aware that a danger lurked, also, at the other extreme. Without sufficient guidance from authority, as the interpreter of tradition, the Christian may become sceptical about his religion. At the time Modernism prevailed, this was certainly more than a remote danger.

The Baron was extremely emphatic on the need for authority as demanded by the very nature of religion. This is well reflected in *The Mystical Element* which was begun during the waning years of the nineteenth century and completed about a year before the encyclical *Pascendi*.[17] Of equal importance is his chapter in *Eternal Life* on institutional religion which, as he told Maude Petre in October 1912, was "written outside of all the excitement or nervous irritation and came, as the preface explains, as an inevitable part of the book's central argument and point."

B. THE ELEMENTS OF RELIGION

In the first chapter of *The Mystical Element*, von Hügel describes three great cultural forces at work in Western civilization. The first is Hellenism, the second, Christianity, and the third, science. He finds Hellenism to be chiefly intellectual and aesthetic, mostly cold and clear, quick and conclusive. It strives for richness and harmony, but it is profoundly abstract and determinist. In it, the will necessarily follows the intellect in exact proportion to the clarity of the information the intellect supplies. Its strength lies in its freshness, completeness, and unity. It is an *ideal* harmonization.

He characterizes Christianity as being directly moral and religious, profound and tender, slow and far-reaching, immensely costly and infinitely strong. It reveals the vast depth and mystery of human personality and freedom.

He judges the contribution of science to be intensely impersonal and determinist, not metaphysical or religious, yet more abstract, even, than the Greek view, and, in a sense, more concrete than Christianity itself.

None of these three forces supplants the others; moreover, they are mutually enriching. Christianity already contained the other two elements within itself, though in varying degrees. It possessed its own mysticism, since, in its own Founder, it is throughout "the Revelation of Personality," both in God and man; it was concerned for nature and historical fact, loosely akin to science; and it manifests a type of philosophy, especially in Paul and John.

After situating Christianity as a cultural force that reveals the value of the human person between the two poles of Hellenism which seeks harmony in development, and science which is deterministic, the Baron proceeds to analyze religion itself. He finds three elements, institutional, intellectual, and mystical.[18] As his thought unfolds, nuances appear that show that the division is as follows: the institutional (historical), the intellectual (speculative and rational), and the mystical (intuitive-emotional-volitional) elements. He verifies the existence of these elements by a study of the growth of the human person, of the constituents of knowledge, of the religions of the world, and of Christianity.

A study of the growth of the human person reveals that the child relies mainly on the senses, on memory, and externals for his religious motivation. An image, a cross, a mother or father, a priest, people belonging to a traditional institution, these are his main motivating forces on the phenomenological level. At this stage the external, authoritative, historical, traditional, and institutional aspects of religion are predominant. The child believes things to be true on the occasion of external influences, but he does not contrast them with error for he has not conceived the possibility of error. When he becomes a youth, the impressiveness of the external world awakens a sense of awe and curiosity. So-called facts have been found to be errors; thus the reasoning, argumentative, abstractive faculties come into play and religion takes on the aspects of thought, system, and philosophy. In maturity, the emotional, volitional, and spiritual powers are set in fuller motion, for man is necessarily a creature of action even more than of sensation and reflection. He acts inwardly and outwardly, and thus the experimental and mystical elements of religion come into play. Religion is loved and lived more than analyzed or reasoned about.[19]

These three elements never exist alone at any stage of growth. There is always an enriching friction among them; but at each stage one or other is predominant.

This general analysis of religion is perhaps von Hügel's most widely accepted insight. A caution, however, is in order. The Baron never held that, when one became a man, one sloughed off the child's attitudes in the sense that, with the development of a broader view, the institutional and traditional aspects became of little importance. We will see his insistence upon this later. His treatment by no means coincides with the popular agnostic positivism of our day, according to which man passes out of "the age of faith" into "the age of reason," which he subsequently deserts for "the age of science." Moreover, the cadres of his division cannot imply, as his general thought shows, that there is a touch of childishness in institutionalism. He would admit that to over-emphasize institutionalism is childish,[20] but he maintained that something childlike must be retained if one is to enter into the Kingdom of heaven. There is nevertheless a germ of distortion in the Baron's parallel between institutionalism and the child's mentality. To be genuinely institutional-directed demands great maturity. Would it not be more true to say that the child is not institutional-directed but, to use Riesman's phrase, "other-directed"? Since the child merely sees "the other," and has no concept of the institution, it is difficult to speak of this at the first stage, and at the last stage the Baron, himself, says it takes great balance to bring the institution into one's life. The mystic, himself, only reaches his true function through the institution: this idea was dear to von Hügel. Thus, a more valid triad would seem to be one in which the first stage was other-directed, the second stage inner-directed, and the last stage mystically-directed (i.e. by God through an institution mystically seized upon). None of the previous stages, however, is excluded.

After positing these three elements in human growth, the Baron then finds them in human knowledge; first, in sensation and memory, second, in the rational, and third, in the ethico-mystical.[21] On the first level we have impressions of the flux of our consciousness as it apprehends sounds, smells, touches, as it rests or moves, as it experiences pleasure or pain—it is "a flux, changeless in its ceaseless change." On the second level we meet the logical order of analysis and the formation of categories. The third level leads to value judgments which move us into a sort of "ethico-mystical" stage. "I have to trust and endorse the intimations of necessity furnished by the second, if anything is to come of the whole movement." Thus we have indubitable sensation and memory, clear thought, and warm faith in and through action. These three aspects correspond to the institutional, intellectual, and mystical elements of religion.

The Baron finds in an analysis of reflex action that it begins in sense impression, the "given" element, moves into mental abstraction and reflection, and ends in a discharge of will and action, in an act of free affirmation, expansion, and love. The first and last links are obscure, the middle link is clear. These also correspond to the three elements of religion. This second approach of the Baron is, in its turn, a valuable analysis, for one would expect religion to correspond in some way with the human powers.

As a third approach, von Hügel quickly examines the great religions to discover if and how they emphasized these three elements. He finds that Brahminism represented an excess of the external, and Buddhism an excess of abstruse reasoning and pessimistic emotion. Mohammedanism combined the three in very imperfect proportions, since it laid great stress on the first, the external element. Judaism was slow to develop the intellectual element, and the mystical element was wholly absent until the exilic period, and became marked only under Hellenistic influence. The Book of Wisdom and Philo developed the three elements almost equally. After that time, we find the severe, external, traditional, authoritative school of the Pharisees, the accommodating school of the Sadducees, and the separated sect of the Essenes which was experimental, ascetical, and mystical. One must leave to an expert an evaluation of these judgments.

The Baron finally considers Christianity. Admitting that he is over-simplifying, he speaks of the predominance of one of these three elements in the "Petrine school" (the synoptics), the "Pauline school" (divided into three stages of development), and the "Johannine school" (his gospel and epistles and the Apocalypse). The Petrine school is predominantly traditional, historic, and external; the Pauline school is chiefly "reasoning, speculative-internal"; and the Johannine school is mainly experimental and mystical-internal.[22] Then he runs through the whole history of Christianity, and finds periods when one or another element dominated.

Von Hügel concludes with an analysis of the factors that cause one element to be denied or suppressed. The basic reason is that the religious temper longs for simplification, but the Baron insists that unity, which must be universally human in all its elements, can be achieved only in a multiplicity of facts and forces. Even ordinary human life teaches us this. The "fighting, administrative, legal, and political" types, which incline to the external and institutional, are never satisfactory in isolation. The medical, mathematical, and natural sciences drive one toward the internal-intellectual in an extreme way. Poetic, artistic, and humanitarian activities lead to the internal-emotional which is dangerous alone.

Our faith itself pleads the same case. We cannot apprehend the unity of God except in multiplicity. In fact, in God there is a sort of multiplicity which loosely corresponds to our own powers. God the Father and Creator, is conceived as corresponding to the sense-perception, imagination, and memory; God the Son and Redeemer, as the Logos, to our reason; God the Holy Spirit, as corresponding to the effective-volitional force. Thus, as in our own selves, so in God there is a unity in multiplicity.

Von Hügel concludes that any of these three elements, operating alone, cripples religion, and that only from their mutual friction and interaction can a healthy, balanced religion result.[23] Catholicism at its best portrays these elements in organic unity.

The Baron's theory of the three elements of religion tolerates all sorts of combinations and rich applications. Through it he challenged the Church of his time to deepen its sense of the mystery of God. This was to be accomplished, not only in the life of the Spirit, but also through a renewed effort at intellectual integrity, and through a reassessment of that element which had come to dominate all else, the institutional element.

C. THE INSTITUTIONAL ELEMENT

Von Hügel was a philosopher of religion, speaking mainly perhaps to non-Catholics about his Church. One hindrance to this dialogue was the institutional element of the Church. Although he was keenly aware of its dangers, he never minimized this element, but insisted strongly on its necessity.

The Baron's theory that Christ believed in a proximate end of the world would seem to make the institutional element of the Church useless, but he insists that this does not follow. The Church, it is true, remained small in the beginning because of this expectation, but Christ's teaching on the Kingdom is organic. Nowhere does it imply that only pure spirit or intellect will survive. Christ Himself selected twelve Apostles and gave them power and authority.

> If the precise term "Church" was, apparently, never uttered by the earthly Jesus, the thing itself is, in its essence, already truly present in the most undeniable of His own words, acts, and organisings.[24]

The parables of Jesus imply a social religious organism and a hierarchy of ordination. There is a movement from the one invisible God down to the one visible Jesus, on to the twelve visible men formed into a single college by Himself, and sent to preach, heal, forgive sins, and solemnly warn those who may refuse to hear them. This visible college is given a visible head by Jesus Himself. The mission of the Apostles, especially, gives the key for the later understanding of the institutional element of the Church. Nowhere does Christ emphasize being "alone with the Alone" as the essence of religion. His teaching is eminently social, and arises from the fact that the Kingdom was at the center of His preaching.

Ultimately, however, the Baron's predominant approach to institutionalism is through his philosophy of religion. His theory of knowledge demands that it begin with the senses, and institutionalism grows from this very fact. Religion is not apprehensible without the use of the senses. He finds Luther's doctrine, that the act and life of faith have nothing to do, in their origins, with the senses, to fly in the face of sound psychology and ordinary human experience: "I kiss my child not only because I love it; I kiss it also in order to love it."

Thus revelation must be manifested in space and time, and thereby becomes embodied in an institution. As institutionalism shrinks to the vanishing point, religion becomes merely a general, vague aspiration. Mysticism, when it shuns the senses and the institution, runs the danger of pantheism. The institution, then, is not a concession to human weakness, but a demand of the very make-up of man. Man must return to "the womb" of the institution if he wishes to be born to a fuller life. The Quaker and the Unitarian, he felt, had a tendency to think it a superior act to rise above these elementary things, but there is thus generated a narrower spirit than is found in institutionalism. George Fox, who rejected institutionalism, unconsciously made use of much that could come only through the institution. Without the Church as an institution, Protestantism itself might cease to be.[25] Even the existence of the papal office is linked by von Hügel to his theory of sense and institution:

> For either the Unity of the Church is constituted by the Spirit only, and then also priest and Bishop are not essential; or the Unity of the Church is constituted by Spirit *and* by sense and then the Pope is as essential as Priest and Bishop.[26]

Together with his doctrine on the non-subjective reality of God, his theory of friction, and his demand for the rights of historical method, this doctrine on institutionalism constituted four of von Hügel's five most recurring themes. (The fifth, the idea of graded revelation, will be treated in the next chapter.)

Dangers in the institutional element.   Although von Hügel insisted that the institutional element was an essential part of religion, he was at pains to assign it what he conceived to be its proper role. It is a coordinating factor between the mystical and intellectual elements. The Baron regarded the Church as an eschatological community. Holding firmly to the Parousia texts, he demanded that the institutional and intellectual elements should never free themselves from the tension generated by that "tip-toe expectancy" of the Parousia which is characteristic of the mystical mind. Without this tension, the intellectual element would degenerate into feverish devotion to a messianic human progress. The institutional element would begin to consider itself an end, not a means, and might try to supplant both the mystical and the intellectual. On the other hand, the Parousia idea itself must be held in tension by the demands of the spirit which requires natural interests and activities in order to operate, and which must seek social justice in order to grow. The whole life of the Church throbs in a rhythmic tension. "Official organisation and authority are . . . ever only a part in what is a dynamic whole—one moment and movement in what is life."

> The lonely, new and daring (if but faithful, reverent and loving) outgoing of the discoverer and investigator are as truly acts of, are as necessary parts of, the Church and her life as his coming back to the Christian hive and community, which latter will then gradually test his contribution by tentative applications to its own life, and will in part assimilate, in part simply tolerate, in part finally reject it.[27]

Thus a rhythmic "inspiration-expiration" operates in the breathing life of the Church.

The Church is thus, ever and everywhere, both progressive and conservative; both reverently free-lance and official; both as it were male and female, creative and re-productive; both daring to the verge of presumption, and prudent to the verge of despair.

The cure for lack of equilibrium is for:

Officials to cultivate in themselves also the non-official, the out-going, lonely and daring, the "expiration" movement of the complete soul and community; and for the pioneers and investigators to keep alive in themselves the recognition and practice of the homing, the "inspiration" movement, the patient referring back and living with the slow-moving, mentally ruminating, socially regulative multitude, and its and their official heads.

The contrast between the movements of inspiration and expiration shows up in the difference of attitude between what he terms "officialism," and that of those who are at least half-awake intellectually.

(1) A man, when he thinks, wills, prays, and adores, produces a new and original act, and from such acts springs creative fruitfulness. They are acts of the present, but at the same time authority will necessarily represent the previous, the what-has-already-been, a past whose infinite variety has been somewhat drained off. (2) The soul in its living religious effort will be lonely and isolated. It will, in a way, be estranged, not only from the majority, but at times from self. In an extended sense it becomes ecstatic; authority, however, will necessarily insist on the religious attitudes of the majority, the average. (3) In these moments, the soul will be immensely active; it will experience the act as rising from its own genuine activity, but also as being from God. Against this, authority necessarily demands a true passivity—it insists upon acting for us. It tends to ask for a repetitive reproduction of its order or action. (4) In these moments the soul necessarily risks and dares much, and is conscious of this risk as it is in all of life. Against this interior dynamic attitude, which is, in itself, a strength, authority insists upon a predominantly external and immediate safety, upon the elimination of risk. (5) At these moments the soul

endeavors to reach truth by an ever-deepening purity of disposition. Against this, authority rightly insists upon objective
truth rather than upon subjective truthfulness, upon truth as
something static and readily transferable, identical with certain
formularies, an orthodoxy, a thing. (6) In these moments the soul
tends to find beauty, truth, goodness, God, in various degrees,
anywhere and everywhere. Authority finds these more in one
particular place. It thus distinguishes good and evil on a
horizontal, geographical plane, and proposes this view in place
of the vertical, geological vision of the soul. (7) The soul
experiences an optimism in and through the pessimism arising
from its own action. Authority is necessarily optimistic throughout, at least as regards its own action, past, present, and future.
It cannot allow the tragic note, nor that of humor:

> In a word, the soul at its deepest is ever profoundly original,
> isolated, active, daring, interior, penetrative and superficially
> pessimist; it moves through suffering on to joy. And official
> authority is, as such, ever repetitive of something past and
> gone; is the voice of the average thoughts of the many; aims at
> limiting the actions of its subjects to a passive reception and
> more or less mechanical execution of its commands; is essentially
> timid; cares necessarily more for outward appearance and
> material output than for interior disposition and form in the
> soul's activity; maps out the very phenomenal world into visible,
> mutually exclusive regions of spiritual light and darkness; ...
> and must at least minimize as much as possible all, even pre-
> liminary present sins, pains and perplexities—at least, those
> of its own creation.

Similar ideas appeared often in his writings. His first major
book, *The Mystical Element of Religion*, began with a nostalgia
for a pre-Tridentine form of Catholicism. The saint he chose for
his study, St. Catherine of Genoa, belonged to a less institution-
alized period. He feared an institutionalism that would diminish
the sense of the mystery of God. To the Catholic who saw the
Church as a great legalistic and institutional structure he said:
"Institutionalism is only one aspect of religion," but to the

liberals, he declared: "Institutionalism is an essential aspect of religion." He balanced the two by asserting that the institution was not only necessary but must also remain "spiritually beneficent."

Von Hügel's thought on the Church is more that of a religious philosopher than of a dogmatic ecclesiologist. In fact, despite his protestations, there is some truth in considering him an apologete.[28]

While the Baron's mystical ideas were not developed into a full theory of the Mystical Body, it would be untrue to say that the idea does not occur in his writing. As we have seen, he strongly proposed the social aspect of Christianity, an aspect that flowers from an organism. This organism has its dynamism in a mysterious person-like identity. Paul, the Baron says, saw that the Last Supper meant a "mystical union of substances," and thus calls the Church the very Body of Christ. Paul proclaims that each organ is part of this great organism. However, each person is not the Bride of Christ, but the whole organism of the Church, and each soul only under the aspect of its union with this organism. For the Baron, the Eucharist is the "very heart of Catholic worship"; the Mass was important to him, but the Eucharistic presence loomed larger than the Sacrifice. His liturgical outlook had none of the dimensions of the modern liturgical revival, but this is merely to say that he shared the views of his time.

We have seen that von Hügel's doctrine on the Church is rich in tensions, but, in general, his writings on the Church lack the magnetism and warmth of his discussions on God.[29] Perhaps the basic reason for this is that he faced the precise problem, the institutional element of the Church. He often seems to be justifying this element as much to himself as to his audience.

It might seem that von Hügel's distinction between the institutional and the mystical elements occasioned a tendency to consider the institutional Church as a sort of external guard to protect one's individual mystical life, rather than as the organism from which it draws that life, but he warned against this conception. He spoke about:

> the priceless conception of the soul's personality being constituted in and through the organism of the religious society—the visible and invisible Church. This Society is no mere congeries of severally self-sufficing units, each exclusively and directly dependent upon God alone; but, as in St. Paul's grand figure of the body, an organism, giving their place and dignity to each several organ, each different, each necessary, and each influencing and influenced by all the others... [Thus we have] that outgoing, social co-operative action and spirit, which, in the more ordinary Christian life, has to form the all but exclusive occupation of the soul [and thus is prevented from] degenerating into mere feverish, distracted "activity."[30]

Von Hügel insisted on the Kingdom as the essence of the Gospel message, and thus underscored the social, community aspect of the Church, but the idea of the Kingdom connotes an eschatology. As the emphasis shifted from Kingdom to Church, Christians to a large extent moved from the concept of a renewed earth to the idea of heaven. Under either of these ideas, the Church remains a prophetic witness against the idea of a divine cosmic process of *universal* redemption. The great eschatological alternative of heaven or hell remains true to the gist of Jesus' teaching. The experience of man in the Church is that of God coming to him in trancendence, and calling for decision.

The Baron's theory of the three elements of religion, though conceived only as a rule of thumb, is useful. The institutional is for the sake of the mystical and intellectual, but these elements are incapable of healthy growth without the institutional. Those who think that the theory of the three elements blocks out areas too neatly are usually endowing the theory with more finality than the Baron attributed to it. It lays the groundwork for movement in a delicate region where precise lines have not been laid out, and may be applied to the Church in general, to one's local community church, to one's personal life. Drawn from reason and the history of religions, and not exclusively from the Catholic faith, it has an ecumenical tone. His early belief that it was a quite acceptable function for the layman or priest to be a discernible influence in the insitutional life of the Church, was cavalierly dismissed as an impertinence, as disloyal diplomacy. Such dismissal often provided a pretext for sidestepping serious consideration of the institutional aspect.

If one is looking for an organic synthesis of ecclesiology, one does not go to von Hügel, but if one is interested in a critique of the contemporary Church situation, von Hügel is rich and incisive. He thought that the approach to ecclesiology in his day too often belittled reality, and he insisted on the rough work preparatory to a new synthesis. Such work, widespread in the Church today, can rightly look back to von Hügel as a forerunner.

CHAPTER TWELVE

THE ENCOUNTER OF THE CHURCH WITH WORLD RELIGIONS

For myself I cannot conceive truth, or rather reality, as a geometrical figure of luminous lines, within which is sheer truth, and outside of which is sheer error; but I have to conceive such reality as light, in its center blindingly luminous, having rings around it of lesser and lesser light, growing dimmer and dimmer until we are left in utter darkness (*RG*, p. 33).

The fifth pillar in von Hügel's thought is that of graded revelation, and in this area it is absolutely necessary that the *context* of his thought be given prime consideration. What does von Hügel mean by the word "revelation"? He frequently speaks of it under the term "givenness"—it is a gift. No religion is to be taken seriously, he said, which does not have some idea of a supernatural givenness. This "givenness" is transmitted by a "condescension," a Patristic idea dear to the Baron; he frequently compares the process to a parent teaching a child. Finally, the result of revelation is primarily "fruitfulness" and richness in religious life.

Von Hügel, however, does not confine his use of the word to the historical revelation given in Christ as described, for example, in the documents of the Vatican Councils. He does not restrict himself to the use of the term in the technical sense of an address by God to man, beginning in the Old Testament, culminating in Christ, and definitively contained in Scripture and tradition. He often uses the word in a wider, looser sense which has Patristic antecedents and is found in St. Thomas.

This use sprang from his desire, not only to discover the essence of pre-Reformation Catholicism, but also to open the Catholic mind to the implications of the post-exploration world. His dialogue, accordingly, was carried on, not only with Protestants, but also with other religions of the world.[1] Catholicism, Protestantism, and long contact with India and the East lay in his memory.[2] He stated that his aim was "to make the Old Church as inhabitable *intellectually* as ever I can." This was to be done by confronting the Church, not only with science, or with the insights of Protestantism, but with the problems posed by the world religions. The science of comparative religion was in its infancy, but despite the fact that its early steps were extremely tentative and subjective, it raised questions demanding answers that would have to be incorporated into ecclesiology, and not treated as mere appendages or corollaries. The manner in which von Hügel moved toward such an undertaking emerges clearly from a synthesis of his scattered statements about revelation. Although they were proposed to audiences of many different religions, they reveal a unified image.

A. REVELATION

Von Hügel liked to compare revelation to the process of teaching children. The teacher presents more and more material for gradual assimilation, and this is the same developmental method he finds in the Bible, and in all religion.[3] The point of departure for a study of this development should be St. Thomas' distinction between nature and supernature, and not the distinction between fallen nature (sin) and redemption.[4] The study of religion in a given individual may begin from an analysis of inner experience, but the same study in history must always begin from the given, the reality. This reality is God who "gives" nature and supernature. To begin with sin is to focus first and foremost on man. We might remark that the Baron's approach is in harmony with his insistence on transcendence and his wariness of immanentism. His aim is to fit all religions into his world view, and to find their inner sense. Thus, the distinction between nature and super-nature gives him a better basis for contrasting religions without denying their proper goodness. To take the sin-redemption duality as the basis of his approach would be to begin with the study of corrosion, whereas he held high hopes for the potential-ities of "natural" religion.[5]

Nature, as reality, reaches us as a kind of self-revealing will. It is dangerous for religion to allow the operations of grace to deaden or deny the beauties of and the duties arising from nature; to do so would be to subtract the material for grace to work on. God and His truth are to be found everywhere; but they are everywhere in different forms, stages, and degrees, and the differences are not only quantative, but also qualitative.[6]

Man has a natural capacity to find the God of nature; he has a natural thirst for God; but in supernature God puts, as it were, salt into our mouths (grace), and we now thirst for what we are experiencing. Thus religion moves from an inchoate stage, where there is a diffused religiosity readily to be discerned in a generous docility present in human souls, to its culmination in historical religion and Jesus Christ. Nowhere does natural religion exist alone. There was always a dispensation of mingled nature and supernature.[7] In the non-Christian religions, men are also touched by the "light that enlighteneth every man that cometh into the world." They are stimulated by a sense of "some, often world-forgotten, historic personality," and they tend toward a real, if "unconscious approximation of His type of life and teaching."[8]

Because of von Hügel's conception of religion as a gradual, ascending development under the impulse of God, the con-temporary presentation of the doctrine of original sin caused him great difficulty. He found that anthropology and ethnology were undermining the evidence for holding a "primitive high level of human knowledge and innocence, and a single, sudden plunge into a fallen state."[9] All our knowledge points to a gradual rise from lowly beginnings. Science, however, leaves undisturbed the truth of faith that man's condition denotes a fall from the Divine intention, and is a parody of God's purpose in history. The Baron admits that he has trouble in understanding Trent's insistence that real sin is inherent in original sin.[10] Without rejecting or accepting the opinion, he cites F. Tennant, who maintained that the Fall was really a refusal of ascent.

Von Hügel, as have seen, was careful to underline the fact that the historical revelation in Christ did not mean that the world before Christ was God-forsaken. This idea gives the significance of his warning against "an excessive Christo-centric theology." In the religions before Christ, and even today, salvation is attained with the help of God's grace by the practice of elements in the religion which "are true and good and originally revealed by God."[11] He sees not only Judaism, but also Hinduism and other religions as preparations by God for the fullest revelation of Himself, and finds in them mixed degrees of light. This does not mean:

> that these various religions are all equally true (or false), and that it does not matter to which you belong (provided only you are in good faith). No: in these deepest and most delicate of all matters, even a little more light, more power, more reality—even what *looks* a little—means, and is, very profoundly, much.[12]

At the center of von Hügel's thinking is the idea that there are grades of Divine self-revelation.[13] He speaks often of the Catholic Church as the fullest and richest form of religion. We must be careful not to misjudge these statements as some have done.[14] Von Hügel was speaking, we might say, as a Catholic phenomenologist or existentialist. He avoided terms like essential, accidental, substantial. He did not say that the Church was essentially the revelation of God, even if it bore accidental blemishes; the dichotomy, essential-accidental, was alien to the non-Catholic mind to which he spoke, and it still is today. He called the revelation in Christ the richest, fullest, unique revelation. Although he was criticized on this point he was not proposing anything unacceptable.[15]

Von Hügel's endeavor was to discover some religious truth in other religions; he struggled with the problem of all men's access to God as much as he did with the problem of a divided Christendom.[16] The Baron's eirenic attitudes were frowned on by many of his co-religionists; this was a natural reaction at the time. In his desire to deal fairly with other religions, the Baron was again a forerunner of modern developments.

It appears that von Hügel never used the phrase, "there is only one true Church." Probably he felt a lack of nuance here. In a letter of Aug. 31, 1909 to Miss Petre he makes it clear that abandonment of the Church could never result, objectively speaking, in the attainment of a fuller truth. He finds the revelation of God "at its fullest and purest" in Christ, and this revelation in Christ is qualitatively different and supremely unique.[17] When, therefore, he says that among the "great Revealers and Incarnations of the prevenient love of the Other-than-ourselves . . . Jesus Christ holds the supreme, indeed the unique place," he is not playing Christ down, but rather trying to appreciate what is noble in other religions. He wrote, toward the end of his life: "What on earth is a simply relatively true religion, how can I live and die for what I admit is but one of many sincere . . . rivals for a similar acceptance."[18]

In an essay on Troeltsch's tri-partite division of Christianity into Church-type, sect-type, and mysticism, he found Catholicism, alone, as fully meeting the demands of the Church-type. He sees the non-Church, mystical type as terminating in an excess of feeling and individualism, and the Christian sect-type as lopsided and unbalanced. Neither of these contained God's ultimate truth.[19]

He looked out even beyond the sect. The great masses of the world who do not know Christ, do they not possess a core of truth? If Catholicism is the "culmination and fullest norm of all religion," it "must find something thus to crown and measure." The dynamism of religion is directed by a teleological force; its movement upwards is not vertical, but rather spiral.[20] As we move backwards down the spiral, we come to a unique, historical intervention of God in the Person of the Word, but as von Hügel moved farther back along that spiral, he reached Buddhism and Confucianism, which he found to be not religions properly so called, but the clearing ground for religion. Buddhism, for example, presented a value judgment in its combination of the Wheel of Reincarnation and Nirvana ideas. The human soul cries out to reach permanence and simultaneity. Primitive Buddhism stood on the bridge between religion and philosophy, but the individual Buddhist, ancient or modern, must not too easily be called an atheist.[21]

It will help to clarify von Hügel's thought on revelation if we gather together his ideas on the act which seizes revelation, that of faith.

B. FAITH

At the roots of our mind there is an impulse to accept knowledge as a true encounter with reality, but this impulse can be resisted. Thus, the very act of knowing requires an act of endorsement, a kind of faith. Consequently, it is not surprising that religious knowledge, too, rests on faith. If there is a God, he must be transcendent, and not merely immanent. Therefore, any religion worth having demands a faith which gives us more than just that which *we* want.[22]

Faith itself is not totally independent of family upbringing. Parents must not only *give* service to their children; they must also *be* tender and out-going, or they block in the young soul the meaning and possibility of a full and normal love. The senses must be developed in order that man be able to reach a healthy love, and whoever cannot love man will find it impossible to love God. Faith itself is connected with love, for there is an "intrinsic loveableness of creatures," and "to forbid such a love is to cut at the very roots of our apprehension of love of God."[23] Thus agnosticism often finds its roots in family training, but agnosticism also draws nourishment from the dishonest actions and unfounded statements of the representatives of religion itself. Apart from environmental factors, agnosticism finds a cause in the will itself. There lies there a contrariness to theism, an obstinacy, and lack of loyalty to the best in oneself.

Agnosticism, however, may not be as widespread as it seems. Much of it is associated with a shallow cleverness which is a quality of youth and immaturity, especially during the years between eighteen and twenty. In fact it seems that, up to the age of thirty, one is unable to make a final negative decision, especially as to the value of institutional religion.[24]

Again, atheism and agnosticism are, at times, mere labels. A dim experience of the Infinite, of God, often underlies what seems to be a complete negation. If this vague sense cannot be suppressed, it cannot constitute even the most elementary faith unless it is endorsed. But endorsement imposes a terrible obligation: to refuse it is to experience the unending disharmony and unappeased longing of the Lost.[25]

Nevertheless, one apparently can deny, in good faith, for many years, the very rudiments of theism.[26] However, while a man may be invincibly ignorant of contingent and historical facts such as the Church and Christ, von Hügel could not see how he could remain permanently in this condition with regard to some notion of God, however dim and unexplicit.[27] In fact, heroic action, coming not from a clear recognition of God at all, can be termed supernatural, but even for an implicit faith the Baron demands that man must co-operate with grace in preparing his dispositions for it. There is a surrender demanded which connotes a Person.[28]

C. NO SALVATION OUTSIDE THE CHURCH

Our discussion of revelation and faith brings us back to consider this formula. Is it a bridge or a wall? Does it invite or repel? Von Hügel sees it as a bridge:

> I have now and then come across thoughtful, scholarly Christians who seem to shrink from the universality of the claim of Christianity, and who incline to think that the way of the intolerable

hardness and exclusion is to look upon all the larger religions as of direct, divine institution, to last unto the end of time each for its own category and degree of followers; but I do not doubt for a moment that such views are mistaken. So little is it true that the claim to universality of itself produces intolerance that we can show, without all too great difficulty, that, where this claim ceases to be taken seriously, there the religion, whatever its past claim, shrinks up into the sacristy; for it is precisely because I hold Christianity in general, and Catholicism in particular, to have a message for all men that my conception of them remains large and many-sided, since "all men" includes an astonishing variety of aptitudes and needs; whilst the very moment I treat Christianity in general, and Catholicism in particular, as just one variety of belief established by God to run concurrently with the others to the end of time, I cease to have any logical reason why I should strive to keep my outlook larger than the particular group, which now adheres to it, presses for readily allows.... It is here, as everywhere else, only the conviction that there is but one God and innumerable variety of sides of life, every one of which, in so far as it is true and good, springs from Him and requires Him, it is only thus that we can keep or require a unity in variety and a sunlight that pierces all, and this is Catholicism and the other is not.[29]

Von Hügel's aim is to interpret the doctrine of no salvation outside the Church in an orthodox fashion, but also in a way that will invite rather than repel. As far back as 1894 he had been struggling with this problem:

Look, Sir [Gore], at our elementary, obligatory doctrine of *Extra Ecclesiam nulla salus*. But Pope Pius IX (allocution of Dec. 9, 1854), after strongly insisting on it as of faith, added: "Yet we must also recognize as certain that those who are, with regard to the true religion, in invincible ignorance, do not bear the guilt of this state in the eyes of the Lord. Now who will dare, in his presumption, to go so far as to mark the limits of this ignorance, according to the character and diversity of peoples, countries, minds, and so many other circumstances?"[30]

In his last work the Baron says that "St. Augustine, the least liberalizing of all the orthodox Fathers, has taught us solemnly that there are many human spirits belonging to the body of the Church who do not belong to its soul, and many human spirits belonging to the soul of the Church who do not belong to its body."[31] The Baron always disagreed with those who held for only an invisible Church. Yet at the same time, he maintained that the Church from Augustine to Pius IX had never clearly identified the visible and the invisible Church. Von Hügel approached the problem by distinguishing the Church into visible and invisible, rather than by distinguishing *types of membership* in the one Church. Pius XII, in the encyclical *Mystici Corporis* (1943), saw that the distinction visible-invisible ran the danger of presenting the visible Church "as a mere human institution with a certain disciplinary code and external ritual, but lacking power to communicate supernatural life." He condemned as an error the contemptuous opposition of the invisible Church of charity to the visible juridical Church, but even during the Modernist crisis, von Hügel never considered the visible church as a mere human institution devoid of supernatural power. His attitude can be summed up in his statement of 1918: "Nothing which falls deliberately short of Visible Unity can or should be the goal."[32]

Von Hügel was an ecumenist in the sense that he endeavored to make the Church understood, by the whole world, indeed, but especially by non-Catholic Christians, both liberal and conservative. He wanted others to join in this task, and he felt that the layman was peculiarly suited for this function since he was in closer contact with circles outside the Church.

D. THE LAYMAN IN THE CHURCH

In the preface to his *Mystical Element of Religion*, von Hügel states that he speaks as a devoted and grateful son of the Roman Church, and as a layman; and as a layman who loves religion, he cannot feel that an interest in other religions could be foreign to him. However, since he has no official authority, he is not bound by traditional, official caution. The "official Church" always has the right and the duty to judge the work of laymen, but the official Church does not operate in a vacuum. It sorts out and eliminates what is false, and proclaims what is true in the preliminary work of its "unofficial" members. In 1895, on the advice of Cardinal Rampolla, von Hügel drew up for Leo XIII a rather favorable memoir on the question of the validity of Anglican orders. Later, he learned through Lord Halifax that Cardinal Ledochowski considered this an "impertinenza" on the part of a layman. In 1906 he was upset by a rumor from Rome that there was a growing "determination to exclude all laymen from theological work and such-like activities."[33] Although the rumor was never crystalized into action, the spirit behind it remained strong until Vatican II.

Edmund Bishop, the great English liturgical scholar who became a Roman Catholic, felt that his productiveness was seriously blocked by what he considered to be the Church's attitude toward the layman. He felt that the role of the layman had been reduced to "be ruled and pay up" or "shut your eyes and open your mouth."[34] He wrote to von Hügel in 1904:

> After six or seven years of Catholic experience in the sixties and seventies, I proposed to myself to give up all interest in, and finish with, studies connected with religion, as not desirable or desired for the layman in my *milieu*. As it is, I listened to the advice of two secular priests . . . who bade me "not to mind but to go on!"[35]

Bishop was nevertheless crushed. In 1908 he wrote to von Hügel: "Truth is *not* to the Catholics a virtue for its own sake," and in 1913 he declared to Miss Petre:

> . . . but for the layman I think now as I have continuously felt— the layman of "sorts"—he is not wanted in our Church, in our day. I neither resist nor rebel . . . but one word seemed to describe the situation for the individual—*inter mortuos liber*.[36]

Von Hügel, however, would have none of this. Just two months before, on Jan. 30, 1913, he wrote to Miss Petre that Edmund

Bishop depressed him

> by his ever recurring insistence upon how, already in 1867, the
> Roman Church finally ruled out all lay work and lay help; how,
> practically, all one's life work is based upon an ignorance or
> ignoring of facts, unchangeable in a special degree and sense.

The Baron was upset by Bishop's insistence that "I was *steadily
ignoring that I was beaten.*" Bishop worked on the principle that
an essential quality for the layman is self-respect. Thus, however
inwardly critical one might be of authority, self-respect
prevented any "wirepulling" to manipulate it.[37]

But the Baron never gave up. In 1913, while rejecting the
attacks on Rome by the Capuchin L. Puecher Passavalli (titular
archbishop of Iconium, d. 1897) which were published in 1911,
he approved his stand as regards

> the large place actually assigned by Providence to the layman
> in the Church—how God can and does use laymen to awaken
> priests as well as laymen to the Christian, the twice-born temper,
> and to the need of a continual renovation of their souls and
> of alertness to the work of God—to the seekings after Him in the
> great world outside. And also this conviction is pierced by sad
> experience—of how there is no recognized position or action of
> such a directly spiritual kind left to the layman in the Roman
> Church of to-day.[38]

The Baron concluded that a monopoly of all influence in the
Church, a monopoly by the clergy of consultation, preparation,
and application, is as uncatholic as is every attempt to have
no clergy, no official heads, administrators, and hierarchical
subordination. (Von Hügel's appreciation of the priesthood and
priestly celibacy was deep and nuanced.)[39] Each extreme position
leads to impoverishment, whereas Catholicism consists in
balance, inclusiveness, and richness. Five years later, in 1918,
he forecasts that the day will come when Rome, having satisfied
not so much Protestant objections as its own good instincts, will
again unite the Christian world. Among those "good instincts"
he undoubtedly included the giving of a greater role to the
layman in the Church.

E. ECUMENICAL ACTIVITY

More and more, in his later years, von Hügel came in contact
with those who had a perplexed interest in the Church. His
recurring guiding principle in such encounters was that no one
should enter the Church unless he knew that he was seriously
sinning unless he did so. In 1909 Tyrrell sent A. A. Cock,
later the author of a critical analysis of the Baron's philosophy
of religion, to visit the Baron. Cock was vaguely interested in
the Roman Catholic Church, and von Hügel discussed with him
the pros and cons of membership in the Church, but advised
Cock that he should not think of changing his church affiliation
unless his conscience clearly told him that he was committing
positive and grievous sin by not changing.[40] Cock did not enter
the Roman Catholic Church. For years the Baron tried hard to
give a sense of institutional Christianity and of religion in
general to his niece, Gwendolen Greene, the daughter of his
brother-in-law by marriage, Hubert Barry. Although she was
thirty-eight years of age, the Baron instructed her as if she
were a child. A good deal of his pedagogy is found in *Letters to a
Niece*, a mine of insight in spiritual direction. But he feared that
his own personality would surrogate for God's. He begged her
not to decide until she had more light, a certainty of avoiding rash
judgments and action:

> I never want to convert any soul that is practising in good faith
> what religion it possesses. I only want to deepen and strengthen
> what the soul has already got. But, on the other hand, when I
> meet a non-practiquant Roman Catholic, I cannot rest for longing
> till I have brought it back to some, if not to the full practice
> of the Roman Faith.[41]

His niece once asked him if he was not indifferent to whether
his friends were Roman Catholics or not. He replied:

> The same thing—how can it be the same thing? My little old
> thing, you do not understand. I love many Anglicans, High
> Church, Broad-Unitarians, Presbyterians—yes—yes—all—many.
> But it is not *the same thing to me*— it can never be the *same thing*.

> I am a child of the Confessional—I am a son of the great Roman Church.[42]

The niece entered the Church in 1926, the year after his death. Another instance: Mrs. Lillie, a medical doctor and the wife of a Chicago professor of biology, had moved over many years from agnosticism to High Church Episcopalianism. The Baron wrote to her:

> You have no business to abandon Protestantism simply because it does not help or satisfy you much; nor to embrace Catholicism because it attracts you much more. You would deserve to find Rome an utter disappointment if you came like that! Your one sufficient, and really compelling motive, would be your feeling that you *must*, that you would be committing sin by not coming.[43]

Mrs. Lillie became a Catholic around 1920, influenced chiefly by her reading of *The Mystical Element of Religion.*

Evelyn Underhill, the great English Anglican writer on mysticism, chose von Hügel as her spiritual director five years before his death. She felt an attraction to Roman Catholicism, but had some deep objections. The Baron, while admitting that he would love to see her simply and completely "one of us," nevertheless advised her to make no move until her conscience told her that she must.[44] Although Miss Underhill under the influence of von Hügel remained an Anglican, she grew in respect for the historical element in Christianity, and for the central role of Christ in the spiritual life.

As Michael Hanbury has pointed out, the Baron's approach was strongly ecumenical;[45] It parallels the modern ecumenical movement which encourages a gradual growth toward unity. He asked Anglicans, at the time of the Modernist crisis, not to make capital out of the Church's position by recruiting Catholics in trouble to Anglicanism. Such tactics, he believed, would only deepen the breach between the two communions. But the Baron made it clear that he did not hold for indifferentism; where the conscience was clear, the obligation was clear.

Von Hügel also based his approach on principles which were rather personal, and more directly concerned with the spiritual life itself than with an ecumenical theory. Whereas he had earlier believed that he was gifted with keen insight into the character of others, in 1914 he wrote that our knowledge of others, even when "near and dear to us," is greatly colored by ourselves, and many times our knowledge is of ourselves alone. "Our knowledge of our fellows is not simple and clear" and great love is needed to surmount this barrier. Thus, towards the end, he told his niece: "The golden rule is to help those we love to escape from us; and never try to begin to help people or influence them, till they ask, but wait for them." He told her that a long list of people who had changed (i.e. been converted) through his influence had later become poor or unpracticing Catholics. He wished he had never talked to them and so unsettled them.[46]

The second reason for the Baron's approach was that he was dealing with highly cultivated English Protestants who loved their liberty. He warned them about difficulties they would have to face in the Church, and treated them most cautiously.[47]

The last reason for his approach is perhaps the most interesting. It concerns the relationship of grace to nature. The Baron was most taken with Benedict XIV's criterion for sanctity, namely, that it must manifest itself in joy, even despite a melancholic natural temperament. He had seen converts became bitter and leave Catholicism. He believed there is great danger when one offers "wares for which there is no conscious wish." Irritation and strain result,[48] a depressing tension that can be fatal to religion.

F. ECUMENICAL TRIBUTES

Von Hügel was rarely praised in Catholic circles. This is entirely understandable, for his involvement in the Modernist crisis, which we evaluate in the following chapter, made him a perplexing figure. Second, a feeling for ecumenical possibilities had not yet sufficiently penetrated into Catholic circles to enable them to distinguish between his valuable religious empathy and his exegetical positions. Yet there are enough hints spread through the literature on von Hügel to suggest that, even within his own Church, he had in certain circles a profound, if quiet, influence. For example, Michael Hanbury relates a remark of Algar Thorold, one time editor of *The Dublin Review:* "To me Algar said it was chiefly through Loisy, whom he had rated very highly, that he had left the Church, and that it was largely through Baron F. von Hügel that he had returned to her fold."[49]

Before we leave the subject of his influence on Catholics, let us say a brief word about influence on his own family. I cannot resist the temptation to describe the Baron's three daughters as the mystical, institutional, and intellectual elements in his family. The youngest, Thekla (born 1886), is today a Carmelite nun in London. The middle daughter, Hildegard (born 1879), worked on Catholic social projects. She founded a Catholic girls' club and associated both with fashionable society and working girls.[50] The eldest daughter, Gertrud (born 1877), was the most intellectual. She suffered problems with her faith because the Baron imprudently exposed her to critical and intellectual pursuits which unsettled her; he grieved over "putting out her eyes." Ironically, it was Tyrrell, more than anyone, who helped her retain the faith, though Huvelin was also a factor. Before she died prematurely in 1915, she had, for a long time, grown deeper and deeper in the faith, and died an admirable death.

Outside the Church von Hügel's influence was almost sensational. In the Synthetic Society (1896–1908) he associated with such men as Canon Gore, Clement Webb, Hastings Rashdall, Alfred Lyall, Pringle-Pattison, William Temple, and Dr. Matineau. He continued his contacts in The London Society for the Study of Religion, which he helped to found. As a pioneer, he envisioned an "ecumenism" within a social, organized cadre, and not on an individual basis alone. Dean Inge, who attended the meetings of the London Society, said: "There is no writer on the Philosophy of religion with whom I am in more general sympathy, and from whom I have learned more, than Friedrich von Hügel."[51] Bishop Gore considered him the most learned man living. Nathan Flew, a nonconformist, wrote a paper in 1952 on the Catholic Church for the World Conference of Faith and Order, since no Catholic was allowed to make a contribution. In the paper, praised by Bernard Leeming for its kindliness and impartial scholarship, Flew said he was indebted to von Hügel as his inspirer.[52] The works of William Temple, Archbishop of York, were influenced by the Baron.[53] Some Anglican circles have looked upon the Baron as almost beyond criticism, especially in his specifically religious publications.[54] Bishop Talbot of Winchester was willing to sit as a "humble learner" at the Baron's feet. Humphrey Johnson, who was a convert at the age of twenty-one, and an acquaintance of the Baron, wrote in 1937 as a Catholic priest:

> It may be doubted whether in the whole history of religion there has been another case of a man who lay under gravest suspicion in his own community, wielding, during his lifetime, an oracular authority over so many members of another. The reverential awe, not merely by intellectually minded High Churchmen, but even by Modernists and Free Churchmen, certainly forms one of the most curious episodes of contemporary religious history.[55]

Johnson, who has been critical of von Hügel's ideas on exegetical questions, mentions that the Baron's influence was particularly felt between the appearance of *The Mystical Element* in 1908 and his death in 1925.

In 1914 von Hügel was given the honorary degree of LL.D. at the University of St. Andrews in Scotland. In 1920 Oxford conferred on him the honorary Doctorate of Divinity, the first Catholic to be so honored since the Reformation. Edinburgh University invited him to deliver the Gifford Lectures for 1924–26, but his final illness intervened. His *Reality of God and Religion and Agnosticism* would have been the basis for these lectures.

Von Hügel, the layman, owed a great deal of his ecumenical insight to a priest, the Father Tyrrell of the early days. They mutually influenced one another, and the Baron's thought owes a great deal to Tyrrell's early work, "The Prospects of Reunion."[56]

What are the *general* lines of von Hügel's thought, as found
in these last two chapters on the Church? He has sketched out
a philosophy of religion which embraces the world religions,
and yet treats Catholicism as the divinely willed means in God's
economy. Although his treatment is weak in its presentation
of an organic mysticism of the Church, it is strong in its outward
thrust. Certain exegetical bases seem false, but the general
treatment is strong, optimistic, and devoid of narrowness. At
the same time the Baron faced up to the problems raised in
his time by comparative religion. Those who have not received
Christian revelation, as well as those outside the Catholic
Church, were not relegated to the state of peripheral problems,
but their situation was envisioned so centrally that the nature
of the Church and of Christian revelation itself is rightly
highlighted.

Von Hügel's idea of a graded "revelation" leads back to
the question of exegesis and authority. The Baron has envisioned
an economy of grades of "revelation" (he uses this last word in
such a way as to bring out the fact that man, outside the Judaeo-
Christian economy, is not left totally without God's word, for
he finds it in nature, grace, and common tradition) which
culminates in the revelation of Christ.[57] Thus, we have a line
of movement up to Christ, but what happens to this movement
after Christ? Does it cease? For von Hügel the revelation in
Christ is the unique and final revelation of God, but the movement does not cease. Just as nature and grace prepared for *the*
revelation, so nature and grace follow revelation and prepare
mankind for a more profound grasp of it. This is all a movement
forward, and in this process there is involved all of man's
world, and all of his tools, nature, science, exegesis, the world
of moral demands, and the experience of charity, the pattern of
Church tradition and magisterial teaching. Thus, there is,
simultaneously, a purification and development in our understanding.

Rather than speak about a development of dogma, the
Baron proposes a providential development in man and in his
environment which in turn develops him again, so that he better

understands revelation. This is exactly the meaning von Hügel drew from the Galileo incident. He saw providence making use of science to purify our idea of what God is saying in the Old Testament. Without science and exegesis, we might have lingered on what He is not saying to us to the detriment of His true word.

We might say that von Hügel envisions a "hominisation" of revelation, a "hominisation" whose thrust is to leave fewer and fewer aspects of revelation fallow and not brought into man's consciousness.

This very process, however, necessarily gives rise to the problem of authority. There will be the danger that man will not "hominise," but humanize, revelation: man may project his ideas into it. The Baron often stated that the Church, which is the guardian and final interpreter of revelation, as well as the mother of our civilization, must not only share man's toil, but must oversee his efforts. The nature of the Church, which is based on the very revelation that it is guarding, *should* finally involve a kind of tension. The believer and scholar should not feel that there is automatically "something wrong with the machinery" because the pattern of authority occasionally presses on him. On the other hand, neither should Church officials feel that this tension is something new, cantankerous, and strange. The author of revelation has His own willed ways, and Catholics cannot be the ones to say, "Would that it were not so."[58]

CHAPTER THIRTEEN

THE EVOLUTION OF
VON HÜGEL'S THOUGHT

Blind obedience to any authority is never equal to enlightened adhesion... [yet] it is not by denying as false what I do not yet see as true, that I give myself the chance of growing in insight (*EA* 1, p. 14, 1920).

A. THE RELATION OF DOGMA TO HISTORY

Léonce de Grandmaison, who was a puzzled admirer of Friedrich von Hügel, wrote in 1926: "He will remain one of the most winning but also one of the most enigmatic figures of contemporary Christendom."[1] Since then some fine studies have been written which have helped to fill out the picture of his personality and thought. Certain aspects, however, of the last period of his life, from about 1910 until 1925, have remained somewhat puzzling.

The evolution of von Hügel's thought may be divided roughly into three periods: a time of groping until about 1900, given mostly to work on the Old Testament and general considerations on biblical scholarship; a period of intense conviction and debate until about 1910, including his early support of Loisy, and his debate with Blondel on the interpretation of the Gospels and the consciousness of Christ; and a period of "transition" from 1910 onwards. We will now attempt to clarify his positions during this last period.

Because of recent historical criticism, von Hügel said, some begin to feel that ideas could remain true even if their historical basis vanished.[2] He considers this position impossible and ruinous. Just as knowledge demands sensation, so Incarnational religion demands factuality. Christianity is not merely a doctrine. The condescension of God, "the penetration of spirit into sense," of the spaceless into space, cannot be relevant or revelant to man if its "happenedness" is known to God alone. Religion, for man, cannot be mere ethics, it demands a "givenness."

Von Hügel held that some dogmas involving history protect a nucleus of historical fact necessary for Christianity, but whatever was phenomenal in these, and therefore open to critical investigation, belongs to history, and not to faith. "My true conviction about the strictly historical-phenomenal character of the Virginal conception and of the bodily Resurrection would not be faith but science."[3] He himself held, in faith, that the Resurrection consisted in objective, i.e., not subjectively induced, apparitions of the glorified Christ to his disciples. He also considered the historical evidence for these to be most strong; he regarded the empty tomb narratives as moderately suasive but secondary. For the gospels in general he insisted on a necessary historical nucleus of facts which, as he put it, would be protected by providence.

The Baron's thought is unclear here. No doubt he did not relinquish to the contingencies of critical investigation a nucleus essential for faith. He constantly rejected the idea that Christian faith can exist without an objective basis of saving events. His position seems to have been that the believer in his faith-encounter with the Father through Christ in His Church adheres by faith to this nucleus involving the Person of Christ. This faith would be both connected with and would safeguard an essential nucleus of scripture, and it would confidently leave scripture open to critical study.

He thought that the dogmas of the descent into hell and of

the Ascension were being re-interpreted in such a way that the faith-content was left unchanged, while the spatial imagery had lost its absolute significance under the pressure of fact and our progress in thought.[4]

Certain aspects of his program are very enlightening, but he allowed himself to apply it, as, for example, with regard to the Virginal conception, in a way which is against the Catholic dogmatic interpretation of Scripture. One is reminded here of the modern movement of "demythologizing." These positions of the Baron have too often been left unrecorded.[5] We have a right to know that a man like von Hügel made these *suggestions*. Only be pointing this out can we draw from our exegetes and theologians a contemporary handling of the matter.

While von Hügel held a non-orthodox position on the relationship between history and dogma, the same cannot be said for his presentation of the connection between the revelation of what is totally beyond history and dogma. Revelation is received in an experience which he calls "the pure gold," which includes an "obscure and vivid apprehension" and a "devoted will." Dogma and theology become the "silver of clear reflexion and reasoning" by which the apprehensions are transmissible to future generations.[6] Dogmas may, indeed, be absent "one remove" from these supra-historical realities apprehended by faith, but this is not to make them totally relative. Dogma is protected in its relation to the Absolute Reality "through the mediation of the Religious Life," which itself is "Evidential, Realist, Metaphysical," but this is not pure pragmatism, for "this Religious Life cannot . . . be divested of its *evidential metaphysical* quality, nor may that quality be treated as always present indeed, but misleading or ignorable."

> And the sense impressions, the sense world, on the one hand, and the Dogmas, on the other hand, would have to be admitted to stand in *some objective* relation, not only to our own minds and souls, but to the Realities conveyed to our minds and souls.[7]

Here von Hügel satisfactorily links revelation and dogma through psychology and metaphysics. Dogma, the finite partial expression of revelation, has its axis in the Absolute through an objective relation. The dogmatic formulation, therefore, has some absolute value. The analogy of being is thus insisted upon. The conceptual dogma and Christian experience are objectively related. At the same time they are not formally identical.[8] In sum, von Hügel has achieved the link between revelation, dogma, and Christian experience.

The Baron never changed in his evaluation of the absolute interior assent demanded by dogmas. This centred on the "necessary realities of religion," and his rather vague nucleus of "historical facts."[9] He did, however, change in his appreciation of the value and need of the Church's disciplinary, practical, and pastoral jurisdiction in so far as this called for "our conditional belief and practical conformity."

Though some of his positions were unacceptable, the Baron raised questions that demand deeper study by Catholic theologians: what is the criterion for determining the essential (or, as Protestant liberals say, "decisive"), and the accidental (as in some spatial images) in dogma? How exactly do spatial and temporal images and happenings differ as regards dogma? Since patristic tradition is certainly a criterion for making the distinction, and since today we differ on some points from patristic exegesis, what, precisely, is unchangeable in patristic consensus? We arrive at von Hügel's question which he applied to Scripture, but which is valid also for tradition: "what precisely is the formal conviction of the author?" Work is being done in this area and it must be deepened. The questions von Hügel asked are the same ones that will be raised as the ecumenical movement progresses. Our Catholic position must be developed in all its depth if it is to make an impact in ecumenical meeting.

B. PAROUSIA AND IMMINENCE

On another important thesis, von Hügel's final position was an admission of uncertainty about the solution. His theory was that Jesus was mistaken on the date of the *parousia*, but that the essence of his message did not lie in the time-prediction (this was a non-essential detail), but in the conviction of the transcendent power of God over the world.

In 1907 von Hügel had written: "Christology is, and probably will long remain, the most important, yet also the most difficult, of the theological problems of the Christian world."[10] In reviewing the pantheistic Christology of the Rev. R. Campbell, he attacked Campbell's solution that all mankind was, at least potentially consubstantial, in some way, with the Father, and that Christ, too, was thus consubstantial with the Father.

> Either, argues Mr. Campbell, Christ's consciousness could not be a limited one, and He be God; or He could be and was God, even though His earthly consciousness was limited. But if these two things, limitation of consciousness and Divinity, could co-exist in Christ, they cannot, he concludes, be intrinsically irreconcilable, they must be capable of combination in any and every human soul.[11]

The Baron however indicated an alternative, and in so doing showed he still believed in a limited consciousness in Christ. He describes this alternative in non-scholastic terms. It is

> a penetration which, in the case of Christ, operates indeed in a unique manner and degree, but which is still best conceived as a penetration, a permeation. For the orthodox conception still holds that in Christ there are human senses, a human imaginative faculty, human reasoning powers, human emotions, and a human will—each of these energies penetrating the others, and all of them permeated by the Spirit, by God Himself—in this case so intensely as to constitute this Spirit, God, their sole ultimate responsible "I."

After this somewhat confusing statement about the divinity of Christ he then moved to the question of the Parousia:

> The element of Transcendence appears plainly in Our Lord's temper and teaching: for what is His poignant insistence upon His proximate Second Coming but a special form and massive

instance of this element? Unless such an element is, in its substance, essential to complete religion, we shall have to admit that an integral part of the primitive Christian life and mind was simply fanatical; whereas if such an element is, in its substance, essential, then that tip-toe expectation, that intense other-worldliness, is in its spiritual significance and operation, part of all deepest religion as revealed by Christianity and a pungent salt of truth and vitality which we must never allow to grow dull.

Von Hügel here presents an idea which he cherished all his life, that the teaching about the proximate Second Coming is really a teaching about the transcendence of God, and the surety of His final victory. The Baron never abandoned the idea that the difficult eschatological texts embodied an extremely important truth. A. Feuillet has said: "The problem of the Parousia is assuredly the most complex and the most arduous of all the problems which the exegesis of the N.T. presents. . . . In reality it is the conviction of the proximity of the Parousia which, rightly understood, gives its true religious sense to the history of humanity as it unfolds today. . . . We have arrived at the last stage which can be very long."[12]

It was characteristic of von Hügel to have been among the first to grapple with a truth whose importance was only gradually recognized. It is essential to notice that he ties the eschatological problem to the notion of transcendence. His interpretation of the eschatological statements of Christ is closely connected with his desire to guard the transcendence of God. The belief in the imminent irruption of God into history and pantheistic immanence are irreconcilable.

Although he disengaged this central truth of the eschato-logical texts, he remained in an exegetical tangle. We may block out his position as follows: (1) Jesus as man (2) was convinced of and taught (3) His proximate (4) second coming. The coming of Christ is treated as something cosmic and visible, and not merely spiritual, up until the very last years of von Hügel's life. Then, as we shall see, he wavered as to the nature of that coming. His thought finally tapers off into a sense of mystery.

We shall look first at the development of his idea, and then, at the legacy of his profoundly rich but never coherently organized insights.

In 1908 the Baron wrote his extensive review of Loisy's *Les Evangiles Synoptiques* for *Rinnovamento*, which he signed "H." After presenting Loisy's analysis of the eschatological texts in the Synoptics, he gives his own conclusions. He says there are two possibilities: either Christ never taught a proximate Parousia, although the first generation held such an idea and had gradually to mitigate it, or Christ taught such an idea precisely because he actually believed it.[13] The first alternative seems to contradict critically established facts, and presents the grave difficulty of the first generation of Christians misunderstanding an important point in Christ's teaching. (This position is held today, for example, by C. Dodd and J. A. T. Robinson.) The problem must be faced with courage; it is not insurmountable.

One might ask, "If Christ is God, how could He ignore the date of His Second Coming?" The question does not take account of the fact that our knowledge of man, of a holy man in particular, is very limited. Second, our knowledge of God is even more limited, and is undefinable. When God and man are uniquely united, our knowledge will be as confused as was knowledge of each of the two united elements.[14] The Baron then cites St. Athanasius who admitted that Christ did not know the date of the Parousia. This ignorance would imply a certain fanaticism in Jesus, for it seems fanatical to conceive as close an event whose date one does not know. Von Hügel admits that this fanaticism would be fatal to our image of Jesus, but he is sure this idea can be avoided. The teaching of Jesus in such matters is typical "of the most profound specifically religious spirit." He believes that Jesus had four convictions about the Parousia. It would be sudden and unforeseen, proximate, social, and individual, and the work of God alone. If Christ was truly man He could not but apprehend and express the eternal reality and truth in the intellectual form, and with something of the images and emotion of people to whom He preached. The action of God is always conceived in the Bible as instantaneous. So, too, the religious soul who believes and hopes ardently conceives what is successive and future under the aspect of simultaneity and eternity; it sees the future as imminent and present. Christ's message thus establishes the certainty that the Kingdom is the work of God alone. The soul of Christ is absorbed in the presence and action of God. He proclaims a message about the Kingdom of God which is incompatible with the idea of total immanence—that Kingdom will break in transcendently from God. This may be a scandal to some, but it is a message which is vital to retain. This is the essence of His message, and not the time prediction.

At first sight this explanation seems to have situated the texts about the Parousia in a literary genre which we might call apocalyptic, eschatological, or prophetic. Yet the Baron continued to hold that Christ was certain about a physical and proximate end of the world. Thus, von Hügel's thinking has not really faced the difficulty of Christ being in error; he simply obscures the time-prediction aspect. He made no distinction, one which many Catholic exegetes find in the texts, between Christ's coming (verified for example in the Resurrection, Pentecost, the end of the Temple which situates the time prediction), and a cosmic end. He has not avoided the difficulty that to leap from passionate hope to passionate conviction is a characteristic of the fanatic. (The Baron never had recourse to the solution that Christ's recurrent words about "this generation" referred to the whole age of mankind.)

On Mar. 20, 1909 von Hügel wrote a letter to his friend Professor Clement Webb which is a gloss on his previous articles. He admits that the conception and inculcation of the Parousia as proximate is a major difficulty in Christology. His solution is that it expresses:

> a deep and abiding, *right* orientation of first-hand and specific spirituality, which, quite clearly, tends, in proportion to its depth and purity, to conceive all *sub specie aeternitatis*, and, in

as much as time is still considered, to apprehend such time as at hand and instantaneous. If Our Lord did not know the date of His Second Coming (and this ignorance He tells us was with Him), then, religious genius that He was, He was bound, as such, to conceive it as proximate and swift as lightning (I have printed something about this; but anonymously, more or less).[15]

Back in 1935, Nédoncelle wondered whether von Hügel might be saved from suspicion of suggesting positive formal error on the part of Christ. The real question, he said, was not that of positive error, but rather of ignorance; the appearance of error comes from the refraction of a profound truth in imaginative and symbolic representations.[16] In the same letter, the Baron speaks of Jesus' "conception and inculcation of His Parousia as proximate." For the Baron, this Parousia was considered, until his last statements, a physical cosmic event. Thus, Christ Himself would have been unaware of any symbolism in His insistent teaching.

With the appearance of *Eternal Life* in 1912, von Hügel began to emphasize a second current. He speaks of Jesus' parables as containing elements that become better understood in time. Further, he says that "Jesus' very presence involves, in a very real degree and way, the presence of the Kingdom" (Lk 4:19, 10:23; Mk 2:19). Thus, Jesus distinguishes between the Kingdom coming in power, and "the Kingdom as already come in obscurity and weakness."[17] Although the Baron reacts against an excessive eschatology in Schweitzer and Loisy, he admits that the imminence of the Kingdom in Our Lord's life and teaching "has, almost from the first, been a grave difficulty for those whom reason and conscience constrain to combine a frank acceptance of the textual evidences with a deep conviction of Our Lord's profound spiritual insight and supreme normality.[18] Thus, he has not yet found a solution. While he has pointed out that Jesus' sayings were in an apocalyptic form, yet he strangely leaves Jesus less conscious of this than were the prophets whom von Hügel elsewhere said were probably aware of a symbolism in their affirmations. He leaves this solution unexplored.

In 1913 von Hügel finds that Biblical criticism raises formidable problems for Christology:

> In Our Lord's own teaching also, the shortness of the persistance of our visible world's present order is implied, taught, solemnly insisted upon. His Proximate Second Coming, with its profound change and conclusion of all earthly conditions, becomes especially emphasized from the great scene with Peter at Philippi onwards.[19]

He believes that even many of the parables insist on the abrupt and proximate end. The prophets, "even the King and Crown of the Prophets, have appeared in the history of the world as so many great stormy petrels, as warning voices, calling man back to God, the Eternal, on the occasion of some national break-up and coming change." From 1912 to the famous essay of 1919 on "The Apocalyptic Element in the Teaching of Jesus," von Hügel's thought remains the same.[20] In this essay he still finds Loisy and Schweitzer somewhat violent in their handling of the texts, in which he discovers that Jesus speaks of three distinct events: His death and resurrection; a divinely effected end of the then extant world with Jesus descending as judge of all mankind; and a national destruction, in that order.

Von Hügel maintains that Jesus was preserved "from all essential error concerning the direct objects of the divine indwelling and condescension." Yet Jesus' truth and insight would, of necessity, show, to minds and hearts of other races and times, imaginative and emotional peculiarities—certain omissions, combinations, stresses, outlines, colorings—characteristic of the race and time of the Revealer. Otherwise, the Revealer would have begun His career by being simply unintelligible to His first hearers, and in the long run even to the large majority of mankind; and He would, in Himself, not be normally, characteristically a man.

In Judaism the Divine action is conceived as instantaneous. "If then Jesus held the present world's present order would be terminated by an act of God, He could not image and propound this act other than as sudden and rapid." But nowhere does the Baron suggest that Christ was aware of the image quality of

His teaching. Everywhere, and without questioning this theory, he presumes that Jesus' idea involves a conception of a cataclysmic, physical end of the cosmos;[21] nevertheless, he states that Jesus Himself had given "unequivocal indications as to how He would envisage, how He would organize, permanent Christian institutions, did the permanence of the world require—as in fact it is now requiring—a corresponding permanence of the Christian organization." "It is really because of Jesus' utter certainty of the unchanging justice and providence of God that, under the pressure of a proximate earthly defeat of the cause of truth and right, He vividly foresees a corresponding exaltation of this same cause." Von Hügel still thinks that Christ foresaw an imminent cosmic event which never came about. He holds that the time element in statements which are specifically religious, and not philosophical, are so secondary that to misjudge it cannot constitute formal error in a religious matter. The Baron has reached an impasse. It is as if he were to say that if Christ proclaimed that He would rise from the dead on the third day, it would satisfy the religious sense if He were to arise only at the end of time.

The Baron, of course, did not feel that he had basically solved the problem. On March 7, 1921, he wrote to Webb, and distinguished between the "Proximate Second Coming, Suffering Messiah . . . . problems *special* to Our Lord" and " . . . exorcisms, catastrophic End of the World," which were problems "taken over and continued by Him."[22] The distinction here between a proximate second coming and a catastrophic end of the world is crucial, but von Hügel never faced its significance. As late as Dec. 22, 1921 he refused to be called an apologist precisely because his essays contain, among other problems, statements like "Jesus Himself taught the proximity of His Second Coming, and we know not how to reconcile this with even a purely religious inerrancy."[23]

Von Hügel's last statements on the subject were recorded by his niece, Gwendolyn Greene, with whom he corresponded.[24] He is against "trying to get rid of the apocalyptic element in

the teaching of Jesus because it raises so many difficulties that
we cannot solve."

> We see everywhere in the Synoptics the immense warnings, and
> texts obviously of Our Lord's own utterance, on the nearness
> of the Judgment, of the sudden coming of the Kingdom, of His
> own coming, in glory and power.... It is not only a Second
> Coming, but a Proximate Second Coming.... It is a teaching
> *peculiar* to Our Lord. The sudden arrival of the Kingdom, the
> choice between good and evil, the immense warnings, the abiding
> consequences of sin, all these are bound up with this great teaching
> of Our Lord.

He cherishes the doctrine for its spiritual significance, because
of its demand for self-purification, and its exhortation to be
ready for the suddenness of God's call, without attempting to
solve the historical and Christological problem. He went on to
make, almost incidentally, a very important observation:

> Our Lord sees something, I do not see clearly what. He is beyond
> me. I know I cannot see what he sees. I do not know that I even
> want to. But I love to accept this great doctrine....[25]

E. Poulat rightly warns that this phrase cannot be taken
to indicate some abrupt change in von Hügel's thinking.[26] It is
nevertheless the first time that von Hügel has even hinted about
confusion as to the content of Our Lord's conviction, though
this was latent in his description of the two currents in Christ's
thought. Of the four elements which we have blocked out: (1)
Jesus as man (2) was convinced of and taught (3) His proximate
(4) second coming, usually the Baron concerned himself with
the problem in the third element; now for the first time he wavers
on the content of the fourth element. "Our Lord sees something,
I do not see clearly what."

In *The Mystical Element of Religion* von Hügel has an
interesting citation:

> [Professor Ward] points out how readily, owing to the ambiguous
> term "consciousness," we confound experience with knowledge;

but holds that experience is the wider term. Knowledge must
fall within experience, and experience extend beyond knowledge.
Thus I am not left to infer my own being from knowing.[27]

Some such idea was doubtless in the back of his mind when
he discussed the growth of Christ's human conceptual
knowledge of his own divinity: it was a stable experience, but
grew with the growth of knowledge. The Baron finds two
elements in human consciousness, a "pure-unitedness and
simultaneity" which "becomes intelligible to us only as a juxta-
position in space and a succession in time."[28] If this is so of
human consciousness in general, it is also true of human consciousness when it realizes the presence of God in mystical
experience.

The Baron points out that St. Theresa always feared delusion
in her visions which she tested only by their fruits. The true
mystic, he says, distinguishes the spiritual reality from "those
realities of an intrinsically spatial—and temporal-seeming—
embodiment." Thus the mystic becomes more aware of the
incomprehensibility of God. The Baron quotes St. John of the
Cross:

> He that will rely on the letter of the divine locutions or on
> the intelligible form of the vision, will of necessity fall into
> delusion, for he does not yield to the Spirit in detachment
> from sense.[29]

This is an eminently sane doctrine; yet the Baron did not
apply to Christ his study of the mystical consciousness. He
did not draw the conclusions his philosophy demanded and thus
hid from himself the impossibility of his position. For if Christ
did not distinguish between the spiritual reality and "those
realities of an intrinsically spatial—and temporal-seeming—
embodiment," He could not fit the Baron's definition of the
mystic who is "great and spiritual." It is evident that von Hügel
was dimly aware of something unsatisfactory in his presentation.
His solution is that Christ had to envision everything *sub specie
aeternitatis* and, in as much as time was *considered at all*, He
had to conceive it as "instantaneous." The Baron's escape from

the impasse is to say that the time-element is not part of the message, but this is impossible, I believe, to reconcile with Jesus' many statements about an event to be experienced by the contemporary generation. The time-element is so important that in 1922 von Hügel has to admit that he does not know how to reconcile this "even with a purely religious inerrancy." It can be conjectured on good grounds that the reasons why von Hügel did not reconcile his exegesis with his sound philosophy of mysticism are three, and they must be taken together: his trust in the "science" of his exegesis, his cushioning theory of friction, and his concentration of the value of *this* exegesis as a transcendental block against an immanent view of God.

Thus, it is interesting that, in his final word on the subject, he abandons *time* as the problem (whatever *it* was, it was to be proximate), and changes the problem to the content of the proximity: "Our Lord sees something, I do not see clearly what." In relaxing his certainty as to the content, he opened the way to a solution already contained in his own thought.

In addition to this last quotation, and to his valuable insights on consciousness and mysticism in *The Mystical Element*, other statements by the Baron should be weighed: that Christ spoke in apocalyptic *form*; that the "little apocalypse" of Mark 13 was artificial and a composite (thus, "all these things" which were to come about are unidentified); that the prophets did not take all the details of their words literally; that Christ Himself made provision for the possible continuance of the community; and that the Kingdom had, in some sense, already come. One can piece together the following theory from statements made by von Hügel at various times.

Christ's experience of His own divine Person, and of His Father, was wider than his conceptual knowledge and cannot be reduced simply to the latter.[30] The eschatological statements were given as moments of intense experience of the certainty of the vindication to the contemporary generation of His work and Person by the Father. The resultant expression was imaged in a vortex or cluster of fused images drawn from Jesus' interpretation of Himself in the context of Jewish literature. Von

Hügel allows for a possible interval between the proximate coming of Jesus and the cosmic end. Although Jesus stressed the immediate proximity of His coming, He nevertheless established the Church in a rudimentary way. Furthermore, the idea of a proximate coming, and a suffering Messiah, were doctrines "*special* to Our Lord," but notions like the "catastrophic end of the world" were merely taken over and continued by Him. Von Hügel thus distinguished what Jesus formally taught as His own message, and what pertained to contemporary religious ideology.

The object of the time element ("this generation") could not be easily identified by the early Christians with any one of the images that were interrelated in an experienced conviction of Divine victory. The question of this identification is still one of the thorniest problems in NewTestament exegesis. Von Hügel said, "Our Lord sees something. I do not see clearly what."

This lack of easy identification has spurred Christian thinkers to make good conjectures about the exact identification in the human mind of Christ. From the text itself no accusation of error can be made, for the Son of Man did come in power in an initial way to "that generation."[31] All the elements for such a solution were presented, at one time or another, by von Hügel. His hard conviction that the coming of Christ had to be identified with a cosmic, cataclysmic end worked at cross purposes to the line of movement in the rest of his thought. But this attitude also made Him the man He was, not "hurrying on" to too facile conclusions.

CHAPTER FOURTEEN

THE EVOLUTION OF
VON HÜGEL'S THOUGHT, 2

A. IMMANENCE AS ADVERSARY

To the degree that imminence was von Hügel's deepest conviction, to the same degree immanence was his bête-noire. At the end of his life von Hügel relates how he had been simultaneously enchanted and dissatisfied with the idea of finding the most adequate formulation of the deepest truths in a more or less idealistic philosophy of an Hegelian type which he thought could be "baptized."

> By "Idealist" I mean any philosophy which is so full of the undoubted activities of the subject as largely to overlook the distinct reality and the influence of the object.[1]

The idea, however, never really influenced his thinking. Some expressions in his article in *La Quinzaine* of 1904 sound Hegelian, but the whole tone of the writing is one of complete devotion to factual objectivity. From the first years of the century, when he began to discern an excessive immanentism in Loisy, to 1909, when he detected a similar trend in many of the Italian modernists as well, his reaction became so strongly adverse that Loisy, toward the end of the Baron's life, thought it had become a psychological obsession, as did Maude Petre. Von Hügel agreed or disagreed with the Italian thinkers precisely on this point. He can agree with Semeria, Crespi, Scotti, Fogazzaro, Genocchi, and Fracassini, but not with Buonaiuti, Murri and Minocchi, and precisely because of immanentist leanings.[2]

The Baron was never an immanentist, but he did shift his emphasis. The chief influence in this shift was the German Lutheran, Ernst Troeltsch. "I never myself realized this originality [of St. Thomas] before Troeltsch taught it to me."[3] His last book, *The Reality of God*, is greatly influenced by St. Thomas' argument from design. The Baron conceived his transition as a movement away from the method of immanence or the logic of action of Blondel and Laberthonnière towards the critical realism of St. Thomas:

> I still admire many such pages of my (always well loved) friends Maurice Blondel and Louis [sic] Laberthonnière; but I have to admit that my fully living interest is now given to thinkers— almost all Germans, English, and Italians—who are on the way of setting up for us a *critico-realist epistemology*.[4]

It would be very unfair to Blondel to consider him an immanentist; his very logic of action was conceived as a means to emphasize the absolute necessity of transcendence.[5] In fact, at the very time at the end of his life when the Baron is demonstrating the transcendence of God, echoes of Blondel, or at least similarities, frequently occur.[6] It is also true that his point of departure is more from the concrete objects of nature, whether it be butterfly or lichen, than from the analysis of the mind's dynamism. The transition may be briefly summed up by a statement in 1923:

> But now I perceive with entire clarity that, though religion cannot even be conceived as extant at all without a human subject humanly apprehending the Object of Religion, the reality of the Object (in itself the Subject of all subjects) and its presence independently of all our apprehension of it—that its Givenness is the central characteristic of all religion worthy of the name. The otherness, the prevenience of God, the one-sided Relation between God and Man, these constitute the deepest measure and touchstone of all religion.[7]

Von Hügel never charged Blondel with being an immanentist; he did, however, in 1921 couple Tyrrell with Loisy as espousing that doctrine.[8] In reply to a letter in which von Hügel warned him of immanentism, Tyrrell wrote:

> Believe me, we are *quite* agreed about the transcendence question. But these gentry think transcendent means *deistic* outsideness, and would justify the notion of a special telegraph between Heaven and the Pope bearing messages no man may control or question. One dare not give them the word to play with. I am sure that it is only in and through the human mind that God speaks to us, but this in no way implies that there is not an infinite *more* behind all he can possibly utter to us. It is like the ocean pressing into a little estuary.[9]

Although Tyrrell laid exaggerated emphasis upon the immanental aspect and the interiority of revelation as experience, he cannot be called an immanentist. On Feb. 18, 1910, von Hügel rejected such an idea in a letter to Miss Petre.

Loisy himself reacted against von Hügel's definition of him as an immanentist. Yet in his diary for 1904, after asserting that he regarded "the personal incarnation of God as a philosophic myth," he wrote: "If I am anything in religion, it is rather a *pantheo-positivo-humanitaire* than a Christian."[10] His thought later revealed touches of deism. He wrote on March 8, 1930, at a time when he considered von Hügel to be psychologically abnormal because of his insistence on transcendence:

> Who leads us? A question almost blasphemous, or at any rate without significance. If there were a *who*, it would be humanity; but it is not humanity because humanity does not walk of itself, it is not a living liberty. Well, then, there is no *who* measurable by its yard-stick. It is nevertheless a fact that this arrogant vermin is solidary with the planet that bears it and the whole universe, of which it is a part, contained and containing. But that with which humanity is solidary and on which it is dependent is not someone as occupied with it as it is with itself. Is it capable of sounding and understanding and defining Him? It may have thought so, but what presumption. . . . To save the future of humanity on the planet might be a more noble occupation if it

> could understand and undertake it, and it might be the only labor that would please the Eternal, if He deigned to regard it.[11]

Von Hügel described the immanentist mentality as that of those who, "when they have made sure of a spatially and temporally finite universe ... had thrown themselves upon it as their God—a God far more admirable and compelling than were the Gods of any of the specifically religious creeds."[12] Loisy, who was quite touchy about being labeled, would undoubtedly have denied that von Hügel's definition fitted him, but the Baron was reacting to positions like Loisy's when he kept insisting on transcendence.

Throughout his life, von Hügel found an immanentist and pantheistic outlook superficially attractive. In fact, he found a provisory value therein, as long as it was transcended. He found a great block resisting pantheism: "A great foot, a pierced foot, prevents that door closing there."[13] But his total view shows that it was not Christ alone who blocked that door for him. Christ never stood in isolation in his thought. The deep, dim apprehension in man of a *who*, and the "givenness" of the intelligent design in the universe also stepped in to prevent that door from closing.

Transcendence was an assertion of an unavoidable knowledge of a *who* rather than a what. He wrote to Tyrrell on May 14, 1907:

> God is certainly not, in any degree or sense, simply (spatially) outside of, or above us; these spatial pictures have indeed all to be interpreted in terms of spiritual experience and spiritual reality. But this experience is *essentially* as truly of God transcendent as of God immanent; of a Spirit indefinitely more spiritual, a reality which is nobler and of a higher nature than our highest, and leaves us with a noble thirst—as well as of this same spirit as penetrating us through and through, and as satisfying our cravings.[14]

When we have purified the spatial image, we are left with something that is not ourselves, not humanity, not the physical cosmos, not sub-personal. In his later stage, von Hügel sees this reality as mind reflected in the created universe, a reflection of order which cannot be conceived as a projection of our own minds. In his earlier period he had said that to hold this reality to be illusion would be to evaluate the artists, the poets, the composers, the saints, the prophets as mere visionaries "in precisely what constitutes their specific greatness."[15] Von Hügel's stress on transcendence is not obsession but vision. No exaggerated enthusiasm is needed to endorse the opinion of von Hügel's friend Clement Webb, no mean philosopher himself, who maintained that von Hügel, "beyond any man that I have known," impressed one with the reality of God.[16]

B. AUTHORITY AND MATURITY

The Baron changed in his appreciation of the value and need of the Church's disciplinary, practical, and pastoral jurisdiction, in so far as this called for "our conditional belief and practical conformity"; he never changed in his idea of the object of absolute interior assent. This centered only on "the necessary realities of religion," and his rather vague "nucleus of historical facts." As Webb said: "... he never failed loyally to follow whithersoever the argument seemed to lead, and was at the end wholly 'impenitent' (as he once said to me) in his adherence to modern critical views of the sacred books."[17]

Closely connected with this was von Hügel's general view of authority and his general application of it. Here he always insisted on the need for a constructive, positive stance. As early as June 4, 1904, he urged Catholics generally to agree with Rome's decisions, rather than to cavil at them.[18] When Maude Petre was forbidden the sacraments in her local church by her bishop, the Baron wrote her on Nov. 12, 1908:

> I see plainly that the question of *principle* is, for the immediate present, easy; the question of policy, difficult. The question of principle is easy, because, after all, we "modernists" [this is the Baron's first use of the word in his own connection that I have found] hold heartily to the "corporate" idea and to the Church

authorities having a considerable voice and a large range for their actions; so that we cannot, I think, deny their right to regulate the *frequency* of such, partly external acts.

On Oct. 24, 1910 he wrote to Miss Petre that unless the negative, destructive, and immanentist approach was guarded against, "Modernism" is "doomed and deserves to be." The same year he wrote also in the *Hibbert Journal*:

[Authority] remains, indeed, divinely ordained and blessed, but not absolute or unlimited. All legitimate authority claimed at first to be absolute because it came from God; but the father of a family has long ceased to hold the life and death of his child in his hands, and the most legitimate head of any modern state no longer proclaims himself, "L'état, c'est moi." The Church and her earthly head doubtless represent the divine authority in ways distinct from those just mentioned. Yet here again the authority, though derived from the infinite God, cannot be treated as itself infinite, cannot ignore or transgress the rights of science, of the individual conscience, of the state, or of the other, though lowlier, constituents of the visible Church, bishops, priests, laity, without producing widespread insincerity and oppression, or revolt and open bitterness. In either case the true object of all authority is stultified.[19]

On Jan. 2, 1914, the Baron wrote to tell Miss Petre that he agreed that "the central problem studied by the 'Modernists' had been that of authority itself." Later, the Baron saw more clearly the need for practical measures on the part of the Church, but the theory remained substantially the same.[20]

The *motu proprio Sacrorum antistitum*[21] of Pius X, dated Sept. 1, 1910, occasioned a letter from Archbishop Mignot of Albi, France, to his friend von Hügel, which situated more clearly the question of the rights of authority.

The *motu proprio* imposed what is popularly known as the anti-modernist oath on all clerics before major orders, professors of sacred subjects in seminaries and religious scholasticates, officials in Roman congregations and episcopal curias, and religious superiors, among others. Usually taken at the same time as the profession of faith required by Pius IV, the oath contains two parts. Part I contains five main propositions: that God can be known and proved by natural reason (drawn from the constitution *Dei Filius* of Vatican I, with the addition of the word "proved"); that the external signs of revelation, especially miracles and prophecies, yield certainty and are adapted to all men and times, even this time (adapted from Vatican I); that the Church was founded by Christ while on earth (treated in *Lamentabili* and *Pascendi*); that one accepts the notion of a deposit of faith, and rejects as heretical the idea of dogmas changing from one sense to another different from that held by the Church (drawn from Vatican I); that faith is not a blind sense welling up from the depths of the subconscious under the impulse of the heart and of a morally formed will, but a real assent of the intellect to truth by hearing from an external source (treated by Vatican I and *Pascendi*). Part II promises submission and assent to *Pascendi* and *Lamentabili*, especially to the rejection of opposition between history and dogma. In the accompanying recommendations, occasioned by the widespread appearance of modernist writing, newspapers and periodicals were forbidden in seminaries, except for special articles to be read to the class. The oath, a formal personal ratification of previous authoritative decisions of Pius X, was aimed at certain clandestine groups thought to be forming after *Pascendi*.

The most violent reaction occurred in Germany. Chiefly because of their position on faculties at State universities where the oath would endanger their position, professors who exercising no pastoral ministry were permitted by Pius X, at the request of the German episcopacy, to be dispensed from the oath. In Italy, the Barnabite G. Semeria, was allowed by the Pope to take the oath with certain reservations. In England, Maude Petre, preparing her work on Tyrrell, refused to take the oath and was deprived of the sacraments in her diocese. Only a very few priests refused the oath; it indeed dealt the death-blow to the Modernist movement.

On Oct. 8, 1910, von Hügel expressed to Miss Petre his "growing sad feeling that my own turn too will not be long in coming," but he was never asked to take the oath. Archbishop

Eudoxe-Irénée Mignot[22] wrote to von Hügel on Oct. 28, 1910 to discuss the meaning of the oath. He felt that any Catholic could accept in conscience the rejection of the errors mentioned, and that only a "global adhesion" to *Lamentabili* and *Pascendi* was required. The delicate difficulty he thought he saw, together with von Hügel, was that:

> The Pope is demanding an absolute assent to formularies which are *not of faith*, at least in all their parts, so that authority *binds us* while *not binding itself*. And so I answer that in doctrinal matters authority can only bind us in the measure in which it binds itself.[23]

Lamentabili and *Pascendi*, he maintained, far from suppressing the rights of theological criticism, have made them more imperative, for one must discern in the teaching the different degrees of certainty. With or without the oath, a complete intellectual (*ex tota mente*) assent does not put all the propositions on the same footing. Accordingly, a duty of respect to every act of ecclesiastical jurisdiction, and a duty of intellectual assent, correlative and proportioned to the order and nature of the truth taught, are demanded. Respect extends to the whole, but internal assent is measured by the nature of the proposition.

Mignot thus implied that the assent to which the oath bound was commensurate with the assent demanded by the sources of Catholic teaching from which it was drawn; with regard to the additions the assent was only that demanded by a *motu proprio* itself. Mignot's letter, a solid though somewhat rapid summary, offered a rudimentary sketch of a sound theology for the interpretation of documents of the magisterium. The Baron's subsequent thought and practice was, to a large extent, worked out along the lines of Mignot's position.[24] Von Hügel grew in respect for non-infallible decrees as demanding "conditional assent and practical conformity."[25]

By 1918 he had developed a theory which he called the seven sets of insights for "Churchmanship"; it was a system for working out the problem of authority in non-infallible areas. The inevitable consequence of belonging to any community is the daily acceptance of limitations and sacrifices. Needless friction must be eliminated, but it must be realized that the faults of Churchmen can disappear only with the disappearance of the Church itself. Second, a Church worthy of the name can never be a society for the promotion of research, for the quest of a still undiscovered good. A Church cannot exist without credal delimitation; but as a vessel of positive religious experience that implies only a rudimentary psychology and philosophy, it continuously risks excessive detail and over-precision. Third, absolute interior assent and conditional belief, nucleus and details, must be distinguished. Fourth, grades of truth must be recognized in other great religions. Churches, however, cannot be considered equally good or interchangeable, for this would make a *teaching* Church *per se* an evil.[26] Fifth, the sect-type of religion must be seen as a functional truth and warning. Sixth, development must be recognized in the Bible, and finally, the unity of God must be reflected in the unity of the One Church.

It is evident from the Baron's statements that he did not conceive the ideal envisioned above as demanding sacrifices from Church officials only and especially from 1919 to the end. He progressively realized that his own scholarship and that of others stood to gain from a reasonable amount of sacrifice. He grew in his appreciation of the part Church appurtenance (as he called it) played in his efforts to interpret the great Biblical texts. He asserted that the institution alone cannot give complete guidance, but that the questions cannot be even *stated* correctly without Church "appurtenance."[27] As to the gain to his own scholarship he wrote:

> I do not cease, thank God, to see and experience that the gain of my Roman Catholic appurtenance is, even simply for the solidity of my freedom, for the balance and reality of my outlook— *just simply even to my life of scholarship and thinking IMMENSE.*[28]

He had obviously felt the pressure of authority, for he apologized to his niece for "thinking of my own case unmanfully, softly, complainingly." His final attitude was summed up almost lyrically in 1924 in an article in *Hochland*, an essay that was his lone publication in German. He wrote about a convert to Christianity, a wandering Hindu monk, Sadhu Sundar Singh, and developed the idea that mysticism can be fulfilled and safeguarded only through the Church. The long passage is worth quoting:

> I was rather disinclined to point out the R.C. Church; since when Sadhu turned toward this great Church, its penetration into his life brought in probably for a long time complications and stoppages, and his mission needed a large measure of intellectual and fruitful liberty; and it would be mean of me who sit in my peaceful study in the face of the conflict to propose something which could involve in wider serious difficulty one already otherwise set in the midst of the battle for the heroic life.
>
> But soon clarity came to me; that I now for fifty years have striven to carry on the life of a critical historian and straightseeing religious philosopher in all conscientiousness; that my membership in the R.C. Church had over a period of ten years cost me hot battles and difficulties; that just exactly when I needed a great measure of liberty to carry on my life's work a temptation pressed me to avoid all such complication through an individualism, as pure as possible, and so to enjoy a complete freedom; that finally membership in the Church protected me from scepticism and psychological self-inflation, and this membership, rightly understood and exercised, was rather well compatible with the healthy liberty which I needed for my work. I also propose nothing whose price I do not know. This price is surely so great that only a stronger belief can pay it. But the gain is high—the highest which such a soul can get, which the gracious God can give.[29]

This little gem appeared just one month before the Baron's death. While mindful of our previous reservations, we can say that this is a finely orchestrated finale for one who fought his way by interior conviction to a bitter-sweet love of authority, and who had been, ironically, called the "lay-bishop" and the "pope" of Modernism.[30] Von Hügel had made a bitter, but not embittered, journey even from as late as 1912, when he saw Lagrange's works prohibited to seminaries as infected with rationalism, to the peace of mind revealed in this passage.[31]

C. MODERNISM AND VON HÜGEL

J. Rivière, author of the first thoroughly documented study of Modernism, called von Hügel the Maecenas of the movement. Our purpose in this study has been not to write a history of Modernism, but rather, after having assessed von Hügel's ideas, to situate him more accurately in relation to the Modernist movement. There is no doubt that he gave impetus to some currents in the movement. But what answer can we give to the question: "Was von Hügel a modernist?" An answer must rest on a clear idea of the essence of Modernism. For a somewhat extended treatment of this the reader is referred to the Appendix.

Briefly, however, it seems correct to say, following a suggestion of de Grandmaison, that at the roots of Modernism lay a triple thesis: a denial of the supernatural as an object of knowledge (in the totally symbolic, non-objective approach to the content of dogma which is related to a type of agnosticism in natural theology); an exclusive immanence of the divine and of revelation ("vital immanence") which also reduced the Church to a simple social civilizing phenomenon; and a total emancipation of scientific research from Church dogma which would allow the continued assertion of faith in dogma with its contradiction on the historical level (as understood in the Modernist presentation of the "Christ of faith/Christ of history," "Church of faith/Church of history" dichotomy).

Let us apply each of these criteria to von Hügel. The first point does not fit his positions. He held an objective relationship between dogma and revelation. (His difficulty arose in the concrete specification in the historical order, which falls under the third point.) Furthermore, his greatest contribution was his insistence upon, and development of, the certainty of God. As to the second point, von Hügel was an arch-enemy of exclusive immanence. In complaining to René Guiran on July 11, 1921, that he feared "labels," but nevertheless had won the label of Modernist from some people, von Hügel pointed out that many, so tagged, had fundamentally different orientations:

> The capital and decisive difference, therefore, now appears to me to be the difference between *Religion conceived as a purely intra-human phenomenon; without evidence beyond the aspirations of the human race; and Religion conceived as essentially evidential, metaphysical, the effect in us of more than us—of more than any purely human facts and desires.*[32]

As to the third point, after 1909 he held himself free, never in published works but only as a private opinion, to interpret the Virgin Birth and the account of the empty tomb in a manner contrary to the unanimous agreement of tradition. (I take it that his final admission of confusion as to the meaning of the Parousia texts must be taken into consideration in this area.)

If Modernism is conceived as springing from only one root, that of vital immanence, then von Hügel would, in no way, be a Modernist, but if it is so restricted, then it is impossible to understand why *Pascendi* was at such pains, and went on at such length to condemn the other two elements in our definition.

If Modernism is seen as having three roots, then it is difficult to find a label for a man whose thinking is related to one (or part of one) root. The safest procedure is to avoid labels, and merely assert that von Hügel shared in one of the ideas officially condemned in the Modernist crisis. It is not totally an academic exercise to endeavor to define Modernism. The encyclical *Pascendi* is a lengthy document, and touches briefly on many issues. It is generally admitted that not every statement made in passing by an encyclical is of equal value to its central thesis or theses. I have suggested the three elements described above as the essence of the condemnation in *Pascendi*.

The Baron, however, claimed that the criterion by which he should be judged should be deeper than that of simple distinctions:

> Hence there is, to my mind, always, for genuine interpreters of any thinker, a duty beyond and above the reaching of what such thinkers think are their ultimate reasons for holding or implying such and such methods, . . . whether, in a word, the thinkers concerned have not got further in their living practice and method, than their attempts at explaining them are compelling . . . . Hence

it will be necessary, I submit, to go behind my explanations, supposing they turn out obscure or contradictory: my instinctive and intuitive practice may be quite right, whilst my explanations might yield ready material for clever refutation.[33]

In 1909 he described himself as "a Catholic born and, I pray, a Catholic to live and die."[34] He had spoken about doing without the sacraments "for a while," meaning that any separation which might be imposed could never be irrevocable for him. He spoke of himself as one "within, and determined to remain within, the Roman Church."[35] In 1918, while defending his thinking, he said that he knew that it required "a continuous purification, correction, supplementation by grace and training within and through the Church."[36] In 1922 he muses over his historical method, and says that Duchesne "taught us critical method," but never showed us, his juniors in trouble, what we lacked in the method.[37] From all that he said, from his love of the Church, it is impossible to come to any conclusion but this: if he had been faced with the choice of giving interior assent to some doctrine or leaving the Church, in utmost probability he would have assented.[38] This was his logic of action. Critique of a person's theology cannot, of course, be ultimately founded on such an approach, but without its mention, theological critique is stunted. Theology even more than other sciences, is bound up with life. If these last considerations are not taken into account, the vignette by his friend, Abbot Butler, makes no sense. He describes von Hügel's daily practice of a long daily visit to the Blessed Sacrament:

> There I would watch him sitting, the great deep eyes fixed on the Tabernacle, the whole being wrapped in absorption of prayer, devotion, contemplation. Those who have not seen him so know only half the man.[39]

The Modernist movement was never interiorly organized in any real sense. It contained too many philosophies, the nuances of which were closely cherished by the sensitive and conflicting personalities who sponsored them, and its principal proponents were geographically too separated for any effective organization. Nevertheless, von Hügel himself tried to conceive of Modernism as a planned movement, and came closest to being its co-ordinator. His meeting with the Italian Modernists at Molveno in the Italian Tyrol during August 1907 found him at its center as they planned their future action. This meeting occurred between the appearance of *Lamentabili* and *Pascendi*. It was simultaneously their greatest and first moment of general contact, and their last moment of anything like agreement.

Many reasons have been adduced why the Baron was never condemned by name. Webb suggested that he was spared, partly because of "his high social position," and because of "the respect which he enjoyed among influential members not of his own communion." Dom Cuthbert Butler (1858–1934), once Abbot of Downside, felt it was because of his spiritual influence on those outside the Church, and because the technical nature of his writing limited the field of readers. Loisy hinted that Cardinal Bourne's personal benevolence played a role.[40] Miss Petre said that she suspected the reason, but never gave it. One should remember, however, that up until 1921, the Baron's signed published work contained only a small number of possibly offensive statements. (His essay of 1904 on authority was published after his death; see bibliography.)

Von Hügel felt that it would take years to assess Modernism.[41] Today, we realize that, just as insights of permanent value lay in the excesses of Protestantism, so did some ultimate good for the Church spring from Modernism. It would be hard to deny that the controversy over Modernism illuminated certain points: the idea of faith *more* as an encounter with God than as an assent to propositions, without ruling out the latter; the increased appreciation of religious experience; the emphasis on the sense of mystery in religion; the distinction between revelation and inspiration; the better realization of pastoral and devotional goals in theology which must not be eclipsed by its speculative bent; a deeper and less mechanical assessment of the meaning of authority; the emphasis on the role of the bishop; the importance of the laity; a greater respect for science; an underlining of a religious anthropology, *gloria Dei homo*.

While the controversy over Modernism may have given later, refined insight into these questions, still the excesses of Modernism caused a reaction which actually retarded the emergence of these insights. Enough of these ideas were being discussed by writers who were not Modernists to make us believe that the values mentioned would have gradually come to the fore if extreme positions had not developed. With a von Hügel *alone*, there would have been no major crisis, but with Loisy whose relatively full-blown Modernism von Hügel was not at first aware of, the situation became a genuine crisis. At the same time the method and reaction on the part of Rome is also open to criticism. This point will be handled in our final chapter.

CHAPTER FIFTEEN

EVALUATION AND CONCLUSION

The period we have studied was a most painful time for Catholic scholars. If they had been obliged to adjust only to the official decrees of the Church, many of which were too sweeping and negative in tone, and over-rigidly interpreted by even otherwise good theologians, this would have been enough of a problem.[1] But an added pressure was exerted by Monsignor Umberto Benigni, a Vatican official as of 1905, a consultor to various papal commissions, and press officer attached to the Secretariat of State. In 1906 he founded *Corrispondenza Romana*, a paper whose title was changed, in 1908, to *La Correspondance de Rome*. (Cardinal Merry del Val, after giving it discreet support, suppressed it in 1913.) He was also the leader of a secret federation of societies called *Sodalitium Pianum*, which had agents throughout Europe from 1909 until 1921.

The history of this group is still being assessed.[2] Benigni saw Modernism as a secret international plot operating in every area, and to counteract it he instigated a campaign of incrimination against anyone suspected of liberal thought; some Catholic theologians, perhaps unwittingly, gave support to such witch-hunting tactics by attributing the highest possible theological note to pronouncements of the magisterium.

In the light of these suspicions and restrictions, it is

remarkable that some Catholics continued creative, if somewhat cautious, work after 1910. They were chiefly those who were in profound sympathy with the decrees, and to a degree, understood better their technical theological import because of their close observation of the Modernist movement. Among these, Rivière mentions de Grandmaison, Lebreton, and Batiffol; Lagrange should certainly be included.[3] It is quite probable that World War I was an important factor in breaking the line of succession. The following generation of scholars, who had not been close to the conflict, apparently proved the axiom *omne ignotum pro magnifico est*. Their remoteness from the real issues provided a seed-bed for greater rigidity and deeper suspicion. Karl Adam's *Das Wesen des Katholizismus* (1924) presaged future possibilities for a more liberal Catholic theology, but the real momentum in that direction did not set in until after World War II.

Loisy. The present writer cannot accept Loisy's major conclusions, such as his interpretation of the meaning of the Parousia texts, and, especially, his denial of Christ's bodily resurrection. However much of the criticism of Loisy's "presuppositions" is not fully convincing unless it be joined to a solid textual analysis of the Bible. But on the resurrection he broke, not just with later dogma, but with New Testament faith.

It cannot be denied, however, that Loisy and von Hügel were pioneers among Catholics in stressing the eschatological ideas of Jesus, and the notion of the final Kingdom of God. They were part of the movement which upset the liberal, simply humanitarian views of so many in the nineteenth century. It was unfortunate that the Church was not better prepared scientifically to lay hold of Loisy's quite valid emphasis, and the same is true of George Tyrrell, all the more since his spirit was not closed to Catholicism as Loisy's was by this time. Tyrrell's thought was not clear even to himself: one stream of it runs to a rather modern and orthodox ecclesiology; the other, which includes his rejection of Trent and Vatican I, flows to a denial of Roman Catholicism. It is difficult to see how the magisterium could have failed to condemn these ideas; further, Tyrrell's published attacks on rather solemn contemporary Church decrees could not have been winked at. Tyrrell's position does not call for further condemnation here, but simply for a lament— a lament, however, that has some relevance today. The climate in the Church at the time was excessively authoritarian, that is, the role of authority on all levels was not sufficiently complemented by the role of intelligence, especially as it evaluates the data of research. Scientific intelligence lagged badly behind pastoral and practical intelligence. When this occurs, the good is often thrown out with the bad.

I cannot, and do not want, to believe as a Catholic that the Church is or should become simply a research society. It should be a hierarchically structured assembly of believers where research is furthered to the fullest possible extent compatible with what is certainly known as essential to revelation. Despite the risks and confusion we experience today, and despite a clear knowledge of the results of walking down the blind alley of ultra-liberal theology—a fact which Protestants who have been down that path warn us about—still a failure of nerve in our search would simply lead us again down another blind alley, along which we have already walked. The antimodernist crusade led to a freezing of the spirit, whereas modern ultra-liberal theology, we feel, leads to a vaporization of Christianity. The lesson of the Modernist period is that we must walk neither of the two blind alleys, but the clear middle road.

The magisterium. There is no doubt that more was at stake in the modernist crisis than the question of measuring out the relative rights of the exegete and the hierarchy. Loisy at least attempted to solve this problem in such a way that the nature of the Church, and consequently the existence of Christian revelation itself, was threatened. It is impossible to see how Church authorities could have avoided some strong action. However, I believe that *Pascendi*, for example, was neither well conceived nor prudently executed. Despite its surface crystal clarity and its fine logical order, it was a *tour de force* against many positions that a good number of modernists did not hold. No doubt it was a fair prophecy of the direction in which Loisy's published work was to lead, but it tried to do too much with one stroke, to tidy up manifold positions in one bundle, and dispose of them. From the subsequent reaction at the time (was Blondel condemned, was Newman?, many wrongly wondered), it is evident that the central condemnations were not clearly indicated, even though, today, we can more easily disengage them. Moreover, its analysis of motives was not justified by the evidence.

A careful analysis of the sixty-five propositions of *Lamentabili* shows that they were worded with great prudence; nevertheless a few were stated quite ambiguously. Proposition sixty-four, for example, reads: "Scientific progress demands that the concepts of Christian doctrine concerning God, creation, revelation, the Person of the Incarnate Word, and Redemption be readjusted (reformentur)." Was this a condemnation of the development of doctrine or of a radical discontinuity in doctrine? At the time, such statements could be only bewildering. The basic problem was rooted in the fact that too many theologians thought that they had some ultimate and final grasp on revelation. However, the decrees of Vatican II in the Constitution on the Church (ch.2), and in the Constitution on Divine Revelation (#8), emphasize growth in insight, not only about the words, but about the realities of revelation. I take it that this demands even some adjustment of concepts, provided a substantial continuity of doctrine is maintained.

There is no intention here to make value judgments about the interior dispositions of the great men who then led the Church. Pius X has been canonized, and one has merely to read his life to be deeply impressed by his profound religious spirit, his tireless charity, and by his pioneering efforts at liturgical and pastoral renewal which enriched the Church up to our time.

A prudent act is the result of weighing unequally good possibilities. As a work of the practical intelligence it discerns the connection between concrete possibilities and a universal aspiration. To make such a value judgment on the past, one would have to consider these possibilities, not as we now see them, but as they were seen in the confusion of the times. After the outcome has been settled, however, we may, at times, draw lessons for our own growth in prudence.

When the Church reverses a previous decree, frequently the new decision includes phrases such as "in view of recent research," "in view of changed times and attitudes," and the like. These phrases imply a general and rightly held presumption in favor of the prudence of past actions. Such a presumption is supported by theological principles, but the possibility of coming to a contrary conclusion on specifics is also left open to the historian. Such a contrary conclusion on several of the points already handled is the result of our study.

Von Hügel.   Dogmatic theology moves from the reality and experience of revelation to clearer conceptualization. Pastoral theology moves from conceptualization to experience. Von Hügel, devoted to an intense sacramental and prayer life and to painstaking research, united these two approaches.

We have already found a surprising consistency in von Hügel's thought, but we have not yet considered that essential something which simultaneously explains his humility, and his daring thrust into the unknown, the quality Wilfrid Ward called his love of riding the crest of a wave. The search for this center of the Baron's aspirations is not particularly arduous, for he reveals it time and again. Basically it is this. Von Hügel was vitally in search, not of the God we would love to have, but of the God who loves us, and this search generated his theory of friction. Friction faces man with the otherness of God, and alone can educate man to be open to all reality. This is the reason for von Hügel's antipathy to pietism which he so often decried; he saw that it sheltered one from the whole reality. He asserted that many have the unfortunate habit of "trying to carry the good God in their pocket."[4] Perhaps no one has insisted more emphatically than von Hügel that God can be known; yet few have emphasized as much as he the religious value of retaining a sense of mystery in God. Our grasp is limited, but our reach is not. Maintaining that God, although transcendent, is not totally other, the Baron avoided Kierkegaardian anguish. Perhaps for this reason he grew more and more in his love of the Church as a community of believers, as God's added means of answering us and easing our search. Yet to the very end he rejected the idea that God's response was supposed to put us to sleep.[5]

The question might be asked: "Why cannot a man who strenuously serves God in virtue and charity simply rest in the knowledge he has of God without seeking further?" The Baron's answer is that although Revelation was given once for all, God is still speaking to us in some way, and we must remain open to Him. He continues to speak to us through science, as well as through the magisterium, tradition, and our life of charity. The whole world of science, including exegesis, is a whispered word, especially to the believer, about God's life and purpose. This concept of science is woven so thoroughly through the Baron's thought that we can truly say that he had developed a spirituality for the scientist.[6] The reality of God speaks out from nature to us who have already been reborn to a second nature. If we close our ears to this voice, we cherish our rebirth, but not totally on His terms. We set up a conflict between the effects of the reality discovered in nature, and the convictions which we believe come from grace, an impossible antinomy. Religion must never perform the functions of science, nor must science ever try to usurp the functions of religion, but von Hügel was aware of the power of science to remold, somewhat, even religious notions. Von Hügel's frequent reflections on the Galileo case suggested to him that God does not direct our minds in the precise way that was once presumed, and he believed that the historical sciences were progressing in a similar direction. He felt that when excessive demands for proof were made of the historical sciences, and were coupled with warnings about subjectivity, there frequently lay hidden in this attitude a fear of being totally open to God and to what He is saying to us.

This hunger and thirst for openness to reality, that is, to God, was Friedrich von Hügel's central aspiration. Thus the man who was characterized as one who loved to ride the crest of the wave, whose temperament seemed to be simply that of a deliberate innovator, turns out upon closer study to be a man whose whole approach was profoundly religious. Though he may have occasionally misjudged what reality actually was, his plea for openness deserves to be heard, for openness and respect for all reality, especially for the believer who accepts revelation, is ultimately an openness to and respect for God.

If we ask the question: "What was von Hügel's plan of operation, what did he want to do in the Church?," we would have to answer that he desired to demonstrate, simultaneously, the non-subjective reality of God and the lack of sufficient respect in the past for the rights of the historian or exegete. And in so far as he was consciously involved in a movement or a crusade, this aspect was uppermost in his mind.

Vatican II, echoing Vatican I, stated that the infallibility of the Church "extends as far as the deposit of divine revelation"; hence the Church's function is to guard, preserve, and transmit revelation. The problem raised by von Hügel's work is this: if the Church, in transmitting revelation, also transmits "all that she herself is, all that she believes," as the Constitution on Revelation of Vatican II states, and if she herself is not yet in full consciousness of herself (she is a mystery because of the presence of the Spirit in her life), then it follows that there must be growth in the conceptual understanding of revelation, that is, of dogma. At the same time, the Church does have an *adequate* grasp of her own nature and of revelation, a grasp sufficient to lead us, according to God's present purpose, to a share in the Trinitarian life—otherwise her existence and infallibility would be meaningless.

Hence the conclusion is that since the Church exists to guard and transmit revelation, but is at the same time dynamically growing both in a knowledge of herself and of the meaning of revelation, her guardianship of revelation should operate in such a way as not, prematurely, to check new possibilities of insight into revelation where they are not clearly contradictory to the present adequate grasp of the essential elements of revelation.

Two difficulties, however, have stood in the way of effective realization of this. First, the static neo-scholasticism of the late nineteenth and early twentieth centuries, under which so many Church leaders were educated, was unable sufficiently to assimilate this idea. Second, the fact was obscured that there are many different tones or accents of certainty in the Church's voice when she issues cautions in order to preserve revelation. The child instinctively knows the meaning of the different tones in its mother's voice, but the faithful had lost a sense of these tones (called by theologians "theological notes" attached to various propositions.) Some examples may illustrate these difficulties. When the Holy Office on Jan. 13, 1897 decreed that one could not "safely" (*tuto*) deny or call in doubt the authenticity of the Johannine comma (I Jn 5:7), it appeared that the matter could not subsequently be safely discussed. Cardinal Vaughan, however, was chagrined because of the decree's effect on English Anglicans, and, undoubtedly after consulting his own exegetes, obtained from "an excellent source" in Rome the interpretation that the decree did not touch the field of Biblical criticism. His very recourse to Rome shows that this was not immediately evident. Furthermore, this interpretation was not publicly sanctioned by Rome until Father Künstle published a dissertation in 1905, bearing the *imprimatur* of the Archbishop of Freiburg, which demonstrated that the verse was composed in Spain around 390 A.D., possibly by the heresiarch, Priscillian. Father Künstle's work was then reviewed favorably (with a note of joy over the episcopal approbation) by Dom L. Janssens, the secretary of the Biblical Commission. Without the later interpretation and the official sanction, it was not clear that the "cannot be safely denied" decree could be interpreted to mean that further research and publication was not forbidden.

Such confusion offers a clear case of the need for discrimination about lesser Church documents, if scholarly work is to develop our understanding of doctrine. The incident helped to clarify for theologians the meaning of the Church's voice.

We find a similar development with regard to the early decrees of the Biblical Commission. It is known that these decrees do not rule out further research and publication provided the decree does not touch the faith directly, but this was not evident to theologians in general at the time.

Similarly, on June 5, 1918 the Holy Office replied negatively to the Sacred Congregation of Seminaries and Universities as to whether certain propositions could be safely taught. It refused to place contemporary theories about the limited knowledge of Christ on the same level as the traditional thesis about His universal knowledge, and stated that the opinion that Christ could have been ignorant of some things could not be called certain. It declared that the "soul of Christ" could not, with certainty, be said to have ignored anything in the *Verbum* from the beginning that related to past, present, and future, that is, all things which God knows by the knowledge of vision.

For perhaps twenty years theologians and exegetes in general did not feel free publicly to discuss the contents of this decree. Yet it was a "cannot be safely taught" decree, which we now know does not forbid further research; moreover, it was very subtly worded and, strictly speaking, applied only to teaching in what we know as seminaries. The subject is now a matter of public scholarly discussion, but for too long the Holy Office's reply was given an overly cautious interpretation.

Theology must continue to grow in insight into what we may call the hermeneutics of magisterial expression. Our contemporary emphasis on faith as an encounter with God more than as an assent to propositions may seem to make this discussion irrelevant. Not so, for if revelation is experienced at least on the deepest level of faith, and if faith is to be intelligent (as it must be), then revelation must contain either propositions or unerring conceptual translations (admittedly not comprehensive or exhaustive) of the essentials of revelation. If this were not so, there could be no *communion* of *believers*. We must, therefore, have sound norms for discerning the precise relationship of magisterial statements to revelation.

Von Hügel, Tyrrell, and Le Roy stressed that dogma was oriented toward life and spirituality.[7] Because Tyrrell and Le Roy seemed to diminish unduly the reality of the knowledge of God as He is in himself, the consequent valid criticism of their positions obscured for too long a time the truth they were emphasizing. It is impossible here to take up the rich analysis of our knowledge of God, as found in St. Thomas; I feel, however, that Tyrrell, if one has the code to understand his language, was for the most part faithful to Aquinas.

What must be pointed out, however, is that both von Hügel and Tyrrell insisted that dogma existed for the sake of prayer, worship, and the life of charity. Too often the impression was given during their time that orthodoxy in belief was the chief, almost exclusive, purpose of revelation. Spirituality was separated from dogmatic theology and taught as a separate tract called "ascetics," if it were taught at all. Our entire discussion of magisterial expression is based on the assumption that true belief is the only avenue to true prayer, worship, and charity. But both Tyrrell and von Hügel warned against devoting so much to discussions of belief that prayer, worship, and charity would seem secondary.

At the same time, to stress the "spiritual life" without giving sufficient attention to the question of belief can lead to attitudes summarized in the glib phrases so common today: faith is not an assent to propositions, but an encounter with God. If the Modernist crisis taught us anything, it should have been the real danger in these expressions even for prayer, life, and worship. The true statement, I believe, is this: Faith is an *encounter* (inter-personal communion) with God *across propositions* (words, the word of God, concepts). Unless the balance is kept between these two movements, we will either fall into a sterile intellectualism divorced from a spirituality of wholeness, or we will slip into a sentimentalism deaf to the demands of the Word of God that teaches us what charity is.

Finally, the Modernist crisis brought to the fore the question of the relation of historical event or historical science to dogma. In view of our earlier discussion, a brief summary here will suffice.

It cannot be denied that a problem still remains in this area. For example, our imaginative grasp of the process of creation has been modified by what we have learned from geology, scientific criticism of the Bible, and other disciplines. Our notion of creation, itself, has not been substantially modified, but if we had none of this new knowledge, if we were not beings with a newly substantiated experience of our past, would we be open to admit the possibility that such new facts need not be in radical disharmony with revelation?

Another example suggests itself. The authoritative, though non-infallible, teaching of the Church at present holds for monogenism rather than polygenism. The teaching authority of the Church warns that it is not apparent that polygenism is reconcilable with the doctrine of original sin, and consequently with the need for redemption by Christ. The magisterium thus presents propositions to guard revelation, in this case the meaning of Christ's life, death, and resurrection. But the teaching authority of the Church has not, with the absolute certainty of faith, closed the door to the assimilation of possible future evidence for polygenism.

Thus, it seems, that within the circle of a dogma itself, there are elements about which we have the assurance of faith that they "belong." Other elements, we feel sure, belong to faith, but not with the absolute assurance of faith itself. The dogma of inspiration and the traditional teaching on biblical inerrancy are other examples of this. The doctrines remain intact, but modern cultural science has brought about a revision in our knowledge of the historical process which, without contradicting the doctrine, has brought about revision in the details of our understanding of it.

This complex process (if it may so be called), is in essence profoundly religious. Modern culture plays a role under Providence in helping the Church to deepen, by purifying, its understanding of revelation. In brief, all humanity's work helps us to understand better what God is saying, what He is communicating to us. In turn, the Church can more relevantly, perhaps even more simply, communicate to that humanity the message of God's loving gift to it in Christ. "While helping the world and receiving many benefits from it, the Church has a single intention: that God's kingdom may come, and that the salvation of the whole human race may come to pass" (Vatican II, Pastoral Constitution on the Church in the Modern World).

When asked about the date of the end of the world, Jesus said He did not know it. Yet He spoke as one having authority. There are many questions which are not of faith, but which are connected in some way with religion to which the Church in the past has attempted to give an answer, but the Church walks by faith, and not by sight. Her Master's action is enlightening. Unless the Church makes clear that her mission pertains to revelation, and admits that she, too, gropes in areas not pertaining to her revelation, but still of great concern to modern man, is there not danger that her certainty in the message of revelation may be misconstrued by some as a similar groping? For the world knows she gropes in many areas, and she has no secret but revelation. It is heartening to see the statement of this idea in the constitution on the Church in the Modern World (#33).

Baron von Hügel, as we have seen, was sometimes called naïve, sometimes complex, but he was not naïve in the sense of not seeing the meaning of his own positions. Much of his thinking, his ideas on our knowledge of God, the theory of grades of "revelation," his concept of friction and tension, much of his thinking on authority, his awareness of the fact that, for too long a time, the historian had not been given his full rights—all these are valuable legacies which suggest the opposite of naïveté.[8]

On May 23, 1927, Isy von Hügel, the wife of Anatole, Friedrich's brother, wrote to Wilfrid Ward's wife, Josephine, the mother of Maisie Ward:

> I have been reading very often—bits at a time—of Freddy's essays: They "give to think" indeed. I read a little of the letters,—but I found that the things of them excited Anatole so deeply that he shut the book away for the present. I hear some really holy people are delighted with them and helped beyond measure,—but I can't help the feeling rising again and again, "Oh: if only he hadn't been deaf, and shut out from the underlying buzz of things"—

and yet when I remember the continuous intense yet at absolute rest look on his face after death, one knows it must mean that his path is the one he had to tread, till the strange visible light was given a chance to shine through the constant looked thinking, thinking—I can't make sense, I must stop.

Caught between the need to be an encyclopedist and a specialist, living by aspiration in the pre-Protestant world, but by necessity in a post-Reformation transitional period, von Hügel in his life was as complex as the very notion of "development" which he cherished. His aspiration could be reconciled with the unrelenting march of history, not by a total return to the past, but by some sort of re-creation. His vision was clear, even if he misjudged some of the lines possible to such an endeavor. He deeply loved God, Christ, and the Church, and it is impossible to say that his life was in any sense a tragedy.

The last word on his life must be the Baron's own. Three months before his death on Jan. 27, 1925, he said farewell to Mrs. Lillie, his American friend, who had been brought to the Catholic Church through reading his *Mystical Element of Religion*: "I am an old man and may never see you again. I do not know much and if I have in any way offended you by what I have said please forgive me and forget it all."

Archbishop Mignot of Albi wrote on Oct. 25, 1893, less than a month before the appearance of *Providentissimus Deus*:

> Let us permit the scholars to debate on those sources which have not as yet been completely studied, those sources whose discovery has caused a bit of trouble for many a soul. Sometimes the sand which is swirled up by the storm obscures the sky for a moment. Then the dust falls and the sun is seen again. After the storm one notices a slight change in the formation of the soil. The particles have subsided differently. Some trees have been carried away, some paths effaced. But the changes are insignificant and the land is the same. So it is with the truth of God. Our agitations hardly graze it and have no other result than to set more clearly in light this fact: *Veritas Domini manet in aeternum.*[9]

This calm reflection could well be the last and best word on the entire period of von Hügel and modernism.

A SHORT SKETCH OF MODERNISM*

Modernism was an ideology that clearly took shape within the Catholic Church at the turn of the twentieth century, whose aim was a revolutionary transmutation of Catholic dogma through the application of historical criticism, either subtly influenced by, or reaching out for a naturalistic evolutionary philosophy, and which was condemned by the Holy Office decree *Lamentabili*, the encyclical *Pascendi*, and definitively brought to an end by the Oath against Modernism. During the short span of twenty years (1890–1910) the Church suffered a convulsion, the exact nature and meaning of which has emerged ever more clearly in recent years. New ideas were broached, old ones were deepened or plundered, almost every basic fundamental of Catholic life and theology was reassessed. Many of these same ideas are once again under the scrutiny of modern theological research. The experiment of Modernism is therefore for the Catholic theologian of today an indispensable source for understanding himself and his work.

The roots.   The roots of Modernism are extremely complex. Four factors may be singled out: in philosophy the prevalence

This sketch is a somewhat revised version of the article Modernism *prepared by Father Heaney for* The New Catholic Encyclopedia *(New York: McGraw-Hill, 1967). It is here printed with permission.*

among Catholics of a shallow eclecticism, combined with the strong influence exerted by the neo-Hegelians, the neo-Kantians, the pragmatists, and the disciples of Schleiermacher; in theology a growing dissatisfaction with a too static neo-scholasticism; in the sciences the development of evolutionary biological theory, and the growth of historical method; and, at least of equal importance, the not yet assimilated, changing relationship between the Church and the socio-political order.

No one of these can be singled out as the sole root of Modernism. We cannot, for example, base Modernism on a sort of back-stairs intrigue against abuse of authority, resulting in a posse hunt of progressives by conservatives, with no deeper intellectual issues at stake. On the other hand, we cannot see it as a conflict in a vacuum of ideas untouched by political and social movements, and even personal sensitivities.

Philosophy and Theology. During most of the nineteenth century an eclecticism under the influence of thinkers like Descartes, Leibnitz, and Rosmini, prevailed in Catholic circles. This was neither profound nor systematic. After the appearance of the encyclical *Aeterni Patris* in 1879, neo-scholasticism began to exercise greater influence from its centers in Rome, Louvain, and in Germany. Many Catholic scholars at the turn of the century, however, had never felt this influence. Furthermore, the categories of neo-scholasticism began to appear inadequate to contain the rich reality suggested by the new work in scripture, history, and a philosophy that accented the aspect of immanence. In general, then, Catholics were left with scattered philosophical insights, but without the depth of a philosophical tradition that could handle the new discoveries.

Contemporary religious thinkers had begun to challenge "scholastic" positions in both Protestantism and Catholicism. Around the beginning of the nineteenth century, F. Schleiermacher developed his theory of experience (the feeling of dependence) as the heart of religion. His later disciples eliminated, perhaps more than Schleiermacher intended, the element of intelligence. Religion was portrayed as a sentiment, an experience beyond the critique of intellectual concepts. To be sure, Schleiermacher's notion of "feeling" includes, not only emotion or sensation, but an intuitive contact with reality that implies some intellectual grasp. Doctrine, however, is not itself religion, but makes explicit what is implicit in religious feeling, and in so doing, becomes more or less distorted, is ever changing and relative.

Similar ideas were being probed in depth by a few Catholic authors. J. Möhler who had steeped himself in the Bible and the Fathers, stressed the fact that the living organism of the Church cannot be fully understood unless it is vitally lived. John Henry Newman, quite independently of Schleiermacher, worked out his own theory of experience as contrasted with notional knowledge, a development that presaged a trend toward greater emphasis on spiritual anthropology. Newman's work on the development of doctrine (1845, revised 1878) had opened new vistas, but its influence on scholastic theology was negligible. Catholic ecclesiology was scarcely influenced by the great mystical and organic insights of Möhler and the Tübingen school, or by Newman.

By 1893, M. Blondel presented, in his *L'Action*, a fully rounded metaphysic of action in which the total man, and not exclusively his intellect, played a vital role in the approach to God, and in the understanding of tradition. Möhler, Newman, and Blondel, to an extent, resembled the Modernists in the questions they posed, but not in their solutions.

In the closing decades of the century the emphasis on growth and development in religion received influential support from neo-Hegelians, like John and Edward Caird in Britain, and from neo-idealists, like R. Eucken in Germany, with his philosophy of activism. In England, the pragmatists, under the influence of W. James, struggled against neo-Hegelianism, but the two streams paradoxically tended to merge. The result was a composite theory of a radical evolution of dogma together with the setting up of a pragmatic norm for finding religious truth, its fruitful life-value, and permanence. This, plus the continued influence of neo-Kantianism, with its separation of thought from reality, brought about a sustained attack on the stability and reality of dogma.

Natural science and history.   The general idea of development in religion was caught up and quickened by the publication (1859) of Darwin's *The Origin of Species*. The same point began to emerge with regard to the Bible through the great archeological work in the Middle East which began around 1850. The scientific development of historical methodology during the eighteenth and nineteenth centuries, especially in Germany, began to leave its mark on the Church towards the end of the nineteenth century, particularly through the work of Döllinger and Acton. Induction and empirical work was set off against the more deductive approach of the scholastics. Subsequent to Döllinger, the split grew between historian and theologian.

Around 1870, the great movement of Biblical exegesis was set in motion by German liberal scholars. New, and often valid, insights as to the formation of the Pentateuch were stimulated by Wellhausen, and the influence of H. Holtzmann's research in the New Testament, the culminating point of liberal exegesis, began to be felt in Catholic circles. The establishment of the Catholic Institutes in France, beginning in 1875, and the contributions of Catholic scripture scholars in Germany and Belgium, around the same period, marked the beginning of renewed exegetical work in the Church. Duchesne began his important historical studies in 1877, and the first work of his pupil, A. Loisy, on the history of the Old Testament Canon, appeared in 1890. In general, however, Catholic exegetical scholarship lagged behind that of liberal Protestants. Many Catholic exegetes were unaware of the lag: an apathy had been created by a lack of historical sense and by an excessive reliance on deductive methods, and a general fear of the new critical method arose in many quarters after it had been used so destructively in E. Renan's *Vie de Jésus* (1863). Further, with some exceptions in Germany and Belgium, where

Catholic faculties received state support, the Church-State struggles had greatly restricted the opportunities for Catholic scholarship. Finally, the belated urge to catch up with scholarly progress entailed the risk of hasty conclusions and the danger of intellectual indigestion.

Culture and politics. The ultimate evolution of the Church's relation to political society was discerned by relatively few of the participants in the bitter struggle between Church and State in the eighteenth and nineteenth centuries. The immediate outcome, at the time of Vatican Council I, in 1870, was the hardening of positions into two camps. Anti-religious and anti-clerical groups opposed Catholics who were religiously and politically conservative, and who supported an extremely simplified view of ultramontanism. Liberal Catholic thought had, in general, been ineffectual. The Church-State struggles had contributed to the destruction of the intellectual structures of the Church, especially in France. The intellectual life of the seminaries had been hampered, although a type of religious piety prospered.

As a reaction to these struggles, a greater centralization of Church authority in Rome gradually emerged. Against this background the decrees of Vatican I on papal infallibility were given a rigid and overriding interpretation by conservative Catholic spokesmen such as L. Veuillot, in France, and W. G. Ward, in England.

In France, political and religious conservatives defended the monarchy, and thus generated the image of a Church rooted in the old order. The Dreyfus affair of 1894 revealed anti-semitism among some of the Catholic conservatives. When C. Maurras founded the *Action Française* movement in 1898, many leading Catholic conservatives, both lay and cleric, rallied around it in their desire to return to the *ancien régime*. At the same time, *Sillon*, under the direction of M. Sangnier, emerged on the left as the liberal, democratic counterpart of *Action Française*. Thus, while Catholic strength was strongly to the right, those most outspoken in the Church in France were radically split in their political and religious thinking.

In Germany, somewhat less touched by political reactionism than France, Reformkatholizismus, especially as represented by F. X. Kraus and H. Schell, began during the nineties to push for reforms in the Latin type of Catholicism and "Romanism." It criticized centralization in the Roman Curia and the use of papal power, and urged that a "religious Catholicism" be substituted for an external and political one. Discussions centered to a large extent on Church discipline and scholarly freedom. The year 1902 marked the appearance of *Hochland*, a periodical whose liberal aim was to bring the Church out of its cultural ghetto.

In Italy, the loss of the temporal power of the Pope, and the unification of the peninsula had inspired many young priests with the vision of a totally new relationship between Church and State. A growing indifference toward the clear-cut philosophies that formed the backdrop of the old conflicts led some Catholics to look with favor at an idealistic philosophy in which the Church was envisioned as merely a powerful cultural force, a totally variable expression of a deeper religious aspiration. At the same time Catholic Action groups began to form in order to inject Catholic social influence into the mainstream of national life. Simultaneously, however, Catholics were forbidden to take part in the political life of a government traditionally opposed to the spirit and demands of the Church. In the matter of social thought and action a tension ensued in the minds of many young Catholics with regard to subordination to bishops and Church discipline in general.

In England, the Church, both numerically and intellectually, was just beginning to exercise any social influence; only in 1895 were Catholics positively permitted to attend the great universities.

In the midst of this complex ebb and flow of philosophies and cultural pressures, Modernism appeared as an abortive and self-destructive attempt at adaptation and rejuvenation. Thinkers, for the most part poorly grounded in philosophy, desperately reached for, and tried to inject into the Church's organism theories not sufficiently analyzed and purified. The outcome was an extremely strong reaction of the magisterium to these undigestible syncretisms.

The movement.   Modernism began as a spontaneous rather than an organized phenomenon. Its four centers of influence were France, England, Italy, and Germany.

France. In 1897 A. Sabatier, a French Huguenot, presented, with force and clarity, many of the ideas of Schleiermacher and Ritschl in his *L'Esquisse d'une philosophie de la religion d'après la psychologie et l'histoire*, a work which was profoundly to influence modernist thinking. The book strongly emphasized an interior religion whose central element was feeling in contrast to an almost totally immutable dogma.

In 1899, the French priest M. Hébert published his *Souvenirs d'Assise*, and, in 1902, the article "La dernière idole." Attacking along broadly Kantian lines the Thomistic demonstration of God's existence, he rejected personality in God, which he saw as merely a way of affirming the reality and objectivity of "the Ideal, the Divine, the Absolute." God is the category of the Ideal, immanent but unknowable. Hébert is sometimes called the herald-philosopher of Modernism within the Church.

From 1890 to around 1900, A. Loisy had been working on the frontiers of the new criticism especially in the Old Testament and had begun to arouse suspicions. It should be mentioned that at the same time M. J. Lagrange's liberal, but solid, positions were, though to a lesser extent, subject to the same suspicions in conservative quarters. In 1893 Loisy lost his position at the Institut Catholique in Paris, and gradually moved toward work on the New Testament. In 1900 he published an article strongly criticizing the notion of inspiration as presented in the encyclical *Providentissimus Deus* of 1893. In 1902 and 1903 he published two books, *L'Evangile et L'Eglise* and *Autour d'un petit livre*, which set off a violent public controversy. Through a selection of the eschatological texts in the synoptic Gospels, Loisy presented the essence of Christ's preaching as a literal teaching of an imminent coming of a physical and visible end-of-the-world Kingdom, a position somewhat similar to that taken in 1892 by the liberal Protestant exegete, J. Weiss, and in 1901 by A. Schweitzer. Loisy concluded that "Jesus announced the Kingdom and it is the Church which came."

Setting up his work as a defence against Harnack's rejection of doctrinal development, Loisy attempted to justify the appearance of a Church which he held Christ never had in mind and to set forth an evolution of its dogma which would be a genuine development. Attacked by Blondel (who presented his theory of vital tradition in action as an avenue of approach to the understanding of the Gospels), and supported by F. von Hügel (at least as to his right to present such a theory as a Catholic), Loisy's work caused great anguish among the intellectual and young clergy in France and Italy. The two works were among the five of Loisy's books placed on the Index in 1903. In 1904, after some ambiguous retractions, Loisy made his submission, an act which rankled afterward.

In 1905, E. Le Roy, a Catholic layman and disciple of Bergson, rejected in an extreme way the intellectual content of dogma in the article, "Qu'est-ce qu'un dogme?" He asserted that since dogma was formulated in relative terms, it could not require an absolute intellectual assent. Rather, it negatively safeguarded against error, and, positively, it prescribed a rule of practical conduct, a personal stance for action in the face of supernatural reality. Thus the dogma of God, as Father, is to be assimilated, not intellectually, but through one's filial action toward Him as Father. In 1902 and 1906 Abbé A. Houtin published studies which were extremely critical of recent Catholic exegetical work, and showed himself favorable to the most extreme positions. Abbé J. Turmel, an historian of dogma who had lost the faith as early as 1886, but wanted to remain in the Church, began, with the turn of the century, to publish numerous pseudonymous articles attacking Catholic dogma. Meanwhile the French Protestant, P. Sabatier, took a leading part in propaganda for the movement.

The Oratorian L. Laberthonnière, many of whose writings were later condemned, and Blondel with his philosophy of action, who were leaders in the contemporary movement of liberal Catholic philosophical thought, from the very beginning reacted against the Modernists' aims, and cannot be considered part of that movement. Similarly, Archbishop E. Mignot of Albi, who was in contact with Loisy, and favored a more liberal attitude toward scholarly work within the Church, was gradually dismayed by the more extreme exegetical positions and by the tendency toward philosophical immanentism.

England. In 1906 G. Tyrrell, who had privately distributed certain works, was dismissed from the Society of Jesus for refusing to retract the ideas in his anonymous *Letter to a Friend, A Professor of Anthropology* (published in Italy without his permission), in which he greatly minimized the function of Church dogma. Privately outlining a blueprint for the Church of the future, he became more and more caught up in controversy. He attacked Papal infallibility, ultramontane and otherwise, and the ecumenicity of Vatican Council I. Until his death in 1909, he developed a theory of the relation of revelation to dogma. Revelation, as the self-manifestation of the Divine in our inward life, was presented as an experience, first, of the Apostolic Church which was normative, and then, of every Christian. Revelation, when communicated biblically, he called dogma or prophetic truth, an imaginative and prophetic "presentment" of Divine reality. Prophetic truth was the living shadow of this reality. Later formulations he termed "theology" or "secondary dogmas," which metaphysically conceptualize the original communication. They were merely protective or illustrative formulae for prophetic truth, could be later contradicted or discarded, and in general were useful, but *totally* relative formulae. Revealed truth (*res*) was still contained in the formula (*enuntiabile*), but since the prophetic imagery was now transferred to scientific language, no absolute value guaranteed to be true could be assigned to the formula. Conciliar pronouncements were to be accepted only through the subsequent acceptance of the entire Church. Having drastically reduced the intellectual element in the original experience, Tyrrell worked out the rest of his system rather consistently, but through a confusing rhetoric. At the end of his life he had espoused the theory of an error by Christ as to the time of the Parousia. Tyrrell never held the doctrine of exclusive immanence as condemned by *Pascendi*, but many of his positions were an evident object of the encyclical's attack.

Tyrrell's friend, F. von Hügel, while rejecting the new immanentist philosophical approach, was a leader in the crusade for untrammeled rights for the exegete, rights, he insisted, that were being infringed by Roman authority. Conferring with various high ranking ecclesiastics in and out of Rome, and keeping up a vast correspondence with the leaders of the new thought, he endeavored to give some coherence and organization to the movement. Maude Petre supported Tyrrell's ideas and published his life history in 1912.

Italy. In Italy, the movement had a more socio-political tone, but discussion of political and social theory continually impinged on the areas of religion and theology. The Italian priest R. Murri, a Christian democrat, founded the *Lega democratica nazionale*, a movement that was to be independent of the hierarchy, and demanded a reform of the Church's institutional and social structure. Anti-clerical in attitude, Murri worked out his ideas from a scholastic basis, but later moved toward an idealism somewhat reminiscent of that of Croce and Gentile; they nevertheless attacked him for equivocation in his positions.

In the exegetical and theological fields, the priest S. Minocchi founded the review *Studi religiosi* in 1901 as a forum for the new thought. He was strongly influenced by Loisy in the exegetical area, and later by Tyrrell with regard to the interpretation of dogma. Another priest, E. Buonaiuti, early enamored of Blondel's philosophy of action, became fascinated by immanentism and moved toward a form of social messianism. He emerged as the leading Italian Modernist, but was anxious to remain within the Church for the working out of his ideas.

More on the edge of Modernism, and ultimately loyal to the Church were the layman, A. Fogazzaro, whose novel *Il Santo* (1905) became the literary symbol of the movement, and the Barnabite G. Semeria, who worked in religious and biblical criticism. In 1907 the journal *Rinnovamento* became an important organ for liberal political and religious opinion.

Germany. In Germany, the review *Das Zwanzigste Jahrhundert*, which was founded in 1901 at Munich by F. Klasen, and continued by Th. Engert, became an organ for Reformkatholizismus. Like the Krausgesellschaft, founded in Munich in 1904, Reformkatholizismus carried out a program of anti-Roman and anti-scholastic sentiment. It attacked political ultramontanism, and insisted on freedom in scientific religious work and the suppression of the Index. It did not totally overlap with Modernism, but remained principally on the level of practical Church discipline. However, the Bavarian priest K. Gebert in 1905 proposed a Kantian and immanentist approach not unlike that reproved by *Pascendi*. Th. Engert, also a priest, demanded the abandonment of the notion of Biblical inerrancy, and the complete revision of the concept of inspiration. Yet it was not until after the condemnations of *Pascendi* that Engert and J. Schnitzer of the University of Munich, who was a supporter of Loisy, emerged as the leaders of a small Modernist extreme. In Germany, Modernism was more localized than in France and Italy, and generated less extreme theological positions than in any of the other major countries involved.

Action of the magisterium. Leo XIII, whose liberal policy was tinctured by serious reserves over the new thought, but who hesitated to take strong action, was succeeded on Aug. 4, 1903 by Pius X. Seeing that the situation was causing anguish and doctrinal confusion, Pius decided that strict action was mandatory. The decree of the Holy Office, placing five works of Loisy on the Index, was approved by Pius X on Dec. 17, 1903. In 1905 he encouraged Catholic Action, but insisted that it must be subordinate to ecclesiastical officials (*Il Fermo Proposito*). In 1906 he warned of insubordination among the clergy in Italy, and declared those priests suspended who became members of the National Democratic League (*Pieni L'Animo*). That same year, Fogazzaro's *Il Santo*, and two works of Laberthonnière, were placed on the Index, and Tyrrell was dismissed by the Jesuits. Murri was suspended on April 15, 1907. On July 3, 1907, the Holy Office's decree *Lamentabili* condemned sixty-five propositions in the area of criticism and dogma. On July 26, Le Roy's *Dogme et Critique* was put on the Index. (During August, Fogazzaro, Murri, Buonaiuti, von Hügel, and others met in northern Italy to limit the terms of their submission.) On Sept. 8, 1907, *Pascendi* presented a global blueprint of the whole Modernist program. It condemned theories on dogma and Biblical criticism which had agnostic, immanentist-evolutionary and anti-intellectualist bases. Constructed from ideas found in the work of various Modernists, the encyclical condemned a system to which not all the Modernists subscribed. As G. Gentile, the Italian idealist, and Maude Petre, the subsequent champion of Modernism, admitted, however, *Pascendi* seized the movement in its totality. At the same time, immanentism, neo-Hegelianism, and agnosticism were the terminal point rather than the *point de départ*, and that for only a few of the participants we have cited. Yet *Pascendi*, which mentioned no names and had the flavor of a theoretical abstraction, was a fair prophecy of the final position of Loisy.

On Nov. 18, 1907, in the *motu proprio Praestantia sacrae scripturae*, Pius X decreed that all were bound in conscience to submit to the decrees of the Biblical Commission, both past and future, in the same way as to the doctrinal decrees issued by the Sacred Congregations and approved by the Pope. (Since 1905 the Biblical Commission had issued a series of generally conservative prudential norms with regard to scriptural interpretation.)

Some loosely organized opposition had developed among the group associated with *Rinnovamento*, but writers and supporters of the review were made subject to excommunication at the end of 1907. Tyrrell (Oct. 1907) and Schnitzer (Feb. 1908) were excommunicated for their opposition to the encyclical.

Minocchi was suspended, and Loisy excommunicated in 1908. Subsequently, Loisy developed his doctrine of the religion of humanity built on a vague agnostic basis. With the death of Tyrrell in 1909 the heart went out of the movement, though small pockets of resistance remained. The requirement of the Oath against Modernism (Sept. 1, 1910), to be taken by professors and pastors of souls, marked the end of the crisis. Maude Petre, deprived of the sacraments in her own diocese, though never singled out for formal excommunication by name, and Buonaiuti, finally excommunicated by name in 1926, continued as champions of Modernism. Le Roy, Semeria, and von Hügel, previously more or less on the margin of Modernism, remained faithful to the Church. Engert became a Protestant, and Houtin rejected the whole Modernist plan and became agnostic. Murri, with reservations on his political and social positions, was received back into the church only in 1943.

Aftermath. After *Pascendi*, there followed a period of unmasking Modernism which caused great anguish. Many incorrectly thought that Newman and Blondel had been condemned. The Committees of Vigilance, set up by the encyclical, were used as a specious support by simplist conservative groups to justify sweeping condemnations. Thought and nuance were rejected in favor of polemics, and the word, Modernism, became a label to be used against whatever was disliked in liberal Catholic thought, in theology, literature, and politics. At the center of this campaign was the association *Sodalitium pianum*, directed by Monsignor U. Benigni, in Italy. A secret code, the counterpart of Modernist anonymity, protected collaborators in various countries. The attacks of *Action Française* (whose condemnation in 1914, four years after the condemnation of *Sillon*, was made public only in 1926), and the intransigence of writers like E. Barbier and J. Fontaine, brought into popularity a counter-label, "integralism." At the beatification of Pius X in 1950, evidence was presented to show that he did not give his support to a great deal of this campaign, but held his hand for fear of encouraging the Modernists. In 1914 Benedict XV's *Ad beatissimi* checked this campaign of unjustified suspicion as World War I broke out.

Definition. Some have defined Modernism as an attempt to retain the form while dropping the content of dogma. Some Modernists, however, desired to drop the form as well. If Modernism is defined very widely, then only its extreme form was condemned (R. Aubert, A. Dansette). Any definition of Modernism must be drawn mainly from *Pascendi*, the most solemn Church condemnation. The loose application of the word Modernism to the development of theological thinking is widely admitted to be an abuse. Further, faint similarities of a position to statements in *Pascendi* can be judged to be fully modernistic only if they are also related to the essential points of condemnation in the encyclical. *Pascendi* stated that it was directly attacking agnostic, immanentist, and evolutionary-naturalistic doctrine.

The following descriptive definition of Modernism is suggested. It was an ideological orientation, tendency, or movement within the Catholic Church, clearly emerging during the waning years of the nineteenth century, and rapidly dying out around the year 1910, after official condemnation. It was only loosely and sporadically organized, characterized by a tone antagonistic to all ecclesiastical authority, and believed, in an adaptation of the Church to what was considered sound in modern thought, even at the expense of radically changing the essence of the Church. At Modernism's core, far beyond liberal Catholic positions on Biblical criticism and theology, lay a triple thesis: a denial of the supernatural as an object of certain knowledge (in the totally symbolic, non-objective approach to the content of dogma which is also related to a type of agnosticism in natural theology); an exclusive immanence of the Divine and of revelation ("vital immanence") reducing the Church to a simple, social, civilizing, phenomenon; and a total emancipation of scientific research from Church dogma which would allow the continued assertion of faith in dogma, with its contradiction on the historical level (as understood in certain presentations of the "Christ of faith, Christ of history," "Church of faith, Church of history" distinctions).

Conclusion. The difficulty in assessing the influence of modernist thinkers on the later Church arises from the fact that these men also fed on, and assimilated many legitimate tendencies which were arising in the contemporary Church. The idea of faith as a personal encounter, the increased appreciation of religious experience and spiritual anthropology, the deeper probing of the relation between psychology and religion, the return to the traditional emphasis on the sense of mystery, the renewed realization of the pastoral function of theology, the less mechanical assessment of the role of authority, the growth in insight into the development of dogma, the underlining of the organic nature of the Church, and the importance of the laity, a greater respect for scriptural scholarship and natural science, a newer framework of Church-State relations, a call to leave a cultural ghetto—many of these insights were already found in the works of scholars like Möhler, Newman, Blondel, Lagrange, and other orthodox thinkers who, by the time of Modernism, had already broached many of these questions. This situation, coupled with the rediscovery of the spirit of a genuine Thomism, might have set the stage, it seems, for fruitful development. It is difficult to see how certain values, said to arise from Modernism, were not actually hampered in their development within the Church by its very appearance, and by the strong medicine deemed necessary to eliminate it.

Through its very excesses, however, Modernism did point out certain areas which called for investigation within a sound theological framework, as in the insights mentioned above. Certain authors, like de Grandmaison, Lagrange, and Lebreton, continued their scholarly contributions. Still, the exaggerated spread of suspicions that followed the condemnation of Modernism probably caused many scholars to shy away from delicate subjects. Only with K. Adam, and after World War II, with scholars like K. Rahner and Y. Congar, did a trend emerge toward a renewed consideration of subjects so destructively and abortively handled by the modernists.

The Modernist crisis retarded Catholic scholarship, and strengthened Catholic discipline. It resulted in a victory that preserved the essential life of the Church, but also postponed an adequate handling of many important religious questions.

NOTES

CHAPTER ONE

1. The best works on von Hügel are: Michael de la Bedoyère, *The Life of Baron von Hügel* (New York, 1952); Maurice Nédoncelle, *La pensée religieuse de Friedrich von Hügel, 1852–1925* (Paris, 1935); English tr.: *Baron Friedrich von Hügel* (N.Y., 1937).

2. *The Mystical Element of Religion as Studied in Saint Catherine of Genoa and her friends* (London, 1908); quotation is from the preface to the first edition, p. xxi in second edition (1909).

3. *The German Soul and its attitude towards Theism and Christianity* (London, 1916), p. 121.

4. J. Rivière, *Le Modernisme dans l'Eglise* (Paris, 1929), p. 105.

5. In what follows, use has been made of "Charles von Hügel," edited and collected by Anatole von Hügel, privately printed, second issue, Julius Wiesmer's account (Cambridge, 1905), p. 25.

6. *Ibid.*, pp. 26, 28. Reumont says further that Carl was a loving husband and father. (See *SL* p. 4). Friedrich's mother, however, querulously tells her son that "her husband had never helped her, or encouraged her or checked her in any way, and that but for conventional Church going on Sunday, he seemed to ignore her having a soul or character." And Friedrich writes to his wife shortly after their marriage, "I was sorry and couldn't say anything for I'm afraid it's a good bit true" (quoted in de la Bedoyère, p. 15). But we must recall that she was thirty-five years younger than her husband.

7. F. von Hügel, "The Story of the Escape of Prince Metternich," *The National Review*, I (1883), 588–604.

8. M. Petre, *Von Hügel and Tyrrell* (London, 1937), 8, 199–203.

9. A. Loisy, *Memoires pour servir à l'histoire religieuse de notre temps*, 3 vols. (Paris, 1931), III, 471.

10. Von Hügel, "The Historical Method and the Documents of the Hexateuch," *Catholic University Bulletin* (Washington, D. C., April, 1898), 199.

11. For example, he claims that the neo-Hegelians' specific English and Scotch antecedents had brought sobriety and sense to their Hegelianism. (*Eternal Life* [Edinburgh, 1912], p. 219.) He speaks about "the ready lucidity of form and comparative indifference to the solidity of the content in the Frenchman's thinking—and ... the probing if often stolid, solidity of mind and the absorption away from questions of form, in the subject matter, so common in the German's rumination." (*EA* II, 259.) He speaks of Hegel as having the great qualities of the Germans, "an intensely professional man," but also their grave defects "in his lack of humour, want of moderation ... something Asiatic that permeates this most western of westerns." (*RG*, pp. 50–51.)

12. M. Ward, *The Wilfrid Wards and the Transition* (London, 1934), pp. 307–308. This quotation would be misleading if it left the reader with the impression that the Baron was fickle in his friendships. He was outstanding in his sense of loyalty to friends. His reactions to these early acquaintances, however, do show us his propensity to undergo waves of enthusiasm.

13. M. Ward, *Insurrection versus Resurrection* (London, 1938), p. 187. For Wilfrid's dying request for spiritual direction from von Hügel see pp. 479 ff.

14. *SL*, pp. 24–25.

15. For example, we must remember that the Ward tradition is influenced by the fact that Wilfrid was himself no expert in scriptural work, that he may have been too anxious in all sincerity to escape from dilemmas. (See de la Bedoyère, p. 291.) It seems there is an excessive tendency to dub as "naïve" his reactions to a critical movement with which this atmosphere was not quite *au courant*. Maude Petre is so closely bound in affection to Tyrrell that she too often finds in von Hügel a scapegoat for Tyrrell's problems (M. Petre, *My Way of Faith* [London, 1937], pp. 286–287). Bernard Holland was a close friend of the Wards and cannot be used as a totally independent source (M. Ward, *Insurrection versus Resurrection*, pp. 479, 526). And Loisy himself, in reverse, naïvely read more agreement with his own views in the Baron than von Hügel actually held (see Nédoncelle, *op. cit.*, p. 34 n. and chapters 2–3 of this study).

16. For example, June 4, 1904 to Tyrrell: "my health is well-nigh breaking down under the strain" (of completing his *Mystical Element*). June 12, 1904 to Tyrrell: "... I have had a succession of nervous attacks and prostrations, of a kind with which my earlier years were

full. ..." Sept. 25, 1909 to Mrs Drew: "... nervous weakness and brain fog that are pursuing me now. ..." Oct. 1, 1909 to Clement Webb: "... a state of brain fog and nervous debility such as I have not known for the last twenty-five years. Loud buzzing in my ears. ..." Nov. 19, 1909 to Mr. Malcom Quinn: "... during some ten weeks now, my nerve and brain force have been painfully low and threatening to break down. ..." July 4, 1910 to Maude Petre: "... ill health—of my present sort especially—makes me realize ... the loneliness of one's special aspirations and apprehensions." Strain and overwork, even more than the modernist crisis, seems to have caused his condition. While ill health never left him, his health seems to have improved until near the 'twenties when, for example, on April 12, 1920 he writes to Dr. Brilioth: "But one of the chief crosses of my life has been my inflammable brain conditions which, when I am working hard, make it almost impossible for me to keep up with my many kind friends." (Cf. *SL* passim.) On June 29, 1922 he writes to his niece, Gwendolen Greene, about a recent nervous breakdown: "such an old acquaintance that! Why from eighteen to nearly thirty my life was pretty well blotted out by such troubles!" (*LTN, op. cit.,* p. 187.) Under such stresses the Baron remained unbelievably balanced.

17. Petre, *My Way of Faith*, p. 257. Miss Petre's judgment is supported by a letter of the Baron to his wife in 1895 where he blames it on his over-intensity "when my friends find me 'too much of a good thing.'" He had even begun to worry that his overwhelming intensity with people was a matter of sex, but Abbé Huvelin, his director, showed him that it really applied to everything that he occupied himself with. (De la Bedoyère, p. 86.) Huvelin's direction freed him from his early "scruple and depression" with regard to purity (*EA* II, 236, [1921]). Issy von Hügel, his sister-in-law, wrote after his death: "... he never lived really in the atmosphere he was trying to be helpful to, and so was unable to appreciate where the people he felt for were different from the picture their works painted of them ... characteristic of him to overdo patience sometimes with word positions." (M. Ward, *Insurrection versus Resurrection*, p. 496.) Perhaps Issy was not in an intellectual position to make the last part of this statement, but the general picture is corroborative. Maisie Ward felt that his deafness and intense absorption tended to limit his field of vision. De la Bedoyère takes a broader and more humorous approach to things which irritated many people. Later in life the Baron seems to have been conscious of this tendency. In 1919 he speaks of encouraging others to be quite different from ourselves (*SL*, p. 289), and "the golden rule is to help those we love to escape from us" (*LTN*, p. xxix).

18. This and the following quotations or paraphrases of Huvelin are contained in *SL*, pp. 57–63.

19. Because of their importance I include a few here. It is not clear what Huvelin meant by "orthodoxy." Probably he meant the agreed teaching of theological manuals when it is not necessarily of faith. We must be careful not to take these following statements as absolutes. Huvelin practiced an adaptive method suited to each individual soul. (J. Rouanet, *L'Abbé Huvelin*, [Toulouse, 1962], pp. 39–41). M.-Th. Louis-Lefebre, in *Un Prêtre, L'Abbé Huvelin*, (Paris, 1956), p. 230, believes that Huvelin's advice kept the Baron from becoming a modernist. Some of the more pertinent sayings were:

IX.   Theologians err at times? I well believe it—they err and *often*. Science and experience have come a long way since theology has been arrested.

X.   Take care with your conscience. Orthodoxy will follow... never wound charity. With you, charity and faith are the same thing. They will sink or rise together.

XXIII.   Yes, you have a horror of "good philosophy," of "orthodox reasoning" because you search the truth, not orthodoxy. Orthodoxy must align itself with truth. That is its affair.

XXVI.   There is no profounder or more dangerous enemy for Christianity than all that makes it shrunken and narrow.

XXVIII.   ... you will never weaken your faith if you search always and only for *the* truth and not *your* truth. You can be sure that if you adhere to an idea only to the degree that, apart from passion and personality, it seems to you true, God will always give you intellectual light on your error, if you are in error.

XXVIII.   Yes, the Church is totally positive, totally independent. This is something a great deal grander than an anti-Protestantism, and anti-rationalism.

XXXI.   I have an antipathy toward miracles.

XXXIII.   You recall the manner of writing history which St. Jerome followed when he treated the famous dispute between Peter and Paul as a staged affair arranged in advance. This is not at all the way to love God. It is not to respect His Providence to thus search, not for the full and living truth which edified by the simple exposition of the Divine permissive will, but for a little proper idea, fabricated quite personally, *a priori*, for which one sacrifices all.

20. This notebook is at St. Andrews University Library, St. Andrews Scotland. Extracts have been published by R. K. Brown, "Newman and von Hügel, A Record of an Early Meeting," *The Month*, (July, 1961), 24–32. There are twenty letters from Newman to the Baron from Jan. 5, 1874 to July 21, 1884 at St. Andrews.

21. Brown, *op. cit.*, p. 32. I am indebted to Mr. Brown for these references and for other insights on von Hügel.

22. *LTN*, p. 114.

23. *EA*, II, 242.

24. It is interesting to notice that the Baron found the poet Milton "doubly cold," incurably Puritan, and without a necessary innocent sensuousness. (The latter he also found lacking in St. Catherine of Genoa.) He also found a Fr. Mackey, O.P. "very depressing, scrupulous, depressed, depressing, unhumorous, generally narrow minded." (See *SL*, p. 274, and M. Ward, *Insurrection versus Resurrection*, p. 145.) "Puritan" versus "innocent sensuousness," and "scruples tending to depression," these terms recur and are of interest. In 1921 the Baron wrote of his earlier discovery on the greater danger of pride than of sex and on the need to respect the body. He concluded: "For the conviction as to purity has freed me from much previous scruple and depression." (*EA*, II, 237.) At the period when he first met Newman, this apparently was a worry (see de la Bedoyère, p. 18). It apparently continued as a worry even after his marriage (*ibid.*, p. 86). Sexual metaphors appear so often in *The Mystical Element* as to become almost a distraction. "Virile" alone as an adjective must occur more than fifty times. All of the previous merely shows that the Baron was a warm human person who had normally strong sexual problems combined with a sensitive nature and need for sympathy. When in this condition he met what he considered a colder personality, there was little emotional harmony. A certain tendency which he had rejected still lurked in him, and began to produce again twinges of depression. Without claiming this theory as a final solution, I suggest it as an explanation of the Baron's antipathy to Newman. It also would have caused him to continue to react against some of Newman's "Predestinarian" doctrines. (See *Der Beständige Aufbruch—Festschrift für Erich Przywara*, undated, p. 55), where Fr. H. Tristam defends Newman against the Baron's statement that Newman could be beatified but only Huvelin could be canonized (*EA*, II [1921], 242). He says that the idea of Newman being "deeply predestinarian" was a figment of the Baron's imagination, and that Dr. Brilioth has suggested that von Hügel himself had feelings of depression.

25. *EL*, pp. 358–360.

26. *ME* I, 65.

27. *On Consulting the Faithful in Matters of Doctrine* (London, 1961 ed.). See also H. F. Davis, "Le role et l'apostolat de la hiérarchie et du laicat dans la théologie de l'Eglise chez Newman," in *L'Ecclesiologie au XIX Siècle*, (Paris, 1960), pp. 329–350, esp. pp. 335–340.

28. M. Ward, *The Wilfrid Wards and the Transition* (London, 1934), pp. 247–249, 302–306. After his article on the laity appeared in the *Rambler*, Newman tried to hold a center position between the extreme criticisms of the hierarchy, written by Acton and Döllinger in the *Rambler*, and the extreme conservatism of W. G. Ward in *The Dublin Review*.

29. Cited in Viscount Charles Halifax, *Leo XIII and Anglican Orders* (London, 1912), p. 218.

30. W. Ward, *The Life of John Henry Cardinal Newman*, 2 vols. (London, 1913), 1, p. 524.

31. A letter by von Hügel, "Louis Duchesne," *Time Literary Supplement* (May 25, 1922), p. 342. Von Hügel was cautious of Duchesne's "brilliant tongue" which, as early as Nov. 1888, was able to express such things in letters to the Baron as: "I am not a theologian; that is why I can praise God with joy." "Among the red and violet soutanes, there are only, with the exception of Lavigerie, the souls of sacristans ... an episcopate composed of imbeciles." Fifty-six of his letters to the Baron are at St. Andrews. On leaving England, once, he told von Hügel that what impressed him most were the ghastly wax figures of the English sovereigns in Westminster Abbey. The Baron took the statement at face value.

32. *RG*, p. 52.

CHAPTER TWO

1. J. Hogan, P.S.S., *Clerical Studies* (Boston, 1898). He pleads for a renewal of genuine scholasticism. For a full, rather personal picture of the period, see M. Ward, *Insurrection Versus Resurrection*, pp. 1–49. For a general picture of the earlier period, see R. Aubert, *Le Pontificat de Pie IX*, pp. 184–224. R. P. Lecanuet, *La vie de l'église sous Leo XIII* (Paris, 1930), esp. ch. vii which throws light on the scholarly deficiencies. A. Dansette, *Religious History of Modern France* (New York, 1961), I, 291–314, shows the relation of this to Modernism.

2. *Ce qu'on va chercher à Rome* (Paris, 1895), pp. 44–45.

3. While admitting the neo-scholastics' "narrowness" and lack of knowledge of contemporary science, we must remember the contributions of such men as Franzelin, Passaglia, Kleutgen at Rome, Heinrich at Mayence, Denzinger and Hettinger at Würzbourg, Scheeben at Colgone.

4. Lecanuet, *La vie de l'église*, p. 319.

5. W. Ward, *The Life and Times of Cardinal Wiseman* (London, 1898.), p. 459.

6. E. Purcell, *Life of Cardinal Manning*, 2 vols. (London, 1895), II, 775.

7. J. G. Snead-Cox, *The Life of Cardinal Vaughan* (London, 1910), II, 85. Robert Hugh Benson, who was thinking of conversion at the turn of the century, complained that in Catholic apologetic books he read, he had been "rendered incapable of appreciating fully the force of the arguments, because it seemed as if the writers desired to bully me." C. C. Martindale, *The Life of Monsignor Robert Hugh Benson* (London, 1916), I, 206.

8. A. Houtin, *La question biblique chez les Catholiques de France au XIX siècle* (Paris, 1902), p. 287. The best work that I have found for giving a feeling for the atmosphere of 1890 among the neo-scholastics in their approach to scripture is J. B. Aubry's *Essai sur la méthode des études ecclesiastiques en France* (Lille, 1890), esp. pp. 378–411. Aubry was a disciple of Franzelin, and brings us into the atmosphere of Rome with Franzelin at the rostrum. Neo-scholastic logic and clarity are evident in the book. But with regard to scripture he says: "Le programme de tout professeur d'Ecriture Sainte doit être rigoureusement celui de S. Thomas: *La recherche du sens dogmatique*, pas autre chose! Une fois ce sens saisi, il possède tout..." And he complains of the recent proliferation of works on the Bible translated from German and English, pp. 382–383.

9. E. Purcell, *Life of Cardinal Manning*, ch. xxvii.

10. In this section abundant use has been made of *L'Ecclésiologie au XIX siècle*, especially Congar's "L'Ecclésiologie de la revolution française au Concile du Vatican, sous le signe de l'affirmation de l'autorité," pp. 77–114.

11. H. Hurter's *Theologicae Dogmaticae* Compendium of 1893 gives to the questions of infallibility in the Church and pontifical authority 34 pages and 120 pages respectively out of 258 pages for the whole of ecclesiology!

CHAPTER THREE

1. *Mémoires*, I, p. 287. Perhaps one sixth of the vast work deals with von Hügel. Although the *Mémoires* evoke a certain feeling of objectivity about Loisy's attitudes, they are radically spoiled at crucial points by a continual reading of others' motives with great assurance and by personal outbreaks of vindictiveness.

2. This was published under the same title, but not until 1930, by Sheed and Ward, London. The friend's name was W. Frere, later to become an Anglican bishop, and to take part in the Malines ecumenical conversations. (See de la Bedoyère, p. 63.)

3. *EA* I, 262–263. In von Hügel's thinking, this will be a genuine and divinely intended development.

4. For d'Hulst's article and the controversy, see A. Baudrillard, *Vie de Mgr. d'Hulst* (Paris, 1914), Ch. xxi. Loisy himself had presented what would, today, be an acceptable treatment on inspiration.

5. *The Spectator* (May 19, 1894), pp. 684–85. Loisy claimed that the Encyclical concerned the method of theological exegesis but ignored the question of historical exegesis, thus bringing about the Christ of history, Christ of faith dichotomy. (*Mém*, I, p. 314.)

6. In *The Spectator* the Baron had said: "If the Bible has as surely a body as the Church has a soul, and it took us up to Pius IX to formally, officially differentiate the latter in one direction, it may take up some time to fully differentiate the former in another." Similar ideas were written to Loisy, Jan. 4, 1894 (*Mém* I, 322–323). In a letter to Bishop Hedley of May 27, 1894 he considers that the Pope's use of the phrase "*communis sermo*" (popular language) explains and limits the meaning of inerrancy, and that Catholics are under an obligation only "to ward off from Scripture ... such relativities as, taken out of their place and time and from their accommodating function in the Bible and changed from simple opinions into formal convictions and systems, would rightly be called error." J. A. Wilson, *The Life of Bishop Hedley*, (London, 1930), p. 215.

7. *The Wilfrid Wards and the Transition*, p. 311.

8. "The Church and the Bible, The Two Stages of Their Interpretation," *The Dublin Review* (Oct. 1894), pp. 313–314; (April, 1895), pp. 306–337; (Oct. 1895), pp. 275–304.

9. Vatican II, in the Constitution on Divine Revelation, says that the Church perpetrates and hands on "all that she herself is, all that she believes" (N. C. W. C. translation, *8).

10. He writes to Ward, May 21, 1894: "You will notice at once that I have gone as far as possible to the right as to the documents and the encyclical's doctrinal importance, as far as possible to the left as to its liberal interpretation. This too I think the wiser course *with an eye to Rome.*"

11. "La methode historique et son application à l'étude des documents de l'Hexateuque," published by Picard (Loisy's publisher) (Paris, 1898), 35 pp. Its English counterpart was published in the *Catholic University Bulletin* (Washington, D.C., April, 1898), pp. 198–26 + 7 pp. appendix. The English translation is very free and differs in a few important sections from the French.

12. "Les sources du Pentateuque," *Revue Biblique* (Jan. 1898), pp. 10–32.

13. Von Hügel's article was reviewed favorably in *Revue Critique d'histoire et de littérature* (Oct. 24, 1898) with the comment that this is the first time that critical methods had been overtly defended by Catholic savants. *The Weekly Register* (Oct. 14, 1899), gives the same impression.

14. The Jesuit, Fr. Méchineau, held that Catholics were not free from the point of view of the faith on the question of the composition of the Pentateuch. In a letter to Tyrrell of Aug. 18, 1900, von Hügel cites an oblate, Fr. Robert Butler, who taught his students that deliberately to harbor thoughts on the possibility of the non-Mosaic authorship of the Pentateuch was a mortal sin. The Biblical Commission on June 27, 1906 (D-S 2000) made some minor allowances for later additions to the Pentateuch, but rejected the theory of non-Mosaic authorship. But on Jan. 16, 1948, in a letter to Cardinal Suhard, the Commission stated: "There is no one today who doubts the existence of these sources or refuses to admit a progressive development of the Mosaic laws due to social and religious conditions of later times, a development which is also manifest in the historical narratives." (Translation from *Rome and the Study of Scripture* [St. Meinrad, 1958], p. 151.)

15. "La Methode historique," p. 4. On May 26, 1896, the Baron wrote to Blondel that he suffered with him in seeing "all that scholasticism spoils and denatures, the history of philosophy, the entire mode of conceiving the role and capacity of human thought, the fashion from one end to the other in which it presents dogma and Christian morality ... a mountain of ice floating in the middle of a southern sea—pagan *intellectualism* even at the heart of Christian morality. And if scholasticism ruins philosophy for me, it is also my implacable enemy on the terrain of history and the Bible. There is no real knowledge of the past stages of human thought... without the three elements of *relativity, development,* and *interiority* ("moralisme") ... The day when scholasticism would accept these, it would cease to be."

16. The Synthetic Society required only an interest in forming a philosophy of theism as a basis for discussion in religious philosophy. See *The Wilfrid Wards and the Transition*, pp. 362–363.

17. *Dogmatic vs Biblical Theology* (Baltimore, 1964), pp. 34 ff.

18. *Mem* I, 297.

CHAPTER FOUR

1. M. Ward, *The Wilfrid Wards and the Transition*, esp. ch. 18–20, and *Insurrection versus Resurrection*, esp. ch. 7–18.

2. Ward's ideas on development are found in *Problems and Persons* (London, 1903), pp. 1–183.

3. *TWW*, p. 300.

4. To von Hügel, Feb. 27, 1900. However on Oct. 7–9, 1900 the Baron wrote to Henri Bremond: "Then the next was Wilfred Ward who came and stayed here for a night and with whom I had three long talks. He was friendly and nice, and had many an interesting bit of information to communicate, and his views on Development of Doctrine, religious philosophy and such like, if somewhat sketchy, are certainly elastic and large. But I got the depressing impression of a soul distinctly *shrunk* and scared since last I met it; of a man living somewhat away from the living springs of light and reality. It saddened me a good bit to find him so sensitively wedded to the contention that the world outside is very largely in hopelessly bad faith, and in a state of fanatical sheer wrongheadedness, before which the Church cannot and must not disarm, and which justifies a substantial 'non possumus,' and excuses the excesses of form and manner which this occasionally takes. This saddens one, because it evidently spells sterility: it is of course the infallible way to stereotype and *fix* those very prejudices which are there, no doubt, but which we have so largely ourselves occasioned, and which if we will excuse ourselves by accusing them as absolutely final, will remain so and be made so by ourselves. The deepest proof of the divinity of Christianity, my dear good Eucken always insists, is its unconquerable *surplusage* over all ignorance, sin and opposition which it finds; a surplusage which actually calls forth, makes the nobility and answering sympathy which it, with a divine authority, presupposes. Religion has disowned itself in the very moment it sinks, in resourcefulness of love and comprehension, to the level of those whom it is there to recreate. And when and where were eggs ever hatched but by warmth?—Still all this with him is part of his present direct apologetic vein; and he is so sincerely good . . . and sees so widely and far when he manages . . . to get away for a little from this impoverishing 'making out a case' activity of mind that I much hope he may again grow out of it. Then Archbishop Ireland kindly came, etc." The Baron's problem with authority is beginning in earnest. (All letters in this study which are quoted without a reference source have been drawn from unpublished matter found listed after Chapter IX.)

5. "The Rigidity of Rome," in *Problems and Persons*, pp. 79–80. A blueprint of today's ecumenical movement is found on pp. 87–98.

6. Feb. 27, 1900. See *TWW*, p. 325. The letters immediately following may be found in the same work, p. 325 ff.

7. *Mém* I, 551.

8. *AAS*, 29 (1896–1897), p. 637.

9. The Baron's opinion of Cardinal Camillo Mazzella was that he was a "neo-scholastic" without a realization "of the special complexity of critical questions and of the wisdom of either studying them carefully or letting them alone." Letter to Ward, May 25, 1898. Mazzella (1853–1900) taught dogmatics at Georgetown and Woodstock from 1867 to 1878 and at the Gregorian from 1878 to 1886 when he was created a cardinal and was at various times Prefect of the Congregation of the Index.

10. *DS* 3681/2198.

11. *TWW*, p. 302.

12. "I am having the strange, very sobering impression that God is designing somehow to use me—me, in my measure, along with others who can and do more, and much more—towards making, not simply registering, history." To Tyrrell (Dec. 18–20, 1901), *SL*, p. 103.

13. On Mar. 4, 1900 he wrote to Tyrrell from Rome: "Brunetière, this spiritually wholly cold and empty theoretician, this panegyrist of an ecclesiastical police ... there is no doubt he represents the type understood here, and again the type we *don't* want. They enormously over-estimate the power of the press for one thing. Then they understand rhetoric, and don't understand specialism, or severe method, critical or any other; and lastly they understand religion as an external institution, a social force, a polity and policy." He finds the major problem around "Merry del Val's drawing room" to be rancor over loss of temporal power. On May 10, 1899 Tyrrell had written him: "In the name of heaven who is the author of all this endeavor to make the shadow go back on the dial? Is Mazzella so omnipotent?"

14. *Vraie et fausse reforme dans l'Eglise* (Paris, 1950), pp. 67–68.

15. In a letter to the Bishop of Limerick, *IVR*, p. 41.

16. He wrote to Ward: "The fact is, no doubt, that these methods and general results have nothing fantastic or arbitrary about them, and though even they (*as indeed what may not, and will not?*) *may, by coming into unprepared minds, work harm instead of good*— yet where the mind is already open or even perplexed beyond the legitimate exigencies of the case, then such first-hand knowledge of the subject, and according to the methods not simply alien to a contemporary mind, will help quiet and relieve the mind." *TWW*, p. 325. (Emphasis added). On June 14, 1894 he had written to Ward that he was aware of the danger of upsetting people's minds. But the ideas were not immediately intended for the majority and were published in specialist reviews.

17. *TWW*, p. 301, letter to Ward.

CHAPTER FIVE

1. *Mém* II, p. 340.

2. The Baron listed these in a letter to Bremond, Nov. 3, 1902: Fogazzaro, later to write *Il Santo*, a novel which was put on the Index; Gallarati-Scotti, Fogazzaro's biographer, "perhaps the most sympathetic mind to your mind of any on my list"; Padre Gazzolo, a Barnabite in Milan, "an admirable mystical-mind, critically trained, most open-minded man of God. I admire him down to the ground. A great admirer of Loisy, and a friend of Semeria. Still a little too intellectualist (à la Rosmini) to altogether please me in philosophy"; Padre Ghignoni, Barnabite, "I think that next to Scotti, you will like this man best of all on my list." Fr. Salvatore Minocchi: "worth knowing, apart from his competence as a Hebrew scholar, because of his knowledge of men and things in Italy; as an instance of the deficiencies of ecclesiastical training; what he knows and sees, he has achieved in spite of his entourage and superiors. And his outlook on life, his philosophy is strangely piece-meal and *naif*. He has, too, notwithstanding all his honesty of principles, a good deal of the curious Italian child's dodginess about him. But an interesting and useful if not a very strong man." Fracassini, "thoroughly open on at least O. T. Scriptural problems." Professor Petrone, the Barnabite Padre Semeria of Genoa, and others are mentioned. Probably he also met Fr. Murri who was later excommunicated.

3. July–August 1901, "A Proposito dell'Abate Loisy," pp. 348–350.

4. The creation of the Commission by Leo XIII's brief *Vigilantiae* on Sept. 27, 1902, followed shortly after von Hügel's discussions with Lepidi. (See M. Petre, *Von Hügel and Tyrrell*, pp. 91–107 for the Baron's remarks on its formation.) De la Bedoyère (pp. 136–137) and Ward (*TWW*, p. 317) both held, and with reason, that the Baron played an important role in the decision to form the Commission.

5. *Mém* II, 79; cf. pp. 70–71.

6. Undated letter to Ward, cited by de la Bedoyère, pp. 137–138. The Commission was established about Jan. 1902 (*Mém* II, 84), but the official promulgation came only at the end of the year (A. A. S. 35, [1902–1903], pp. 234–238).

7. In this resumé I have been aided by Grandmaison's analysis in *Etudes (Religieuses)* (Jan. 20, 1903), pp. 143–154, which was praised by Loisy (*Mém* II, 198).

8. Cf. *Mém* II, 170, 173. By Jan. 1, 1903 Blondel writes the Baron about the "uneasiness" he felt with the book, though he respected

Loisy. Loisy lists other supporters, including Mignot, in *Mém* II, 172–173. The difficulty was that while Christ did preach a *proximate* kingdom, Loisy's conception of the exact nature of this event was veiled in his book.

9. Letter to Tyrrell (Nov. 28, 1902), cited in Petre, *Von Hügel and Tyrrell*, pp. 108–110. In this letter the Baron says that there has to be a constant re-interpretation of the original message, but he presumes that this can be done because *the proximity* of the Kingdom as a world-ending event is not of the substance of the original message.

10. *Mém* I, 444. This throws light on what is meant in *L'Evangile et L'Eglise* when he says that the eschatology for the Church would also be a symbol, always perfectible. This symbolizing effectively empties the Parousia idea of any content. On this point Loisy does not differ much from Harnack; where he does is in the demand for some external organization. But this organization, discontinuous with the Gospel which is locked in its false eschatology, is simply human, and we are already on the road to Loisy's later idea of the religion of humanity.

11. Cf. *Mém* II, 179. Caird's article appeared in *The New World*, VI, 21 (March 1897), pp. 1–13. He points out that we cannot totally translate ourselves into the past with its thousands of details without escaping from our conflicts today, and this latter is impossible. Christ wanted us to reach Him through a society, the Church. While Caird verbally admits the value of Biblical criticism, in his article he swings to an extreme and says we must treat Christ as an idea, a spirit. E. Caird was a disciple of Hegel. With regard to E. Caird, Tyrrell wrote to Bremond on Sept. 18, 1902: "The Baron has come and gone . . . were it not for men like Caird and Eucken I don't know where I should be. Doubtless God speaks in history, but it is a polysyllabic word of which we miss the ends and therewith the meaning; and unless He is to be found within each soul He is practically unfindable." Cited in *Von Hügel and Tyrrell*, p. 117.

12. For such a critique, see J. Guitton, *La Pensée moderne et le Catholicisme*, III, *La Pensée de M. Loisy* (Paris, 1936); see also his *The Problem of Jesus* for a phenomenological analysis. See Poulat, *La crise moderniste*, pp. 190–232 for reactions at the time. See *The Jerusalem Bible* for modern explanations of the eschatological texts. For present positions cf. B. Rigaux, "La seconde venue de Jesus," *La Venue du Messie* (Paris, 1962), pp. 173–216.

13. *SL*, p. 120 (April 25, 1903). He formulated an objection by Gardner: how can you who see Papacy, Episcopacy, etc., as of very mediately divine or Christian origin, reject other combinations today (Protestant) which are to all appearances just as suited to their age?

The Baron answered, "I willingly accept the appeal to life and results." (*SL*, p. 119.)

14. See short biographies of the *dramatis personae* of the crisis in *Alfred Loisy, sa vie, son oeuvre*, pp. 325–409. This collection is one of the immense contributions by E. Poulat to the study of the period.

15. The articles used are: a) "The Case of the Abbé Loisy," *The Pilot* (Jan. 9, 1904), pp. 30–31. b) Von Hügel on the case of M. Loisy, *The Pilot* (Jan. 23, 1904), p. 94. c) "The Abbé Loisy and the Holy Office," *The Times* (Mar. 2, 1904), p. 15, signed "Romanus," a reply to an article of Jan. 25 and signed "Catholicus" (Fr. David Fleming of the Biblical Commission, perhaps with the aid of Lagrange, *Mém* II, 325). d) An article in *Il Giornale d'Italia*, (Mar. 11, 1904) and reproduced in *Le chrétien Français* (Apr. 2, 1904). The article was sent under a pseudonym but the editor demanded his name. e) An anonymous introduction to letters of B. Saunders and of Loisy (retouched by the Baron), *The Times* (Apr. 30, 1904), p. 6. Article C is anonymous because "I have already . . . shown my colours," "I really must now avoid prodding or worrying the powers that be," and because of worry over involving the reputation of his wife and daughters. The handwriting of the letters to Tyrrell at this period deteriorates remarkably. On Jan. 28, 1904 he says he is "on the verge of breaking down." The letter was published in *Von Hügel and Tyrrell*, pp. 142–144.

16. *Von Hügel and Tyrrell*, p. 144.

17. These articles, "Lettres Romaines," *Annales de philosophie chrétienne* (Jan. to Mar. 1904), pp. 349–359, 473–488, 601–620, were written anonymously by "N.C." In Italy they were attributed to von Hügel. Loisy, and now Poulat, in a good treatment (*La crise moderniste*, pp. 671–672) rightly believed Genocchi to be the author. The Baron retouched these articles. (cf. e.g. p. 483 bottom—484 top).

18. *EA* II, pp. 18–19.

19. *Von Hügel and Tyrrell*, p. 144, a letter to Tyrrell of Feb. 5, 1904.

20. *EA* II, p. 21. This article was a private paper written with the aid of Tyrrell in 1904. Published after his death, its tone does not reflect his later thought.

CHAPTER SIX

1. "Professor Eucken on the Struggle for the Spiritual Life," *The Spectator* (Nov. 14, 1896), pp. 679–681.

2. But the idea came from the German, Kraus to Reuter, to Eucken, according to the Baron. "The Religious Philosophy of

Rudolph Eucken," *Hibbert Journal* (April 1912), pp. 660–677; cf. pp. 664, 675.

3. *SL*, p. 72, letter to Tyrell of Sept. 25, 1898. Four days earlier Tyrrell had written him, "as the heart is capable of indefinite purification, so God is indefinitely apprehensible. ...." It is interesting to note that while the Baron begins from God, Tyrrell begins from the human heart.

4. *CB*, article 1, pp. 315–18. Von Hügel points out, with Scheeben, that most probably the incomprehensibility of God applies also to the soul of Christ. He follows the Scotists in holding that happiness consists specifically in acts of the will, in love, consequent upon sight.

5. The Baron continually uses this dichotomy but it is evident that his "conflict" is basically interior. Also, he speaks of "purification" in many places as if it were a synonymn for tension and friction, whereas it is really the result. All through I have endeavored to clarify his thought without changing his meaning.

6. To Tyrrell (Dec. 4, 1899). *SL*, p. 88. 7 8

7. To Maude Petre (Sept. 26, 1900). *SL,* pp. 94–95.

8. *EA* II, 14.

9. *Von Hügel and Tyrrell*, p. 152. (Emphasis added).

10. *EL* (1912), p. 200, 370; *EA I*, 39 (1909), 119 (1919).

11. *EA* I, xii, 120 (1919).

12. *EA* I, 11. I have found about one hundred independent references to friction in the von Hügel works. Judaism, Islamism, Eckhart, Kempis, Schleiermacher, Bergson, are all criticized for lacking tension in some way. The principle is applied to mysticism and religion in *The Mystical Element* (1908). The principle is present in its most *moving*, and perhaps *paradoxical*, form in *Eternal Life* (1912), e.g. "everywhere we have to watch to maintain the friction, the pain, and the cost of the spiritual in and around the material, and of the Eternal in the Temporal and Spatial" (p. 357). It is most *maturely* present in *The Reality of God* (shortly before death in 1925).

13. *Von Hügel and Tyrrell* (June 22, 1908).

14. *RG*, p. 31. Grandmaison in his critique of *L'Evangile et L'Eglise* (*Etudes* [Jan–March 1930], p. 158) reacts against a Hegelianism in which the idea progresses from an opposition of contradictories to a higher synthesis which absorbs and goes beyond the contradiction. The Baron's thought is not on this level, since he always rejected Hegel's self-developing God, and he denied that there were real contradictories present.

15. "Experience and Transcendence," *The Dublin Review* (April 1906), p. 373. *ME* II, p. 346.

16. Batiffol published a critique in 1903–04, but the Baron felt Batiffol could not be trusted and thus would be unlikely to be influenced by it. Lepin published a good, moderate theory which excluded error in Christ, but only in 1905. (See *La crise moderniste*, pp. 379 ff., 499 ff.)

17. The clear distinction begins to show up in his writings of 1905 or shortly after. (Cf. *EA* II, 32; *ME* II, 382; *SL*, p. 135). In 1904 he is writing about "becoming what we know" (*EA* II, 8). At the end of his life he is pointing out that what we know in history on the origins of religion depends partly on what we are. (*RG*, pp. 161, 197, 254).

18. De la Bedoyère, p. 118, a letter to his daughter Hildegard.

CHAPTER SEVEN

1. Before the appearance of Loisy's little red books, he had read J. Weiss, *Die Predigt Jesu vom Reiche Gottes*. (Weiss held that Jesus centered, in His person, the hopes of His contemporaries, that He was conscious of being a judge of men, and that He preached the proximate coming of the Kingdom, but did not dream of a Church.) The Baron also was reading, in 1893–94, Hermann Schell's *Katolische Dogmatik* which proposed a theory of limited knowledge on the part of Christ (pp. 142–147; see *Mém* I, 378, 500). But in details Heinrich Holtzmann had the greatest influence on the Baron. It is probable but not certain that Loisy was influenced by J. Weiss; see Lagrange, *M. Loisy et le modernisme* (Paris, 1932), pp. 184, 236–237.

2. *Revue Biblique* (1896), pp. 452–454. Lagrange warned of the peril of seeing Christ as playing a role. He said we must respect Scripture. But he asked, could Christ's soul not see the essence of God without penetrating the secrets of His will?

3. Marlé, *Au coeur de crise moderniste*, p. 221.

4. Jan. to July, 1896. (See *The Letter on Apologetics and History and Dogma*, presented and translated by A. Dru and I. Trethowan [New York 1964], a partial reproduction of *Les premiers écrits de Maurice Blondel* [Paris, 1956].)

5. April 12, 1896, letter to Blondel. A good part of von Hügel's correspondence with Blondel has been published by R. Marlé, *Au coeur de la crise moderniste* (Paris, 1960). When this is complemented with the citations found in Part VI of E. Poulat's *Histoire, dogme et critique dans le crise moderniste* (Paris, 1962), one has the most valuable parts of the correspondence.

6. For a pertinent analysis of the *Lettre* and of *L'Action*, see H.

Bouillard, *Blondel et le christianisme* (Paris, 1961), esp. pp. 32–33, 71–109.

7. *La Quinzaine* (June 1, 1904), pp. 285–312, cited as *CE*. It was translated into French by Bremond.

8. Marlé, *op. cit.*, p. 138, letter to von Hügel (Feb. 19, 1903).

9. Marlé (April 2, 1903), p. 144; *CE*, p. 195. In his later article in the *Encyclopaedia Britannica* on St. John's Gospel (XV, 452–458), the Baron will say that John handles traditional material with sovereign freedom. He considers Cana a symbol and the resurrection of Lazarus an allegory.

10. See Marlé, pp. 93 (to Loisy), 133, 134, 137 (to von Hügel), 148 (to Wehrlé).

11. Distinctions similar to these were made by Blondel after this immediate debate in his article "De la valeur historique du dogme," *Premiers Écrits*, pp. 229–245. See Poulat, *op. cit.*, pp. 601–603, for an analysis.

12. Marlé, p. 137. Remember the Baron has not yet, in his exegetical thinking, sufficiently separated phenomena in science from those in history, despite the letter to Miss Petre which we have just seen.

13. *The Letter on Apologetics*, pp. 240–241.

14. *CE*, p. 305.

15. *CE*, pp. 290, 305. He claims the same position for Loisy (p. 305). M. Ward in *Insurrection Versus Resurrection*, p. 505, says that the article by von Hügel "contains no suggestion of revelation as the Catholic understands it." But this is not accurate. Some of the Baron's phrases, it is true, if isolated, give a false impression. For example, he says on p. 290: "Our soul wakes up to the presence of spiritual realities only when a contingent and historical stimulus reaches it from the outside" (see p. 294). Such statements might give the impression that the Revelation, lying immanent within us, is aroused only by historical reality. But his point is that the soul is *awakened* as to the depth of its aspirations by Christian history, not that it already immanently contains the Revelation. (See p. 290, where he says that without *revelation-history* there can be no Christianity.) This is a central point in the Baron's thought. While his expressions seem to be a bit colored by E. Caird's Hegelianism, his thought is satisfactory.

16. *CE*, p. 291.

17. *CE*, pp. 301–302, 304. What von Hügel meant by "the Christ-object" was what can be known by criticism, by "the Christ-subject," what can be known by faith. But we have here excessive separation of history and faith. Blondel's distinction between the

"passible" Christ and the glorious Christ is the exact one. (See Marlé, p. 147.)

An ambiguity arose out of the fact that the Baron was really applying his distinction to the problem of Christ's human *knowledge*. His knowledge before and after the Resurrection. Blondel, looking at the matter from a more universal plane *of being*, criticized it on this plane.

18. See E. B. Allo, *Seconde épitre aux Corinthiens* (Paris, 1937), p. 168.

19. The value of this distinction is that it avoids the creation of a dichotomy in Christ since the two elements, the phenomena of Christ and the Person of Christ, overlap as to material object. Yet in preserving a distinction of formal aspect, it preserves a distinction of method, i.e. between exegesis whose primary, but not exclusive, formal object is the phenomena and theology whose primary formal object is the metaphysical Person. Historical method reaches phenomena, but does not deny that the metaphysical Person is there. In fact, in studying phenomena, it arrives at the Person under the functional aspect. Thus the reflex and metaphysical evaluation, which follows with the appearance of theology, has already been implied in exegesis. Theology on the other hand studies the *Person* of Christ. Yet since the metaphysical Person included body, action, and expression in time, theology itself must deal with phenomena, at least obliquely, though they are not its primary formal object. Accordingly, a distinction which partially overlaps is demanded.

20. *CE*, p. 309.

21. *Lettres Romaines, Critique, histoire et foi chrétienne, An PC* (Jan. to March, 1904), pp. 475, 351. It is interesting to note the similarities between this article, which was almost certainly written by the Italian, Padre Genocchi, and Gore's *Dissertations*, pp. 94–97.

22. Marlé, p. 243.

23. Marlé, pp. 353–354.

24. *CE*, p. 310.

25. The metaphysical problem was afterwards handled by Lepin and others. See J. Mouroux, "Maurice Blondel et la conscience du Christ," in *L'Homme devant Dieu: mélanges offerts au Père de Lubac*, pp. 185–208.

CHAPTER EIGHT

1. Marlé, pp. 55. 135.

2. In *Lettres romaines*, the author held that Jesus was in the *error* of His time, for error derives fatally from ignorance (p. 486).

But this is not true. I may be ignorant as to when I will finish my present work, but I am not fated to error because I have hopes of finishing it soon. My very ignorance makes me withhold my judgment as to the date of completion. Tyrrell expressed the same thought in *Essays on Faith and Immortality*, pp. 43–46.

3. Marlé, pp. 245–246.

4. *Jésus, Messie et Fils de Dieu* (Paris, 1905), pp. 417–419, Poulat's *Histoire, dogme* has a section on the knowledge of Christ where he has analyzed various theories at the time. For Lepin, see pp. 501–502. For contemporary treatment, see K. Rahner in *Dogmatic vs. Biblical Theology* (Baltimore, 1964), pp. 241–268; E. Gutwenger, "The Problem of Christ's Knowledge," *Concilium*, 11 (N.Y., 1966).

5. Marlé, p. 123.

6. See *Letter on Apologetics and History and Dogma*, pp. 249–250, my translation.

7. Marlé, pp. 179–180. For a further development by an exegete of the period, see Lepin, *Jesus, Messie et Fils de Dieu d'apres les Evangiles Synoptiques* (Paris, 1905), pp. 410–411. When Christ's prophecy about the destruction to the temple (which had been intermingled with the prophecy about the Parousia) was fulfilled, it caused the Christians to see that the destruction and the Parousia were separate events and thus they re-thought the message in depth.

8. See M. J. Congar, *La Tradition et les traditions* (Paris, 1960), p. 266, who finds his master lines in Blondel. Also Marlé, p. 351, who finds it the most powerful systematic essay yet written on the subject. See H. Holstein, *La Tradition dans l'Eglise* (Paris, 1960), pp. 134–140, 287–299. For my development I am partially indebted to William Scott, S.J., who has since published his synthesis, "The Notion of Tradition in Maurice Blondel," *Theological Studies* (Sept., 1966), pp. 384–400.

9. Marlé, p. 201. Blondel says his position is a living synthesis of all the forces, speculative and ascetic, a resumé of the data of history, the effort of reason, and the experience of faithful action.

10. Abbé Wehrlé in his reply to von Hügel suggested Constantinople II in 553 as opposed to a psychological human *person* in Christ. But the question about the human *consciousness* of Christ is hotly debated theologically today. Though the term, a psychological human person, has been rejected by the Holy See, the idea of a human consciousness has not. Cf. H. M. Diepen, *La Théologie de l'Emmanuel* (Paris, 1960), esp. 263.

11. *Letter on Apologetics*, p. 246.

12. The logic of action demands that life have a meaning, and man a destiny. The Judaeo-Christian idea of Providence adds greater

clarification and a rich content to this. It has not been shown, I believe, that the conclusions of Loisy, for example, would be in harmony with either of these two ideas, destiny or Providence. The very logic of action of the early Christians in ridding themselves of what Loisy considered central, the imminence of a visible Parousia, would present the Church as unable to accept the central thrust of the teachings of the Messiah, the Representative of God for the people, precisely because of the continued ongoing of a history moving toward the Absolute, God.

13. Some of the exegetes, at the time, made many valuable points. See Poulat, *Histoire, dogme, passim* on Batiffol, Lagrange, and Portalié, esp. pp. 383–394, 605–609. Also, de Veiga Coutinho, *Tradition et histoire*, pp. 112–152.

14. *Bulletin de littérature ecclesiastique* (Feb.-March, 1905), pp. 61–77. Reprinted in *Les premiers écrits*, pp. 229–245. See Poulat, *Histoire, dogme*, p. 599. In the following pages Poulat gives an analysis of Blondel's article. See M. Nédoncelle, "Histoire et dogme, ou l'exigence de tradition active," *Giornale di Metafisica* (Sept.-Oct., 1961), pp. 576–590, for a critical evaluation of Blondel's thought.

15. The Baron fell into this distinction to explain the differences between Christ's actions in John and in the Synoptics.

Wehrlé, in his reply to von Hügel ("Le Christ et le conscience catholique," *La Quinzaine* [Aug. 16, 1904]), pointed out the impossibility of the Baron's celestial-terrestial distinction. Space does not permit a thorough discussion of this article. It made many excellent points especially with regard to the Baron's expressions. But his approach is that of a driving logic. Instead of forcing the Baron into an almost heretical corner on this distinction of celestial-terrestrial, he could have pointed out conflicting statements in the Baron's work, and demanded a choice, for there is a series of totally orthodox statements in von Hügel's work precisely in connection with this distinction.

Wehrlé himself suggested that the Baron consult *Revue de la Clergé Français* (July 15, 1903) to find what could be legitimately held on the knowledge of Christ. The article in question (pp. 338–365 by a "Docteur en Théologie") is a good study. What is incredible, however, is that the author *makes a point* of distinguishing between the question of limited knowledge in Christ, and the question of error. The former (p. 361) he opposes, but will not absolutely reject (p. 362) after citing numberless Fathers. But this major distinction nowhere appears for purposes of clarification in Wehrlé's attack. He says that if we distinguish the question of general consciousness from that of knowledge, the latter is of secondary importance and bypasses it totally. (The "Docteur en Théologie" was Abbé F. Dubois [see Poulat, p. 675]).

CHAPTER NINE

1. See Maude D. Petre, *Autobiography and Life of George Tyrrell*, 2 vols. (London, 1912). Miss Petre's work has great value if read with discrimination. Born in 1863, she died during the war in 1942, after performing much social and charitable work. Maisie Ward told me that she found her most refreshingly direct and forthright. For ten years she was Provincial of the Daughters of Mary and left with honor. Until her death at 80, her theological position was quite similar to Tyrrell's. Her devotion to Tyrrell, while above suspicion or insinuation, unduly colors some of her treatment of the period. While I feel that Miss Petre's remarks have been generally underrated, still one can hardly expect objectivity where such devotion colored her view.

Her friend James A. Walker remarked of her after her death: "Hard as a diamond and more tender than a mother." (*Alfred Loisy* [Cambridge, 1944].) She had a camera eye for personality analysis. She held that von Hügel betrayed his foreign office ancestry, and Loisy his agricultural descent (p. 30). But Loisy esteemed her highly and von Hügel, also, deeply appreciated her, although he unconsciously trampled on her sensitivities with his labored planning and effort to brake Tyrrell's impetuosity. Once the Baron warned her that Canon Lilley's "judgment about persons is frequently not of the best" (letter of Dec. 16, 1910). On Feb. 16, 1911, however, he is fumbling with an apology because Lilley has just dedicated his book to her. Perhaps von Hügel summed her up best: "A loving woman's heart appears there with much of a man's head, and the combination is as rare as it is beautiful" (letter of April 20, 1902). Most of the Baron's letters to her which I will cite, as well as some of his letters to Tyrrell, are unpublished.

2. *Mém* III, 470. Von Hügel had certain reserves about Vol. I of Miss Petre's work which contains Tyrrell's autobiography up to 1885. He said Tyrrell showed "astonishing self-detachment" there, but that the autobiography did not give the "picture of the whole of him during the times depicted" nor did it show Tyrrell at his deepest. (Letters to M. Petre, Jan. 18 and Jan. 30, 1913.)

3. M. Petre, *My Way of Faith* (London, 1937), p. 271. The chapter on Tyrrell in this book is a frank description of their relationship. Tyrrell in 1900 told her: ". . . it is not the femininities of a woman that attract me; nor the clinging dependence; nor can I care for a love that is not critical and intelligent" (p. 275). From this time on, Miss Petre's friendship took on the character of a "spiritual vocation."

4. F. von Húgel, "Father Tyrrell: Some Memorials of the Last Twelve Years of His Life," *The Hibbert Journal* (Jan. 1910), pp. 233–252. The Baron adds that Tyrrell was "too sensitively dependent

on the sympathy of his interlocutors to impress much in conversation."
Tyrrell himself said: "I have a certain simplicity and trustfulness,
for which nobody who knows me will give me the least credit. I fall
a victim to a very positive and dogmatic manner in others. The self-
confident can gull me over and over again." *Autobiography* I, 201.

5. *SL*, p. 132. "*Mentally* you apprehend ... the exceeding variety
in unity of all reality ... whereas *emotively* you are a *prime sauteur*
[sic], *hic et nunc*, neck-or-nothing to an equally rare degree" (June
12, 1905).

6. *SL*, p. 141 (Oct. 1, 1907).

7. *Alfred Loisy, sa vie, son oeuvre*, p. 42. It is interesting to
note that both Tyrrell and Loisy lacked paternal influence in their
religious upbringing. (Tyrrell's father died just before he was born.)

8. *Through Scylla and Charybdis* (London, 1907), p. 364.

9. *Von Hügel and Tyrrell*. (London, 1937), p. 116, Dec. 4, 1902.

10. Miss Petre held that the introduction of Tyrrell to exegetical
problems was a tragic mistake. Von Hügel "impelled an incautious man
into the fight and then expected him to exercise restraint" (*My Way of
Life*, p. 291).

11. *Ibid*. II, 398. Schweitzer praises Tyrrell's use of his insights in
Christianity at the Crossroads, in *Out of My Life and Thought* (New
York, 1933), p. 44.

12. *Through Scylla and Charybdis*, p. 202.

13. *Ibid*., p. 203.

14. *Ibid*., p. 205.

15. *Ibid*., pp. 285, 207.

16. *Ibid*., p. 302; *A Much Abused Letter*, p. 34.

17. *Ibid*., p. 234. When he had definitively moved to the
eschatological school, Tyrrell held that the people who made these
prophetic utterances actually took them rather literally. See *Autobiography* II, 400.

18. *Through Scylla and Charybdis*, pp. 342–343.

19. *Medievalism*, p. 85.

20. *Ibid*., p. 55.

21. *Ibid*., p. 79. Many of these ideas of the Vatican Council
are reflections of Anglican, Orthodox, and Old Catholic positions.
At this time he had a momentary attraction for Anglicanism and
Old Catholicism. In 1908 he was dickering with Dr. Matthew, the
Old Catholic Bishop. These letters are now in Farm Street archives,
London. Miss Petre judged that since they were written "in shirt
sleeves," they would not be suitable for publication. One letter of

Sept. 30, 1908 (?) is typical: "Yet one sees that Rome cares for nothing so little as for souls, that her whole effort is to win power and authority—as though that were an end in itself; and that she is cynically indifferent to all these horrors of celibacy so long as they remain in the dark and no scandal is raised." Von Hügel was upset by these leanings and drew from Tyrrell the response: "Do you know I sometimes think...that you would rather see me an atheist than an Anglican?"

22. "Father Tyrrell," *Hibbert Journal* (Jan. 1910), p. 234. Miss Petre thought that the Baron had blundered, but she admitted that Tyrrell would have had occasional trouble merely from his own temperament. (*Von Hügel and Tyrrell*, p. 119.) His earliest letters to the Baron contain flashes of anger at authority. Many of his reactions had nothing to do with Scripture and the Baron cannot bear the blame for these.

23. For example, with regard to Tyrrell's article in an Italian journal, von Hügel wrote: "I think I find a note, at least a more marked note—of bitterness" than was present in the original draft. He asked him to avoid "those touches" (Sept. 30, 1907). *After* Tyrrell's deprivation of the sacraments, he wrote on Nov. 15, 1907: "*Perhaps* the ideal, all-round man should be able to hate and pursue destructively, with the same directness and fulness, with which he would love and construct. *Perhaps*, though I am far from sure, even of this. But I am very sure that, in any case, George Tyrrell is not that kind of man. A dominant hatred and determination to destroy even a set of men or an institution predominantly evil; such a disposition would, the writer of this scribble is absolutely certain, shrivel up and evaporate all the true power, all the deep and glorious helpfulness of G.T., long before he had done any serious execution on his enemies." He warns him of "sterilising negation and feverish hate." *S. L.*, p. 145. See de la Bedoyère, pp. 213–228.

24. See *SL*, pp. 131, 139. In 1907 he is warning Tyrrell against reformulating God's transcendence in an immanental fashion. *Oil and Wine* (1906) he had found to have touches of excessive immanence (see *SL*, p. 335).

25. Letter to Miss Petre of Feb. 18, 1910. *The Church and the Future* presents in a milder form what we have seen in *Medievalism*. The Church is seen as a democratic rather than a monarchic structure. The *sensus fidelium* controls the Councils rather than vice versa (pp. 108–110). He denies a "miraculous" charism for the pope. At the same time some of the ideas have a very modern ring to them.

26. *SL*, p. 166, to Canon Newsom (Sept. 7, 1909), and p. 139 (May 14, 1907) to Tyrrell.

27. Cited in *Von Hügel and Tyrrell*, p. 181.

28. This concerns an article by Tyrrell in *The Home and Foreign Review*. The Baron suggested that, in dealing with the Vatican Council, Tyrrell should have quoted "that saving clause in the decree as to the universal and direct episcopate of the pope, that affirms the apostolic authority, of non-delegational kind, appertaining to bishops." "I know well that this is practically denied by the Roman policy; and that it is probable, if the other, the direct Papal authority conception be pressed (and Rome presses it), hopelessly out of place in this system. Yet, even so, would it not be well to use this saving clause against the rest? And if it shows that the defining bishops did recognise other rights besides the pope's, ought they not to be given the credit of this?" *SL*, p. 150 (April 16, 1908). The Baron's approval of *The Church and the Future* is based on the same idea: "After all, you showed in the 'Ch. and the F.' so finely, I thought, how these decrees are capable of a . . . Catholic interpretation" (to Tyrrell, Mar. 25, 1908).

29. *SL*, p. 152. The Baron is apprehensive over the forthcoming *Medievalism*. He is against prodding too much "since the other side are beginning to discover the immense difficulties of *their* position. . . . I ever feel that (brilliant as are your controversial, polemical hits) God has made you for something greater and deeper."

30. "Father Tyrrell," *Hibbert Journal* (Jan. 1910), p. 252.

31. *SL*, p. 24.

32. The correspondence between von Hügel and Tyrrell at times reveals the Baron in the role of the guiding father, "Now I want my beloved Celt to do this," etc. When Tyrrell reacts a bit, the Baron becomes sensitive about his own approach. (M. Petre "noticed a certain drifting apart between Fr. T. and myself" as early as October 1906.) With Miss Petre, too, he is sensitive to the differences which his approach caused: "*I could not exaggerate the importance I attach to your kind trust and friendship:* and I hope that God will punish me by their withdrawal." (Nov. 12, 1909).

33. *SL*, p. 133.

34. *SL*, p. 165 (July 17, 1909) to Edmund Gardner. Cardinal Bourne refused to condemn Tyrrell because he felt he was suffering from disease, according to S. Leslie, *Cardinal Gasquet* (London, 1953), p. 188.

35. Von Hügel said Tyrrell held much more strenuously for the divinity in his *Christianity at the Crossroads* than previously.

36. *EA* 2, p. 232. In 1909 he spoke of ". . . this profoundly important point of the Papacy (yes, but not an absolute one, taking the place of the other legitimate forces and authorities within and

without the Church)," *SL*, p. 175. His orthodoxy, for those who have doubted it, is shown by *EA* I, 232 (1913); 275 (1918); II, 248 (1921).

37. *EA* 2, p. 22 (1904).

38. *Ibid.*, p. 21. As late as 1911 the same idea shows up in his "Loisy" article in the *Encyclopaedia Britannica.* The 1904 essay owed something to Tyrrell. On Feb. 13, 1907, Tyrrell wrote about his revisions of an article by the Baron on "Official Authority." "I think I have made it quite clear with no more than a number of small tinkerings. . . . As to the Christology at the end (not to speak of lesser audacities about authority) I have put in little loopholes of escape; but still its frank Loisyism remains. Everyone who knows you knows quite well that you agree with Loisy. Still they cannot put your unwritten views on the Index as they can an article." This apparently is the present article.

CHAPTER TEN

1. Dec. 18, 1906 to Tyrrell. He also believed that the Curia was too absorbed in a mechanistic presentation of Christianity. He suggested to his friend Humphrey Johnson that Pius X attached an exaggerated importance to the external aspect of religion. (H. Johnson, *Anglicanism in Transition* [London, 1937], p. 155.)

2. Cited from de la Bedoyère, p. 97. On the Johannine Comma, cf. A. Houtin, *La question biblique . . . au XIXe siècle* (Paris, 1902), pp. 224–241. On the meaning of authentic, cf. *DS* note before 3681.

3. Translated from J. Rivière, *La modernisme dans l'Eglise*, p. 231.

4. Translation as found in *Rome and the Study of Scripture* (St. Meinrad, 1962), pp. 118–119. *DS* 3394/1997.

5. Undated letter to W. Ward at the time.

6. Published in London and N. Y., 1906. In 1907 it appeared in French as *La Commission Pontificale et la Pentateuque* (Paris).

7. Cf. A. Robert, *Introduction à la Bible* (New York, 1965), for the present state of the question. The Mosaic exodus is held to be around 1290–1250. Von Hügel's statement about the book of the Law is still debated. That "P", the priestly document, was not completed before the fifth century seems generally accepted. The question of fixing dates is still in a very fluid condition, and one tends to speak more of "stages" than documents. The system of Wellhausen upon which the Baron relied heavily had many defects and *a priori* weaknesses. But he never accepted a Wellhausen naturalism.

Thus there is some doubt that he "was mixing philosophical and theological questions with critical ones" (p. 311).

8. The secretary of the Biblical Commission in his letter to Cardinal Suhard (Jan. 16, 1948) said: "There is no longer anyone today who puts in doubt the existence of these sources, and who does not admit a progressive growth of the Mosaic laws which is due to the social and religious conditions of later times." *DS* 3862/2302 ff.

Wilfrid Ward, who by this time told von Hügel that he had less confidence than the Baron in the "scientific" conclusions of Loisy, wrote an interesting review of the Briggs-von Hügel book. He approved the Baron's optimism for the future. ". . . a Catholic approaching such a decision should always bear in mind the rule observed by authority in such cases—namely, that a time-honoured tradition is not officially displaced until it is, by the practically universal consent of specialists, admitted to be mistaken. It is as it were driven out bit by bit. . . .

The first formal toleration of freer views will be suggested rather than emphasized in such a document. And we take the answer of the commission to the last *dubium* (which includes that the Pentateuch as we know it may include later additions to any work which Moses wrote or planned) as being such a suggestion. . . .

The transition from a conservative view to a more progressive view is often inevitably effected through a temporary position of indeterminateness or even apparent inconsistency, in which the inadequacy of the former is recognized while the limits which are safe and true in the newer are not yet generally agreed upon. The extreme to which Rome in the past carried her official conservatism supplies the law or interpretation for fresh cases.

The decree against Galileo was not suspended until 1757. Leo XIII gave formal permission as late as the year 1822 for Catholics to teach the Copernican theory. No intelligent Catholic then alive had ever doubted this theory. This is an extreme instance, but it illustrates the better what we are pointing out—that official recognition by Rome of a change in traditional theology is by a custom, which, we may add, has its roots in the nature of things, belated. Nearly all the force of original thought is on the side of change. Authority is, in the first place, the "counsel for the defence" of tradition. Its decrees must be interpreted in the light of this fact." (*Dublin Review*, 22 [1907], 214–216, found in the Baron's notes at St. Andrews, Scotland).

9. The Letter says that a "Commission of competent men" is now established. They will have as their "function to direct all their care and effort that the Divine Scriptures may find generally among our (exegetes) that more careful treatment which our times demand,

and that they may be preserved not only from all breath of error but even from every rash opinion." If they find some drifting towards the heterodox, "they will lead them by persuasion to follow and listen faithfully to the Church's teaching." Its duty is to regulate certain questions "now by the light of its judgment, now by the weight of its authority." Thus it will give the Holy See a favorable opportunity for declaring what must be held, what needs more research and what is free. In general, the letter is most encouraging for exegetes. (*Actes de Léon XIII* [Paris], pp. 132–141.)

10. Reviews of the book were kept by von Hügel and are at St. Andrews, Scotland. They give a picture of the time, *Manchester Guardian* (Mar. 20, 1907): praise for emphasis on need for the Church in Biblical work. *Jewish Chronicle* (Dec. 14, 1906): favorable. *Oxford Magazine:* shows "the uncomplimentary truth" that Rome will yield when it has to. *British Friend* (Quaker) (Jan. 1907): "Rome has shown a marvellous facility of readjustment, and it will be interesting to see whether her hand has lost its cunning." *Church Times* (Dec. 7, 1906): change has been made before, "it will be done again." *The Methodist Quarterly Review* (Jan. 12, 1907): almost the same as the previous. *The Evening Post* (N.Y., May 11): "This correspondence is another illustration of the impotency of ecclesiastical authority, whether Protestant or Catholic, to affect the course of critical opinion.

Meanwhile in Catholic circles, *The Month* (Jan. 1907), says that the Baron contributes nothing towards solving the problem of inspiration which his position raises (p. 100). *The Universe* (R.C. weekly, Dec. 28, 1906) merely regrets finding the Baron side by side with Briggs.

But on the favorable side, besides Ward, Archbishop Mignot thoroughly approved of the book (de la Bedoyère, p. 187). Le Roy, author of *Dogme et critique*, which was later put on the Index, wrote the Baron: "The recent decision of the Biblical Commission seems to me also simply grotesque." (Aug. 30, 1906).

L. Venard, in *Revue du Clergé* Français (March, 1907), pp. 55–71 is favorable. This review is very important. Venard uses also E. Mangenot, *L'Authenticité mosaique du pentateuque* (Paris, 1907), cf. especially pp. 309, 320–323, 327–328 of this book. Mangenot was a consultor for the Biblical Commission. Mangenot, who thus had a particular authority though he was not speaking for the Commission, defended the recent decrees, but said that they were not obligatory in faith. Later he explains that the Mosaic authorship allows "more or less numerous" later insertions and glosses in the text. Venard points out that non-Catholics have only a vague knowledge of the value of different Church decrees. He says that the Commission gives *official* (the italics show that this is a technical word) Church teaching, but that, while it demands respectful submission, it is only *directive*.

Citing Condamin, he suggests that its authority comes from the theological and exegetical competence of the members. Mangenot on the other hand tries to leave the door open for liberal opinions, but admits that the decree *could* be said to give theological certainty. But von Hügel had showed that Hummelauer, Lagrange, Clarke, van den Biesen, van Hoonacker and Poel, all held rather large later additions to the Pentateuch. "Theological certainty" is a word to be used with caution.

11. Text in Italian and French in A. Vermeersch, *De Modernismo* (Rome, 1910), pp. 46–47. The letter asked Cardinal Ferrari of Milan to demand that the review *Rinnovamento* cease publication either entirely or at least of a type of article which had been appearing. (The ambiguity is evident in the later interpretations of this censure.)

12. To Tyrrell he wrote: "a piece of administrative rhetoric— something intended not to define a reality but to affect a situation." (May 8, 1907.)

13. A fine treatment is found in Rivière, *Le Modernisme . . .*, pp. 333–348. There were two classes of ideas in the decree. The first re-emphasized truths already taught by the Magisterium. The second concerned propositions which had not previously been touched by a magisterial decree, such as the nature of the integrity and veracity of the Gospels, the historicity of St. John (13–18), the continuity between Scripture and the traditional Christology and Soteriology, general sacramental dogma and the nature of the Church (27–54). Cf. R. Aubert, "Aux origines de la réaction antimoderniste deux documents inédits." *Ephemerides Théologicae Lovanienses* (May-Sept., 1961), pp. 557–578.

14. *Forma communi* means that a decree, although approved by the Pope, draws its force immediately from the Congregation, and only mediately from the Pope, and it is the Congregation which is juridically responsible. When a decree is approved in *forma specifica*, while not involving infallibility, it becomes a strictly Papal decree since the Pope makes it his own. (Choupin, *Valeur des Décisions* [Paris, 1928], pp. 71–75 and 177–181.)

15. Fleming was an Irish Franciscan who had been Provincial in England. He played an important role in the formation of the Biblical Commission in 1901 and was first Secretary in 1903. (Cf., Poulat, *Alfred Loisy*, p. 351.) "His letters supplied the gossip of Rome," "on . . . every question of the Curia he retailed the latest anecdote. He was always fighting 'Frenchers' and foreigners. He seemed to think he was the chosen instrument to steer the Church." "Irish of blood, with the style of an English schoolboy, he amused Leo XIII. . . ." (Shane Leslie, *Cardinal Gasquet* [London, 1953], p. 191.) In 1903 he favored

condemning Loisy only "for reasons of expediency" and did not favor Cardinal Merry del Val (p. 199). He was replaced as Secretary of the Commission in 1905, remaining as consultor. After *Lamentabili's* appearance von Hügel saw Fleming and said he was "outspoken." A description of the two types of sessions of the Holy Office is found in F. Grimaldi, *Les Congregations Romaines* (Siena, 1890), p. 170. The Wednesday session was presided over by the Pope. The Thursday session was rarely called and only for the gravest matters. Fleming's expressions, "feria quarta, feria quinta" seems to have been a popular way of speaking of in *Forma communi* and *in forma specifica* decrees, though the first can by no means "go into the wastepaper basket."

16. The Sulpician M. Lepin wrote a commentary on *Lamentabili* in 1908 (*Christologie, commentarie des propositions XXVII–XXXVIII,* Paris). On #27 he says that the decree means that the Divinity of Christ "is not a dogma which the Christian consciousness *had itself conceived* in deducing it from the notion of Messias, but that this dogma had its authorized foundation in the Gospels, namely in the personal affirmations of Jesus related in these documents, which are equivalent and identical, at last in some manner, to the Christological doctrine of the Apostles and Councils." (P. 33, emphasis added.) This interpretation would not necessarily condemn the Baron's idea of "pressing the Messiaship" so that it spontaneously shows the idea of Divinity. He did not hold that it was the Christian conscience alone that supplied the idea of Divinity. But the second statement in the text (#29) he said is "the contradictory of Loisy's persistent contention."

17. The contemporary Lepin showed that the first sentence (#32) means that Jesus is not susceptible of any error (p. 54). With regard to sentence two (#33), he said the decree takes no position with regard to the *character* of the proximate coming. He said that it is not merely the glorious kingdom of the last days that Jesus preached, but also an anticipated kingdom in an initial phase (p. 61). When Jesus spoke of "this generation," Lepin held he was thinking of the destruction of Jerusalem. The confused impression of the Apostles, however, was salutary. Sentence number three (#34), he said, demands that one attribute unlimited knowledge to Chirst, without this being against history or moral sense. Christ's human "knowledge of God" is not the infinite knowledge which the critics decry. The knowledge is unlimited because it *can* be extended to all that a creature is capable of. He admitted a growth in Jesus' human consciousness of His mission (p. 75).

18. Benigni led a vociferous campaign against the Modernism which he saw everywhere (Rivière, pp. 350 ff., 469). This campaign

was recalled at the time of the beatification of St. Pius X, when evidence was presented to show that the Pope had not favored Benigni's excesses. (P. Fernessole, *Pie X* [Paris, 1953], II, 228–251, 526.) Merry del Val said the Pope deplored the excesses of many journals and exhorted them to moderation, but that he did not want to disavow them publicly to avoid giving a handle to the Modernist adversaries (p. 236).

19. This is mentioned in a letter to Archbishop Mignot, (Oct. 7, 1907).

20. An effort was made to organize this, but for some unknown reason, it never fructified. Cf. Rivière, p. 363; Fernessole, *Pie X*, pp. 210–211.

21. M. Ward's *Insurrection Versus Resurrection*, Ch. XV, gives a fine first hand account. Rivière, pp. 374–427. Rivière says that in naming no one, the Encyclical is a sort of impersonal abstraction. What is most important in it is its large lines (p. 368). If one should say that the modernism of the Encyclical, in the formal sense of the word, is a creation, still "it is not at all created *ex nihilo*, but . . . the religious literature of the epoch furnished all the elements" (p. 369). It unmasks the latent principles (p. 370). M. Petre admitted that it apprehended the "movement in its totality" (*Modernism*, p. 115).

22. *Insurrection Versus Resurrection*, pp. 274–276. Newman was exonerated. (Cf. Bishop E. O'Dwyer, *Cardinal Newman and the Encyclical Pascendi* [London, 1908].) Cardinal Merry del Val, the Secretary of State, once wrote to Gasquet: "Newman had declared that he was not a theologian . . . I must say I should not have styled him a theologian" (*Cardinal Gasquet* [London, 1953], p. 186).

23. *Simples Réflexions* (Chez l'Auteur, 1908), a point by point attack on *Lamentabili* and *Pascendi*. With regard to Blondel, the Baron wrote to Tyrrell on Oct. 24, 1907: "Poor Blondel is down-rightly ill nervously; he has a physical horror of condemnations, etc. and there is a curiously sacristan, seminarist side to the man. . . . Yet Laberthonnière and Blondel are fine fellows in spite of these (?) poor failings; and we will interpret them as kindly as we can." The reference to Laberthonnière refers to his retraction. But the Baron found *Simples Réflexions* "egotistical in tone" and said it would be well if it disappeared. (To Tyrrell, Mar. 18, 1908.)

24. To Tyrrell, Oct. 17, 1907.

25. With regard to the strong expressions, we may find light in a saying of an author unknown to me: "The trouble with Encyclicals is that they are composed by Italians with a flair for hyperbole and read by Englishmen with a habit of understatement."

26. Cardinal Ferrari of Milan made the excommunication not only with ordinary power but with delegated Pontifical authority. *Civiltà Cattolica*, LIX, I, 240 ff.

27. De la Bedoyère, p. 205.

28. To be "bound in conscience" by the decrees of the Biblical Commission did not mean that von Hügel had to hold *internally* that the Biblical decrees were correct. Genocchi told the Baron that the Pope admitted to him that one could hold different opinions on the Mosaic authorship but should resign as a professor if he did. De la Bedoyère, p. 207.

29. *Mém.* II, 595. On Bonomelli, cf., A. Poulat's *Alfred Loisy*, p. 333. He was associated with the French liberal theological elements, including Mignot, Lacroix, but was early disquieted by Loisy's evolution. An early religio-political tract had been put on the Index. He wrote 18 volumes of pastoral and apologetical works. His position which the Baron here espoused would deny the possibility of the *latae sententiae* (automatic) excommunications which Canon Law holds. Is it certain, in the light of this opinion, that the Baron was excommunicated? De la Bedoyère and Fenton say yes. But in censures *odiosa sunt restringenda*. One element required is a grave fault, both internal and external (Capello, *De Censuris* [Turin, 1925], pp. 26 ff.). There was grave external fault. No writer is competent to judge the sincerity of his action. Back in London he continued to go to communion and we know nothing further of his interior life. However, in the external forum he would be considered to have incurred the excommunication.

30. For not signing his work in *Rinnovamento* except as "H", a "non-tell-tale letter," the Baron gives as a reason: "After all it is of importance to me, with my book now coming that I should not rile and irritate them more than I can help." (To Tyrrell, Mar. 25, 1908, *Von Hügel and Tyrrell*, p. 168). The editors would not let him sign the *Hibbert Journal* article on Loisy's new book with only an "H".

31. *Von Hügel and Tyrrell* (Dec. 7, 1908), pp. 181–182.

32. Cf., Nédoncelle's treatment, *La pensée religieuse*, pp, 203–205. The English edition adds a footnote of extra caution to what was already found in the French work. (*Baron Friedrich von Hügel*, p. 190).

33. "L'Abate Loisy e il Problema dei Vangeli Sinottici," *Il Rinnovamento* (Milan, 1908), III, 209–234; IV, 1–44; (1909), V, 229–272, 396–423, signed "H".

34. It is worth noting that the Baron says that Loisy's work has flaws, that it is only for the serious student and that his own review is subject to the authority of the Church. He rejoices in Loisy's acceptance of a two source theory which includes eye-witnesses.

35. Cf., footnote 38; Vol. V, pp. 419–420.

36. *Ibid.*, Vol. III, p. 224. It should be noted that the Baron is not referring to virginity *in partu* but to the Virginal conception.

37. *Ibid.*, Vol. V, p. 258.

38. *Ibid.*, Vol. V, p. 413. Since the Baron thinks along the lines of a logic of action, for him the words "spiritual orientation" include a definite element of knowledge and truth.

39. Cf., *Informations catholiques internationales* (Paris, Dec. 1, 1962), pp. 29–31—where Tyrrell's ideas are criticized along these lines. The nuances of the general question are well treated by F. Crowe, S.J., "Development of Doctrine and the Ecumenical Problem," *Theological Studies* (March, 1962), pp. 27–46.

40. In *Humani Generis* Pius XII warned about speaking of the mysteries of faith as being expressed in "only approximative and ever changeable notions" but he continued "in which the truth is to some extent expressed but is necessarily distorted." *DS* 3882/2310. Von Hügel did not see an approximation which would mean distortion.

41. *DS* 301/148. Cf., also, Lateran IV, *DS* 801, 429. A thoroughly referenced summary is found in J. de Aldama, *Sacrae Theologiae Summa* (Madrid, 1950), III, 340–346. Cf., also, C. Dillenschneider, *Le sens de la foi et le progrès dogmatique du mystère marial* (Rome, 1954). H. Crouzel, S.J., *Homélies sur S. Luc, Origène, Sources Chrétiennes* (Paris, 1962), pp. 22–30, has a fine treatment on Origen's views.

42. On Feb. 13, 1907 Tyrrell had written a long and extremely important letter to the Baron. In this letter he said that the considered "the Virgin Birth as a far other *kind* of crux than the physical resurrection." (He suggested that they talk the matter over.) The factualness of the Resurrection was of capital importance. "The historicity of His passion is all-important, the factualness of His resurrection equally so. But the mode not equally so. What imports is the triumph of the Gospel through His death." (I believe Tyrrell did not, and certainly the Baron did not, hold this last sentence in the Bultmanian sense which we will mention in a moment.) But the re-interpretation of the Virgin birth would present the faithful with a Church which had "blundered in a way to forfeit all credit as a doctrinal guide and as a director of worship and devotion." "In other words, its denial as historic fact involves that complete revolution in our conception of what dogma is for which Loisy and Le Roy are preparing the way—a kill-or-cure remedy to which, however, we are simply *forced* by the results of the historico-critical method."

"Of that symbolic and imaginative construction"—prophetic truth—"the Virgin Birth is an integral part." "That He was born of a Virgin and ascended into heaven may be but a 'visiblising' of the truth of His transcendence as divine." "The Virgin birth may but teach the same truth as "He who does the will of my Father is My Mother, 'i.e. the soul which impregnated by the Holy Spirit, reproduces Christ in its own bosom." The fact of Mary's virginity seems to add little to its spiritual value." "The irregularity of His physical conception might symbolize, but could it possibly constitute the dignity of His person" "Can this symbolism square with currently approved ideas of what dogma is? The answer is an emphatic No." (Letter quoted in M. Petre, *George Tyrrell's Letters* [London, 1920], pp. 56–61.)

43. Fr. Raymond Brown, S. S., has recently defended the traditional position on the empty tomb. At the same time he writes: "... we should make clear that the empty tomb is not an object of faith; we believe in the risen Christ." *Jesus. Commonweal Papers: 2, Commonweal* (Nov. 24, 1967), p. 234.

44. *Kerygma and Myth*, Ed. H. Bartsch (1953), p. 39. The Baron opposed "the *present* large class of Germans in search of a faith free from historical contingencies, metaphysical subtleties, mystical exaltations and priestly oppressions—a combination of Christ and Kant." *EA* I (1914), 148.

45. He referred to a letter "pp. 55–61." He suggested changing "Zeiller to "Z" twice. The only letter to fit this description is the one we have cited.

CHAPTER ELEVEN

1. "God leads to Christ, and Christ leads to the Church; and inversely, the Church leads to Christ, and Christ leads to God. Or, better, the Church always involves Christ, and Christ always involves the Church." (Aug. 1919, to Gwendolen Greene, *SL*, p. 285.) In 1921, he writes: "But God is God, already apart from His occupation with us ... We will thus retain a strong sense that not even Jesus Christ and His Redemption exhaust God ... Christian prayer, indeed Christian theology, are not thus Soteriology, practical or theoretical." He urges a tender devotion to Christ "free from all excessive Christocentrism." (*EA* II, p. 218). Even Our Lord must not be made into "so exclusive a center and home of all that is divine, as to cause Him to come into an entirely God-forsaken world." (*ME* II, p. 267). The best exposition of the idea is found in *SL*, p. 200 ff, (1912) to Canon Newsom. "My Faith in God and in Christ is necessary for my faith in the Church, but the Church is necessary for a full faith in God and Christ. But my faith is not simply "passive in the hands of Churchmen." Cf., also, p. 318, (1920): "We require God and Christ

and Church; each in and with the other." He called this "intimate interpenetration" the "trinity in Unity" of his study, *EA* I, xvii, (1921).

2. The best summary of these works is to be found in J. Steinmann, *Friedrich von Hügel*, pp. 245–310, 376–394, 544–559.

3. *EA* I, p. 46 (1909).

4. *SL*, p. 269, (1919) to Gwendolen Greene.

5. *EA* II, p. 7, (1904).

6. *Ibid.* p. 6. It is characteristic that the first quotation (note 41) which brings out the *positive* value of the "skeleton" definition is from 1919, while the quotation which expresses what it *lacks* is from 1904.

7. Dakin calls him "the old wizard" in the sense that he often begs the question. But Dakin seems unaware of the real force of his approach. He looks for a scientific proof and then misses the power of what is there. (*Von Hügel and the Supernatural*, [London, 1924], p. 82).

8. *EL* p. 231, (1912); *EA* II, p. 53, (1905).

9. *EA* II, p. 6, (1904); *EL* p. 232.

10. *EA* I, p. 296, (1920). Blondel had not said that men in general were conscious of this sense, but that the logic of action could be used to explicate it for them. The Baron finds the consciousness present proportionate to the degree to which man is "awake" to reality. Cf., Scoppola, *Crisi Modernista*, pp. 379–384.

11. "The Religious Philosophy of Rudolph Eucken," *Hibbert Journal* (April 1912), p. 670. Religion begins as dissatisfaction. It thirsts not for an idea but for reality. The Baron was discontented with Eucken for not bringing out the uniqueness of Christ (p. 672).

12. *LTN*, p. xxxl.

13. *SL*, (1910) p. 182, to Webb. Cf. *Von Hügel and Tyrrell*, (March 4, 1900) p. 127, to Tyrrell; *EL*, p. 339; *ME* I, pp. 44–46.

14. *RG* pp. 188, 6. Whereas in 1902 the Baron said that he found the traditional proofs of reason for the divine personality cold and static (though he did not deny them), by 1925 he is speaking about St. Thomas' argument from design. (Compare *SL*, p. 104 written to Hebért, with *RG*, chapter V, "Intimations of the Reality of God in Nature and in the Human Mind."

15. For example in his latter years he tells his niece: "Religion is like a cuckoo in some people's nest," that is, it is a little compartment remotely set aside, a phrase from Tyrrell, "They do not understand man's need. No man is satisfied in a swimming bath; he knocks his knees and elbows and thirsts for the ocean, for God." *LTN*, p. xxxi.

16. Tyrrell had written to the Baron on Feb. 16, 1898 at the time when he was helping the Baron's daughter, Gertrud, with her problems on faith which may have been generated by her father's imprudence. He said that there are many people "who do not know you well enough to understand that it is just because your faith is so much stronger than theirs that you can afford to make so many concessions, to allow the existence of so many adverse facts and difficulties. A man who stands on firm ground can enjoy a freedom of movement impossible on a tight-rope." (Cited in *SL*, p. 12.)

17. On Oct. 19, 1906 he wrote to Miss Petre that he had not yet finished the Preface to *The Mystical Element* but that the book itself was completed.

18. *ME* I, pp. 51–82. The Baron came to find that this chapter was the most popular part of his book, but he himself preferred volume II where he treated of mysticism and the doctrine of St. Catherine of Genoa, which was the core of his work and part of its title, *The Mystical Element of Religion as Studied in Saint Catherine of Genoa and Her Friends.* (Cf. *LTN*, p. 78). A.A. Cock found the triple division a little too neat and schematic. He found small place for the aesthetic element as part of the mystical. (*A Critical Examination of von Hugel's Philosophy of Religion*, [London, no date], p. 26). P.F. Chambers suggests a fourth element, the practical element found in active people. (*A Little Book of Baron von Hugel*, [London 1945], p. 38). Since the Baron admitted writing with broad strokes, I think we can find enough elasticity to fit the suggestions of Cock and Chambers under the mystical (intuitive, emotional, volitional) element.

19. *ME* I, pp. 51–53. The Baron said that W. James (*The Will to Believe*, [N.Y. 1904], p. 113) influenced him in choosing his triad. James said: "The structural unit of the nervous system is in fact a triad ... the sensory element exists only for the sake of awaking the central process of reflection, and the central process of reflection exists only for the sake of calling forth the final act ... the middle stage of thinking is only a place of transit ... both whose ends have their point of application in the outer world. ... Perception and thinking are only there for behavior's sake."

20. He conceded this to Anglicans when they spoke of their religion as an adult religion. Laberthonnière in 1903 had warned about an external authoritarian catechetics for children, *Essais de philosophie religieuse*, pp. 233–292 (put on Index 1906).

21. *ME* I, p. 56.

22. *ME* I, pp. 61–65, 28–39.

23. Cf., *ME* 2, pp. 387–396 for a fine summary of the entire process.

24. *EA* I, p. 261, (1918); cf., also pp. 129, 250, and *EL* 327. Von Hügel holds that Peter was made chief of the Apostles by Christ. However, the "rock" text in Matthew and the Lucan text where Christ says he will pray for Peter, the Baron believes are "later constituents." *EA* I, p. 262, (1918).

25. *SL*, p. 301, (1920) to Mrs. Lillie. Cf., also *EA* II, 246, 70–71, 85, *ME* I, 75, *RG* 138–139.

26. *EA* II, p. 248 (1921).

27. *EA*, II, pp. 6–11, 17, (1904).

28. The Baron said he was not an apologete. To put him in that role, he said, was like giving a dog first prize among cats. (He loved dogs). I understand apologetics in a modern sense as the intellectual scrutiny of the credentials of one's faith, both for oneself and for others. He certainly aimed at this. He said he wanted to make this Church an intellectually habitable place. And a good deal of his writing was aimed at reducing the intellectual scandal for those outside, though he knew the Church must ultimately be a scandal of some sort for the unbeliever. (*The Times Literary Supplement* [Dec. 22, 1921], p. 860.)

29. *ME* II, pp. 355–356. The Blessed Mother is almost totally absent in von Hügel's thought. He said a decade of the Rosary every day to keep his spiritual life "from losing touch with the devotion of the people." His idea was that to honor the Son is to honor the Mother. (*Rinnovamento*, IV, p. 21). Abbot Butler said that the Baron on his deathbed recited his beads devoutly and that he always had a deep devotion to Our Lady. Humphrey Johnson says that the Baron told him that he did not believe in Our Lady's corporal Assumption though he feared it would be defined along with the Immaculate Conception of St. Joseph! (*Studies*, [Dec. 1950], p. 376, n. 2.).

30. *ME* II, pp. 355–356.

CHAPTER TWELVE

1. Dom Cuthbert Butler said that he appealed especially to the intellectual "either outside the pale of Christianity, or on its borderland" and that there his influence was extraordinary. *Religions of Authority and the Religion of the Spirit* (London, 1930), pp. 180–181. The best article on von Hügel's attitude is Michael Hanbury, "Baron

von Hügel and the Ecumenical Movement," *The Month* (March, 1963) 140.

2. The von Hügel family had always been Catholic. But Friedrich's mother, Elizabeth Farquharson, was born in India, bred a Presbyterian and converted after her marriage. His wife, Mary, was converted shortly after her own mother, Lady Herbert of Lea, who had been a friend of Newman and Vaughan. Friedrich's father had traveled widely and written on Kashmir and the Sikh Kingdom. His maternal grandfather had spent forty years in India, and his good friend, Sir Alfred Lyall, was an expert on Indian religion (*RG*, p. 156).

3. *EA* I, p. 88, (1916). He gives a beautiful development of the idea of eternal life in Israel in *EL*, ch. II. For his finest summary, cf., *EA* I, pp. 72–80, (1916).

4. *EA* I, p. 88 (1916); p. 163 (1914).

5. Von Hügel is peculiarly sensitive to anything he finds depressive. As symbols of the growth of Christian insight he chooses the Synoptics, John, Augustine and Thomas. (*EA* I, pp. 80ff., [1916]). Of the four, Augustine is in disfavor. He finds him rigorist. Paul he bypasses with the suggestion that he was too juridical. We have seen, in ch. 1, that von Hügel found Newman depressing because of his "predestinarian" tendencies. Recall that Newman was a convert. Von Hügel now speaks of a rigorism connected with conversion which he found in Paul and Augustine. People have compared von Hügel to Kierkegaard. It is true that von Hügel goes part of the way with Kierkegaard's "otherness in God" but it is mainly on the epistemological level. While von Hügel's God demands sacrifice, he is not the flaming utterly other who agonizes souls.

6. *EA* II, p. 39 (1905); *EA* I, pp. 278–298 (1920).

7. *EA* I, p. xiv (1921).

8. *ME* II, p. 267; *EA* II, p. 76.

9. *ME* II, p. 299.

10. *Ibid.*, p. 300. He felt that science was reducing to a postulate of theology the idea of a sudden fall, not only from knowledge but also from innocence. The evidence for this he does not mention. He quotes without rejecting it the idea that the fall is a picture *sub specie historiae* of the conflict of freedom and conscience. But he makes no thesis for his idea and is quite hesitant. His proposition was basically that comparative religion was raising questions for which he could not as yet see the answers.

11. *EA* I, p. 63 (1909); p. 252 (1917). The Baron refers here, as frequently to de Lugo, De Fide, Disputatio 11, no. 50.

12. *SL*, pp. 257–258, to his niece.

13. *SL*, p. 350, (1921) to a lady (i.e. Evelyn Underhill). His friend, the philosopher C. Webb said: "No one can appreciate von Hügel's theology aright who does not realize the importance in it of a conception of graded revelations, each embodied in a religious organization, which he found—or rather read into Cardinal de Lugo." (*Blackfriars,* [July 1937], p. 340.)

14. Cf., e.g., Msgr. Fenton, "Von Hügel and Spiritual Direction," *American Ecclesiastical Review* (Aug. 1955), 117–121. Msgr. Fenton said also that for the Baron revelation was not a *locutio Dei ad homines* but a necessary condition of religion as sincere and experienced. Our present discussion belies this. What would Fenton make of the following statement: "All real actual Religion is ever an act of submission to some fact or truth conceived as not only true but obligatory, as coming from God, and hence as beyond and above our purely subjective fancies, opinings and wishes" (*ME* I, p. 60). Cf., also, *EL*, pp. 228–230. Vatican II has freed us from this sort of quibbling.

15. Loisy saw a condemnation of these statements of von Hügel in *Pascendi* but distorts his ideas (*Mem.* II, p. 577). The Encyclical said: "In the conflict between religions, the most that the Modernists can maintain is that the Catholic has more truth because it is more vivid, and that it deserves with more reason the name of Christian because it corresponds more fully with the origins of Christianity." (DB, 2082) The Baron held that Christianity was the unique revelation. He uses "more and less" only to bring out the truth that those outside the visible Church are not left without truth.

16. Cf., M. Hanbury, *The Month*, pp. 143–144. He cites G. Baum and C. Davis and shows their similarity to the Baron's approach as regards dissident Christians.

17. *EA*, II, p. 39 (1905).

18. *RG*, p. 146.

19. *EA*, I, pp. 177–194 (1914).

20. *EA*, II, p. 38 (1905); *ME*, I, p. xxv.

21. *EA*, I, p. 89 (1916); *RG*, p. 215; p. 218; *EA*, II, p. 158 (1920).

22. *RG*, p. 15; *ME*, II, p. 276.

23. Letter to Tyrrell (Dec. 31, 1898). Also *RG*, 192, 209.

24. *SL*, pp. 281, 268, to his niece (1919); *RG*, 190–194; *SL*, 341.

25. *EA*, I, p. 221 (1917). The Baron holds that hell is unending, but that there might be a type of mitigation in that the soul may have a diminished consciousness of the supernatural call, and a lesser awakenness. But hell still remains hell, *the* loss of life, the loss of

the meaning of life, the painful loss of the Reality of life. Cf., *ME,* II, 338; *EA* I, 221.

26. *EA*, I, p. 4 (1920). The Baron referred to the death of the French positivist Emile Littré, a description of which he had from Huvelin. (Cf. J. F. Six, *Littré devant Dieu* [Paris, 1962], pp. 163–168. "If the abbé (Huvelin) had demanded an explicit adhesion to the dogma of the Trinity, or that of the divinity of Our Lord, he would not have received it; and if he had persevered in his demand, M. Littré *would have shown him to the door.* However he did not die, as Mill, without faith, and only with hope; he already believed in an absolute manner ... in the existence of an invisible world and in the *"persistence"* of his soul." Littré was baptized by his wife.)

27. *SL*, p. 234, to Professor Sonnenschein (1916); *EA* I, pp. 200–201 (1917).

28. *ME*, I. pp. 72, 60.

29. *RG*, p. 151.

30. *The Spectator* (May 19, 1894), p. 685.

31. *RG*, p. 149.

32. *EA*, I, p. 276.

33. Letter to Miss Petre (April 17, 1906).

34. N. Abercrombie, *The Life and Work of Edmund Bishop* (London, 1959), p. 443. The citation is merely a marginal note to his copy of Petre's life of Tyrrell.

35. *Ibid.*, p. 45.

36. M. Petre, *My Way of Faith* (London, 1936), p. 213.

37. His inward attitude is found in the marginal notation to his copy of the life of Tyrrell: "Rome" is "an embodied and *organized egotism:* one of the greatest ... the world has ever seen." Abercrombie, *op. cit.*, p. 443. For his attitude against wirepulling in the external forum, see, N. Abercrombie, "Von Hügel and Edmund Bishop," *Dublin Review*, third quarter (1953), p. 288. The four issues of 1953 contain the correspondence between the two men. Bishop's attitude toward von Hügel was frequently unfavorable.

38. *EA*, I, p. 232. The Baron frequently used the expression "twice-born" of the Christian. The totally optimistic religions where there is no thought of self-imperfection he termed "once-born." The expression he found in W. James, *The Varieties of Religious Experience* (1902), Mentor edition (New York, 1958), cf., p. 78.

39. *SL*, p. 238, (1916) to C. Montefiore. Before an Edinburgh audience in 1914 he said that a priest, Richard Simon, and a layman,

Jean Astruc, laid the foundations of Pentateuchal criticism. (*EA*, II, p. 104.) He often points out that Christ was more in conflict with laymen, the Pharisees, than with the priests. (*EA*, II, p. 66, [1913]). He is strong on the great value of priestly celibacy. (*EA*, I, p. 232, [1913]; *EA*, II, p. 93, [1914]; *EA*, I, p. 286, [1920]; *SL*, pp. 142, 184, 209, 327.) "Celibacy can and ought, thus, to remain, as the heroic exemplification of that self-restraint which married and single, we all so greatly require" (To M. Petre, Dec. 16, 1910). But he also thought some reform was desirable. He felt that a priest who had unwisely undertaken this obligation, should be allowed to marry and retire into "a specially honored position among the lay communicants of the Church" (*EA*, II, p. 94 etc.).

40. *SL*, p. 162, to Tyrrell.

41. *LTN*, p. xxxix.

42. *Ibid.*, p. xlii.

43. *SL*, p. 302. On Mrs. Lillie, see de la Bedoyère, p. 326.

44. M. Cropper, *Evelyn Underhill* (London, 1958), pp. 68–69, 82. The Baron's letters in this book are a treasury of spiritual direction.

45. "Baron von Hügel and the Ecumenical Movement," *The Month*, pp. 144–147.

46. *LTN*, 47, p. xxix. Msgr. Fenton takes the word "change" in the context to mean that people changed for the worse because of his influence. This is impossible both from the context and from the Baron's history. Fenton goes on to make up a list using his false interpretation. Even then, the list is fantastic: Hébert (whose immanence the Baron always disliked!), Loisy (!), Addis (de la Bedoyère, p. 59, documents the opposite position), Fawkes (the opposite in de la Bedoyère, p. 219), the old Catholic Bishop Matthew, who left Catholicism (I have found no dealings of von Hügel with him, but he did dislike Tyrrell's dealing with Matthew), Buonaiuti (in his letters to M. Petre the Baron is continually warning her about his negative influence and he shows that the only reason he did not discriminate himself publically from the Italian modernist was for fear of bringing public dissension into the ranks). To this list of priests, Fenton adds Tyrrell.

47. *SL*, (1911), p. 187 to a lady; (1921), p. 344 to a lady. (The latter is Evelyn Underhill.)

48. Among other places see *EA*, I, (1920); p. 18 *SL* (1920), p. 301 to Mrs. Lillie. *SL* (1911) p. 188, to J. M.; de la Bedoyère, p. 28, to his wife.

49. M. Hanbury, "Algar Thorold," *The Dublin Review*, first quarter (1955), 12.

50. "A Hitherto Unpublished Letter from Baron von Hügel" (on religion written to a young girl), *The Dublin Review* (1951), 452, 1–11. The author describes Hildegard's work. She also shows Lady Mary, the Baron's "lovable and eccentric wife," as the center of an artistic and musical world. Cf., Hildegard's notes on her father in *SL*, pp. 66–67.

51. W. Inge, *God and the Astronomers* (London, 1933), p. 120.

52. *The Nature of the Church* (London, 1952), p. 17. Hanbury, *The Month* (March, 1963), pp. 148–149 gives Leeming's remarks.

53. For von Hügel's influence on Anglican theology, see Archbishop Ramsey, *From Gore to Temple*, pp. 59, 164–165.

54. Cf., J. Mozley, *Some Tendencies in British Theology*, pp. 53–55. Also, A. Vidler, *The Modernist Movement in the Roman Church*, p. 254.

55. *Anglicanism in Transition* (London, 1937), p. 155. Times have changed since J. Rivière spoke of the "interconfessional coquetry" which was of common occurrence in England, *Le Modernisme*, p. 448.

56. *The Faith of the Millions*, I (London, 1904), e.g., pp. 55–61. This, together with "Theology and Devotion" (*The Faith of the Millions*, I), and "From God or From Men?" (*Scylla and Charybdis*), were von Hügel's favorites. "I love these papers through and through." (*SL*, p. 166 (1909) to Canon Newsom.)

57. It should be pointed out that von Hügel also insisted that outside Christian Revelation there are many major deviations from God's design (e.g. *ME* I, pp. 60–61). Also, the Baron's use of the word revelation is paralleled with his use of the word "givenness" (*EA*, I, xiv). There is also a givenness in the non Judaeo-Christian world through grace. By the word "givenness" he does not mean the fact of creation. The reason why he uses this word so often is to emphasize that there is something behind or at the ground of reality which is not ourselves. (Cf., *EA*, I, 56). He uses the word "givenness" in reaction against exclusive immanence. "Givenness" brings out the fact that there is a source distinct from us, "a source itself loving, Itself a Lover" (*EA*, I, p. 114 [1914]).

58. *EA*, I, p. 267 (1918).

CHAPTER THIRTEEN

1. "Bulletin de littérature religieuse," *Recherches de Science Religieuse*, 16 (1926), p. 166.

2. *EA* II, pp. 105 and ff. (1914).

3. *Rinnovamento*, III (1908), p. 224.

4. *Rinnovamento*, V (1909), p. 399; III (1908), pp. 225–226.

5. Since they were first quoted by M. Nédoncelle in 1935, they have been mentioned again only once, by H. J. Johnson, "Baron von Hügel and the Catholic Religion," *Studies*, XXXIX (1950), p. 377.

6. *Rinnovamento*, V (1909), pp. 419–420.

7. Cited in de la Bedoyère, letter of Aug. 15, 1921, p. 338. Von Hügel's "fruitfulness" of dogma is not doctrinaire pragmatism. *EA* II, p. 102. There are similarities here between von Hügel and one of the two currents in Tyrrell's thought. The Tyrrell who constantly embodied his thought in an overstated rhetoric to serve his attack on the theological handling of dogma claimed that dogma *as theology* was fallible and thoroughly mutable. It is infallible only in its practical and approximative spiritual orientation. Theology must treat revelation exclusively as experience and not as statement. (*Through Scylla and Charybdis*, pp. 209–210, 229, 238.)

This would lead to the conclusion that no infallible statement can be made about the faith experience. But this is contradicted by the second stream in Tyrrell. Here Tyrrell says that a revelation which ignores the check of theology (he includes dogma here) is sterile (*Through Scylla*, p. 238). There is a theology implicit in revelation as theory is implied in experience (p. 289). A metaphysics can be deduced from life and conduct (pp. 198–199). The truth in "prophetic utterance" (either scripture or dogma) is a symbolic presentiment of supernatural reality and secondarily has a consequent efficacy in shaping our spiritual life (p. 326).

Thus there is infallible truth that can be expressed about revelation though it involves image or symbol or what scholasticism calls analogous truth. At least on the relation betweeen dogmas and supra-historical reality, von Hügel is in harmony with this second current in Tyrrell's thought. We have not yet had a treatment of Tyrrell which by disengaging this aspect of his thought would show what Tyrrell was basically after in many of his incorrect and misleading overstatements, an emphasis on the analogous quality of dogmatic statements about the supra-historical in revelation.

8. A group of Dutch theologians recently presented a similar development. "The faith in a dogma therefore does not aim only at the representative and conceptual factors fixed by the Church, but also and in the first place it aims at the mystical, irrepresentable aspect of the same reality which we attain through the representation. The religious notions and the dogmatic formulas *are* the reality of Salvation in so far as we know it according to the mode of our modern objective knowledge. In this sense, the conceptual element itself

of dogmatic formulas forms a part of the dogma." Translated from *Informations catholiques internationales* (Dec. 1962), p. 31.

9. The only place where he gives a possible rough content for this nucleus is in *EA* II, p. 106. He includes the Sermon on the Mount, the cures, the conversions, the Passion, "indeed the very Person of Jesus, as so many actual happenednesses and at one time visible and audible facts." To this he would add the post-resurrection apparitions.

10. "The Relations between God and Man in 'The New Theology,' of Rev. R. Cambpell," *The Albany Review* (formerly *The Independent Review*) (Sept. 1907), pp. 650–668, p. 652.

11. *Ibid.*, p. 655.

12. *Dictionnaire de la Bible, Supplément*, VI (Paris, 1960), cols. 1411, 1412.

13. *Rinnovamento*, IV (1908), pp. 34–44 on the Parousia, esp. pp. 41–43.

14. K. Rahner has made similar suggestions but has stated the problem with more careful nuance in "Zur Theologie der Menschwerdung," *Catholica*, 12 (1958), pp. 1–16.

15. *SL*, pp. 158–159. Later on, von Hügel took the avowal of ignorance by Our Lord as to the date of the end to be a later addition to the text.

16. *Baron Friedrich von Hügel*, p. 106. A word is in place here on the distinction between error and ignorance. Ignorance is generally the lack of some knowledge which implies no defect. For example we certainly may hold that Christ in His *human* intellect was unaware of the heliocentric theory or of the exact composition of the atom. Ignorance may entail negative error, i.e. material mistakes through lack of knowledge. Positive error, however, is a formal conviction, certainty, or teaching as to what is false, reached through the rejection of one or more alternatives. Such an undue adherence is a defect in ordinary human action. If Jesus made a formal assertion about a proximate end of the physical world, He would have fallen into formal error in rejecting one of two alternatives, end of the world now, no end of the world now. But if Christ's statements were symbolic and imaginative, their formal conviction would center, not on the alternative—end of the physical world or its continuation, but on the alternative—inruption of the Kingdom or no inruption. The element of dating would not be a consideration and the formal conviction would be true. This is along the lines of Nédoncelle's suggestion. And Jesus would still had admitted ignorance about the date of a specific final event. (Tyrrell

said that ignorance on anything implies error about everything because of the harmony of the universe, *Essays on Faith and Immortality*, pp. 44–45. But his thinking would equate formal teaching of error with ordinary lack of knowledge in areas outside one's intended affirmation. It would follow from his discussion that the Christian who, before Galileo, said that the sun rises, even though he had given no thought to any alternative, such as that the earth circles the sun, would be in error in the same way as a modern astronomer who formally held that the sun circles the earth.)

17. *EL*, pp. 61–62.

18. *EL*, p. 58.

19. *EA* II, p. 81. In 1914 he again emphasizes the proximate second coming. *EA* II, p. 189.

20. *EA* I, pp. 119–143. Cf., also, *EA* I, pp. 159, 180 (1914); p. 82 (1916). Fr. Grandmaison found the essay on the Apocalyptic Element to be "incomplète, discutable mais profond et original." *Jesus Christ,* II (Paris, 1928), p. 456.

21. Cf., pp. 127–128, 137–138, 142.

22. *SL*, p. 326 (Mar. 7, 1921). The idea appears again in a letter to Webb of May 1921, p. 329.

23. *The Times Literary Supplement*, p. 860.

24. The following quotations are from "Thoughts from Baron von Hügel," *The Dublin Review* (April 1931), pp. 254–260. The thoughts are no doubt abridged.

25. *Ibid.*, p. 259.

26. *Histoire, dogme,* p. 591. Poulat takes exception to Nédoncelle's suggestion that von Hügel "renewed and amended this thesis in a definitive manner" (p. 114). "Definitive" would certainly be true in the sense of von Hügel's final statement on the subject. But it is more of a glimpse of a new insight whose significance the Baron did not fully comprehend than a really definitive position. The proximate Second Coming is still a doctrine "I cannot wholly explain and understand." (Cf., the same in *EA* I, x, [1921]. Both Nédoncelle and Poulat are right from their points of view. Nédoncelle is interested in showing that von Hügel's final thought cannot be totally rejected as wholly unorthodox on this point. Poulat seems interested in maintaining that von Hügel never rejected his movement toward a total respect for his idea of historical criticism in his approach to Christology.

27. Vol. 2, p. 279.

28. *ME* II, p. 248.

29. *ME*, p. 51.

30. *EA* I, p. 126 (1919). The distinction between intuitive experienced apprehension and concept or perception is very frequent, e.g., *RG* 41, 71–73, 82–83, *SL*, 138.

31. For a survey of recent positions on the question, see G. Lundström, *The Kingdom of God in the Teaching of Jesus* (Richmond, 1963); N. Perrin, *The Kingdom of God in the Teaching of Jesus* (Phila., 1963); the best Catholic work, endorsed by Lundström, is R. Schnackenburg, *God's Rule and Kingdom* (N.Y., 1963); Cf., also, A. Feuillet, *Dictionnaire de la Bible, Supplément*, VI (Paris, 1960), "Parousia," col. 1349, and B. Rigaux, *La Attente du Messie* (Paris, 1962), pp. 173–216.

CHAPTER FOURTEEN

1. *RG*, p. 3.

2. His reaction is conveniently found in de la Bedoyère, pp. 238–239. However the same ideas are sprinkled all through the correspondence with Miss Petre. The same consistent picture emerges from Scoppola's *Crisi Modernista*, e.g., pp. 202, 224, 243, 303 (a long tribute to von Hügel by Fracassini where the Baron is "nostro padre e maestro" on this point), 306.

3. *SL*, p. 215, to Miss Petre (Dec. 30, 1914). Troeltsch "brought me back to a full . . . admiration of the Golden Middle Age." *LTN*, p. 176. He also attributed the change to the influence of the Scottish and younger Oxford philosophers. His transition also coincides with the transition from nineteenth century individualism to a sense of community.

4. *SL*, p. 334, to Professor René Guiran (July 11, 1921). Norman Kemp Smith of Edinburgh was also very influential in the transition. Von Hügel finds it paradoxical that he now is more helped in his Catholicism by the Lutheran Troeltsch and the Calvinist Smith than by Blondel and Laberthonnière. But Blondel himself was also in transition. Cf., C. Tresmontant, *Introduction a la metaphysique de Maurice Blondel* (Paris, 1963).

5. "In fact the study of the connected system of our ideas makes evident that the very notion of immanence is realized in our conscience only by the effective presence of the notion of the transcendent." "Exigences de la pensée contemporaine," *Les premiers écrits* (1896), p. 40.

6. E.g., *EA* I, p. 47 (1909); *EA* II, p. 144 (1918); *RG*'s many passages on the original dim apprehension of God. Von Hügel had

long felt dissatisfied with Blondel's appreciation of history. On March 18, 1914 he wrote to Miss Petre comparing Blondel, Laberthonnière and Le Roy. He said that Laberthonnière was the "greatest spiritual writer" of the three, Blondel is the "ampler, richer philosopher" but that Le Roy better recognizes historical problems, "a sealed book to Laberthonnière and Blondel." *RG*, p. 254, the third last page he ever wrote is redolent of Blondel, and it concerns historical method. The Baron early appreciated Blondel's method, but felt Blondel did not give facts their due. He more deeply assimilated Eucken than Blondel.

7. *ME*, preface to second edition, p. xvi.

8. *SL*, p. 334 (July 11, 1921) to Guiran.

9. Letter of May 15, 1907.

10. Alfred Loisy, *Sa vie, son oeuvre*, ed., E. Poulat (Paris, 1960), p. 129.

11. M. Petre, *Alfred Loisy*, p. 38. Cf., also, pp. 35, 38, 87, 89. Loisy himself denied that he was agnostic, *Mém.* III, p. 352; cf., also, pp. 20–21, 24, 141, 164.

12. *RG*, p. 57.

13. *LTN*, p. 36.

14. *SL*, p. 139.

15. *EA* I, p. 38 (1909).

16. "Baron Friedrich von Hügel and His Contribution to Religious Philosophy," *The Harvard Theological Review* (Jan. 1949), p. 18.

17. *The Harvard Theological Review* (Jan. 1949), p. 7.

18. *SL*, pp. 126–127, to Mrs. Henry Drew.

19. "Father Tyrrell: Some memorials of the last twelve years of his life" (Jan. 1910), p. 251.

20. De la Bedoyère nicely brings out the permanence of the Baron's positions, p. 329. Earlier he had said that von Hügel gradually awoke "to find himself a normally orthodox Catholic in all the points for which he stood *as public witness and teacher* in the later part of his life" (p. 247). While the Baron's published treatment of the Parousia texts of course did not make him heretical, still it would be hard to say that he was normally orthodox in them. But my underlining points out the careful choice of words, and there is a real point to them. In his published works "as public witness and teacher," i.e. in all his signed articles, in fact in everything after 1909, he tried to write with the Church documents in mind, and apparently he even believed that he was doing so on the Parousia texts.

I feel that the final portions of de la Bedoyère's biography (a generally superb work) fail to capture the inner consistency of the Baron's positions. Certain documents, as the *Rinnovamento* articles, were not cited.

21. *AAS* II (1910), p. 669 f, *D-S* 2145–2147.

22. Mignot (1842–1918) was a staunch friend both of von Hügel and Loisy. Courageous, generous and intelligent, he stood out among the hierarchy in championing freedom of research. But he was not a modernist and while retaining Loisy's friendship was greatly saddened by his revelation in 1913 as to his true positions. Only of late has his correspondence become available and a final evaluation must remain for the future. Cf., M. Bécamel's publication of letters of Loisy and von Hügel in *Bulletin de Littérature Ecclesiastique* (Jan.-Mar. 1966), 3–44, (April–June), 81–144, (July– Sept), 170–193, (Oct–Dec), 257–285.

23. Cf., de la Bedoyère, pp. 210–211 for Mignot's full treatment.

24. A good piece of evidence is the Baron's letter to an anonymous mother published by de la Bedoyère: "Certainly it will be well ... if you can get *yourself habitually to see*, feel and practise a catholicism which recognizes *itself bound* to two things, but to two things only:

a) the acceptance, *ex animo*, of all the solemn definitions and condemnations of the Church, and

b) the avoidance of ignoring or contravening even lesser ecclesiastical decisions (e.g. Pius Xth's Encyclicals and the Decisions of the Biblical Commission) without serious reasons and real careful study and knowledge of the subject matters, or without restraint, and, wherever possible, silence. ... Certain it is that any attempt to force our minds *to a final, unhesitating, interior assent to professions, to which the authorities themselves do not so bind themselves* can only end in unreality and scepticism" (1912), p. 265.

25. *EA* I (1918), p. 266 f.

26. *EA* I, p. 268; *RG*, p. 14.

27. *LTN* (May 30, 1921), p. 137.

28. *LTN* (Feb. 22, 1921), p. 128.

29. "Der Mystiker und die Kirche aus Anlass des Sadhu," *Hochland* (Dec. 1924), p. 330. The monk never became a Catholic. Some of his mystical adventures he had to admit were exaggerations.

30. The first title was bestowed by Paul Sabatier, *Les Modernistes* (Paris, 1909), p. li, the second by Salomon Reinach. De la Bedoyère says that "Von Hügel himself, together with Sabatier, came nearest to being a leader through his indefatigable liaison work," p. 193.

31. *SL*, to Webb, (Sept. 26, 1912) p. 197. For a discussion of the Lagrange decree (*AAS* [1912], p. 530 ff.) see F.-M. Braun, O.P., *The Work of Père Lagrange* (Milwaukee, 1962), pp. 92 ff.

32. *SL*, p. 334.

33. A letter to Thorold from early in 1921, cited by de la Bedoyère pp. 331–332.

34. "Father Tyrrell," *The Hibbert Journal* (Jan. 1910), p. 235.

35. *SL*, (Nov. 17, 1909), p. 173, to Malcom Quin.

36. "Eudoxe Irenée Mignot," *Contemporary Review* (May, 1918), p. 520.

37. "Louis Duchesne," *The Times Literary Supplement* (May 25, 1922), p. 342.

38. Even Loisy said that at the height of the crisis von Hügel would have submitted but "with great anguish of soul." *Mém.* II. p. 416.

39. *IVR*, p. 506.

40. Cardinal Bourne certainly showed indulgence to his subject, von Hügel. The diary tells us that the Baron first visited Archbishop Bourne of Westminster on Oct. 23, 1903, during his first year in office. They talked about Abbé Hogan (who had been Bourne's superior when he had been a student at St. Sulpice and encouraged an openness to modern research), Semeria, Duchesne, and the Biblical Commission, as well as Tyrrell's *Oil and Wine* (which Tyrrell had tried to publish in 1901).

His second visit was on Jan. 11, 1904. For this visit he recorded in the diary: "wholly (?, i.e., word illegible) satisfactory talk about Loisy." On Dec. 9, 1909 the Baron wrote to Miss Petre and passed on Bourne's message to him through Thekla: "that he trusted I did not interpret his silence toward me as a want of appreciation of my motives and the substance of my labors. I believe this to be quite sincere, and to include you as really as myself." (In 1907 the Baron had published his books on the *Mystical Element* and on the Pentateuch without the *Imprimatur*.) On Jan. 18, 1913 he assured Miss Petre that Bourne would not cause her trouble. The documentation on Bourne's role apparently is not available, but what we have suggests a very tolerent attitude toward von Hügel.

As to the *Imprimatur*, although in 1753 Benedict XIV had demanded it for all books, as of 1883 there was a liberal interpretation that demanded it only for the books of Scripture, their annotations and commentaries. (J. Tephany, *Constitution Apostolicae Sedis de Sa Sainteté Pie IX limitant les censures latae sententiae* [Paris 1883], pp. 418–424). But in 1897 the *Officiorum ac Munerum* of Leo XIII demanded the Imprimatur for all books touching matters of religion or morality. Article 49 said that the Bishop should make reprimands according to the degree of culpability in those who transgressed the law. (A. Boudinhon, *La Nouvelle Législation de L'Index* [Paris, 1899], p. 321.)

41. *SL*, (Dec. 3, 1919) p. 298 to Webb. He considered a discussion of Modernism to be "at a date still too early, I think, to do much good."

CHAPTER FIFTEEN

1. A. Vermeersch, for example, held that the *Motu proprio* of Nov. 18, 1907 made the doctrinal portions of *Pascendi* (parts of which he admitted were disciplinary) and all of *Lamentabili* infallible. He admitted that the infallibility did not necessarily concern something divinely revealed, apparently accepting the idea of "ecclesiastical faith." He cited L. Choupin as dissenting about infallibility in *Etudes*, 114, pp. 119–120. (*De Modernismo* [1910], pp. 62–64.)

2. For a short accessible introduction with references, see, Gerald J. O'Brien, S.J., "Anti-Modernism: The Integralist Campaign," *Continuum*, Summer (1965), pp. 187–200. Also, Jean Madiran, *L'Intégrisme, histoire d'une histoire* (Paris, Nouvelles Editions Latines, 1964) (strongly criticized by R. Aubert, *Historical Investigations, Concilium,* 17 [N.Y., 1966], "Recent Literature on the Modernist Movement," pp. 91–108.) Cf., also, P. Fernessole, *Pie X, essai historique* II (Paris, 1953), 244, ff., 526. Benigni had a secret code in which the Pope was mamma, Merry del Val was George, bishops were aunts, priests were nephews, etc.

3. *Le Modernisme*, p. 476. For Lagrange's publications see the bibliography in F. Braun, *The Work of Père Lagrange* (Milwaukee, 1962). Rivière himself might be included in this list, even though his articles on the knowledge of Christ (*Bulletin de littérature ecclesiastique* [1915–1916], pp. 241–261, 289–314, 337–364) contained theory which was rejected by the Holy Office decree of June 5, 1918 as not safe teaching. He was removed from the seminary at Albi and went to teach at Strasbourg. Wilfrid Ward summed up well the delicacy of the general problem when he wrote to Cardinal Bourne in 1906: "The principle that the thoroughly Catholic attitude is to keep as far as possible from what has been condemned would have made it a part of Catholic loyalty to become a Monophysite when Nestorianism was pronounced heretical; and that of course was what some people did, making the further condemnation of their excesses on the other side necessary." Cited in *IVR*, p. 216.

4. Letter to Bremond (Jan. 31, 1899), cited by R. Marlé, *Au Coeur de la crise moderniste*, p. 29. On pietism, cf., *RG*, p. 31; *LTN*, p. xxxii.

5. *RG*, pp. 14–15.

6. E.g., *EA* I, p. 238; *ME* II, pp. 367–386, his longest treatment. Von Hügel's spirituality insists that one cannot find God in all things unless one clearly situate the "thing" and respect its "thingness".

7. Le Roy held that dogma had two senses, one negative and one positive. The negative sense means that dogma safeguards against possible errors without defining the positive truth of the reality. The positive sense is in the fact that dogma gives a rule of practical conduct. That is, for example, the dogma that God is personal rules out subpersonal notions of God and demands a personal reaction to Him without giving us metaphysical information about God. This presentation, I believe, is ultimately inadequate.

8. Before we end our study, let us mention that the Baron totally accepted the Church's teaching on moral questions. Miss Petre said: "It was a very marked characteristic of the Baron's mind that his readiness to converse on any or every mental problem of the modern mind was not extended to moral questions. He was not, so far as most of us knew him, open to any discussion of established moral laws, nor even conventions; any revolutionary inroads of tentative psychology into the moral domain, any easy-going resolution of moral restrictions, was to him objectionable, reprehensible and inexcusably dangerous. He would always have been the most patient and charitable listener to a tale of sheer temptation, to a confession of failure and sin; but he would have been frankly intolerant of any attempt to fit the moral law to modern inclinations or exigencies. In these matters F. von Hügel was not what the world calls 'large-minded', though the application of the term might well be disputed. . . . Hence he was able to ignore and discount certain problems from which the most ordinary confessor cannot escape." *Hibbert Journal* (Oct. 1925), p. 79. His niece, Gwendolen Greene, specifically mentions the Baron's staunch opposition to divorce and birth control, *Dublin Review* (1931) p. 26.

9. *Dictionnaire de la Bible* (Paris, 1895), preface p. lvii.

BIBLIOGRAPHY OF
VON HÜGEL'S WORKS

This list completes the bibliographies of A. H. Dakin and M. Nédoncelle by adding material obtained since 1937. However Nédoncelle's listing is still of value for references to philosophical and mystical research on von Hügel since I have not included these here. My brief comments on various works are not to be taken as definitive judgments, but merely as aids for future research on the period.

THE WORKS OF FRIEDRICH VON HÜGEL

1. "The Story of the Escape of Prince Metternich," *The National Review*, I (March-August 1883), 588–604. A selection by Friedrich from the papers of his father, the late Baron Karl von Hügel, traveller and diplomatist, 1795–1870, with commentary. Karl: "Scarcely a day (in Vienna) when I did not see him" (Metternich). See my Ch. 1, and 15 below.
2. Booknotes and Comments, *Bulletin Critique* (May 1, 1885), 175–178 (from notes on new books on Bible texts and manuscripts, to the need to protect Paris monuments, to the use of pagan pseudonyms among the Jews in support of Jewish belief). Similarly notes for the issues of March 15, 1886, pp. 117–118 (philological books reviewed), April 1, 1886, p. 135 (Harnack and Lightfoot on St. Ignatius of Antioch), Dec. 15, 1886, pp. 477–478 (books on archeology and philology). All were signed "F.H."

3. "The Spiritual Writings of Père Grou, S.J." *The Tablet*, (December 21, 28, 1889), 990–991, 1029–1031. Two articles of review on Grou's work, on the occasion of an English translation of *Manuel des Ames Intérieures*. The need of spiritual childhood in facing trials and the advantages of hard intellectual work for the maintenance of the spiritual life. "In heaven we will have a very imperfect comprehension of that which we shall see." The need of guidance: "A book which is dangerous for you at 20, will not be so at 30 or 35."

4. *Notes Addressed to the Very Reverend H.I.D.R. upon the subject of Biblical Inspiration and Inerrancy*, privately printed (July 1891). Sent to Fr. Ryder of the Oratory, an opponent of the conservative extremes of W. G. Ward, and of the liberal "extremes" as approved even by Manning. Uses and modifies Fr. Dausch, *Die Schriftinspiration* (Freiburg, 1891). Praises Ryder's statement: "I am well aware that the opinion safest theologically is not always the wisest, and that the true road may often run along the verge of the precipice." According to Dausch, the Fathers confounded Revelation and its scriptural transmission, the theory of Revelation and that of Inspiration (p. 5). Critical inadequacy of Franzelin and Kleutgen (p. 7). Revising Dausch, says "auctor" is wider than our "author" (p. 9). Influence of Holy Ghost in ideas of their times. Inspiration is the absolutely new spirit which animates the narration although the form may have existed among neighboring peoples (pp. 9–11). Not intermittent inspiration, no *obiter dicta* outside of it. Excludes: subjective error, objective error in faith, morals, and the substance of the history of revelation, and "the Divine non-intendedness of such growths and changes in this history as could be fairly argued to be compatible with subjective truthfulness" and yet to be not of the substance of this history (p. 12). Inerrancy not limited to faith and morals (p. 13). The changes, as in understanding of Johannine Comma, suggest future development in our idea of Inspiration (p. 14).

5. *Some Notes on the Petrine Claims* (London, 1930), 103 pp. Written through a friend "Rhoda" for the later Anglican Bishop, W. Frere, who subsequently took part in the Malines dialogues. Defense of the *Tu es Petrus* text. For full meaning of the text, later Church must also be taken into account. Written (September 2–7, 1893).

6. "The Papal Encyclical and Mr. Gore," letter to *The Spectator*

(May 19, 1894), 684–685. Allying himself with Loisy, he defends *Providentissimus* against Gore. Opposes placing *obiter dicta* outside inspiration and inerrancy, pleads for a sense of development and a search for what expresses "the formal convictions" of the inspired writers. Development in understanding of Church doctrine, e.g. as regards *Nulla Salus*, parallels development in understanding of Biblical Inerrancy. Similarly, Pope's silence on Pentateuch inquiry probably intentional.

7. "The Church and the Bible, the two stages of their Interrelation," three articles in *The Dublin Review* (October 1894), 313–341; (April 1895), 306–337; (October 1895), 275–304. A harmonizing of contemporary liberal work with Leo XIII's *Providentissimus Deus*.

8. Transpositions in the Gospel of St. Luke. A communication to the Roman Society of Biblical Studies (March 5, 1896) found in Mgr. Battandier's *Analecta iuris pontifici* (1896), and printed in *Revue Biblique*, 5 (1896), 470–472. Luke's intention to write the facts "in order" did not exclude an ordering which was mainly geographical, logical, or theological. (Cardinal Parocchi, who presided, warned Catholics against thinking that because they had an infallible teacher they were dispensed from critical studies of the sources of Revelation.)

9. "Professor Eucken on the Struggle for the Spiritual Life," *The Spectator* (November 14, 1896), 679–681. Article unsigned. The system of Production of Personality clears up uses and abuses of historical method. Caution on Eucken's attitude toward positive historical religion. (To be completed with #33.)

10. "La Méthode historique et son application à l'étude des documents de l'Hexateuque" (Paris, 1898), 35 pp. A paper read at the fourth Catholic International Scientific Congress, Fribourg, Switzerland (August 16–20, 1897). Slightly revised and published in English in *The Catholic University Bulletin* (Washington, D.C., April 1898), 198–226 + vii as *The Historical Method and the Documents of the Hexateuch*.

11. "Impressions of Elizabeth Rundle Charles" (1827–1896). *The Hampstead Annual*, ed. Ernest Rhys (1897), 52–62. Reminiscences on a friend.

12. "Caterina Fiesca Adorna, the Saint of Genoa," *The Hampstead Annual* (1898). The Baron's first biographical sketch of St. Catherine. Some of his insight attributed to Blondel and

Eucken, p. 79, "that the highest and ultimate form of knowledge is experience, and of reality personality; that this personality is most fully developed within us, and apprehended and approached without us, not by the exercises of reason, but by the dispositions of character." Action distinguished from feverishness and activity.

13. Notes on Wilfrid Ward's idea of authority. Delivered January 27, 1899 to the Synthetic Society. Published in *Papers Read Before the Synthetic Society* (London, 1909), 235–239. On the occasion of the apprehension of the phenomenal, there arises irresistibly the impression of a permanent, infinite Reality. "Authority can never be a simple substitute, and ought never to supplant, but can and does and ought everywhere to supplement the individual experience."

14. "A Proposito dell' Abate Loisy," *Studi Religiosi* (July and August, 1901), 348–350. Happy to be mentioned with Lagrange as a representative of historical method. Defends Loisy, who though he may be defective on individual points, has made great contributions even before *Providentissimus Deus* and has not been condemned. Says Loisy rightly affirms that the Bible must be considered as an historical and contingent work before it is considered dogmatically and as inspired.

15. In Karl von Hügel, April 25, 1785 to June 2, 1870, privately printed (Cambridge, 1903), 31–49, translation of biographical sketch by Alfred von Reumont. Re-issued 1905. Also contains accounts of Karl by Julius Wiesmer and Lady Fullerton.

16. "Experience and Transcendence," *The Dublin Review* (April, 1906), 357–379. The article was originally an address to the Synthetic Society on May 28, 1903, and was translated in *Studi Religiosi*. Considered of great importance by Nédoncelle: "In it von Hügel shows himself a more moderate transcendentalist than Kierkegaard; a realist without the agnostic elements of the Pseudo-Dionysius, and a believer in an immanence which he does not confuse with certain pantheistic aspirations of Jacopone di Todi." (See also, Nédoncelle, *R SC Rel,* XXXVI [1962], 154).

17. "The Case of the Abbé Loisy," *The (London) Pilot* (January 9, 1904), 30–31; translated in *Rassegna Nazionale* (Feb. 16, 1904); reprinted in *The Living Age* (February 20, 1904). After the decree on Loisy, an admission of possible mistakes but a plea for critical method and liberty. Compares to case of Aristotelianism in Middle Ages and of Galileo.

18. A letter to *The Pilot* (January 23, 1904). Loisy's submission sincere but not without "some reasonable and necessary reservation in the matter of his historian's conscience and critical method." After Loisy's books were placed on Index.

19. "The Abbé Loisy and the Holy Office," *The Times* (March 2, 1904), 15. Signed "Romanus" in reply to an article by Fr. Fleming signed "Catholicus" (January 25). (See Poulat, *Histoire, dogme*, 650.) An interpretation of Loisy, important for insight into vH's thought at this time.

20. A letter to *Il Giornale d'Italia* (March 11, 1904); reproduced in *Le Chrétien Français* (April 2, 1904). An answer to Professor Labanca on Loisy. The conflict between faith and criticism is only apparent, temporary and transitory.

21. A short anonymous introduction to a letter of B. Saunders and of Loisy in *The Times* (April 30, 1904), *6. "Not a renunciation of his (Loisy's) entire historico-critical conscience."

22. "Du Christ éternel et de nos christologies successives," *La Quinzaine* (Paris, June 1, 1904), 285–312. A part of the preamble was cut out for editorial reasons where he said that the small amount of philosophy in Loisy's system did not justify the introduction of a philosophy so special as Blondel's. (See, *Mem.* II, 408.) Abbé Wehrlé's reply appeared in the August 15 issue.

23. A letter to *La Quinzaine* (September 16, 1904), 276–277, in reply to Wehrlé.

24. *The Papal Commission and the Pentateuch* (London, 1906), 64 pp. Translated in *Il Rinnovamento* (January, 1907), 86–112; and as *La Commission pontificale et le Pentateuque* (Paris, 1907). An exchange of letters with Charles Briggs, an eminent Presbyterian exegete who had been censured by his Church for his views. VH gives reasons why Catholic Church might change its stand.

25. "The Relations Between God and Man in 'The New Theology' of Rev. R. J. Campbell," *The Albany Review* (previously *The Independent Review*) (September, 1907), 650–668. Against Campbell's immanence, he proposes a transcendence which demands that Christ be unique, with God His "sole ultimate responsible 'I', yet undergoing limitations in some way.

26. Letter in *The Tablet*, on Loisy (March 1, 1908), 378–379. The Baron tries to rectify an impression which had been created that Loisy considered his distinction between faith and historical matters as a mere rhetorical distinction. Loisy "has undoubtedly no intention of leaving the Church."

27. *The Mystical Element of Religion as Studied in Saint Catherine of Genoa and her friends*, 2 vols. (London, 1908), 888 pp. (Portions translated in *Les Annales de Philosophie Chrétienne* [February and March 1909], 450–461, 561–577.) Second edition of 1923 (re-issued 1961) has a new preface, vii-xix, with remarks on reviews of the book. Vol. I: Religion in general, Critical biography of St. Catherine, her doctrine, Vol. II: critical study of Catherine's mysticism, and mysticism in general, here eschatology, conclusion on religion, mysticism and the scientific habit. A major work. (Tyrrell had given a good deal of assistance with the volumes especially in improving the style and clarifying some ideas but agreed with vH not to have his name in the work.)

28. "L'Abate Loisy e il problema dei Vangeli Sinottici," *Il Rinnovamento*, III (Milan, 1908), 209–234; IV, 1–44 (1909); V, 229–272, 396–423. Signed "H", an initial which vH felt did not hide his identity except officially. A book length review of Loisy's *Evangiles Synoptiques* presented in submission to the Church but as proposing problems which must be faced. Opposes Loisy's "joyous destructivity" in his preface.

29. Review of Loisy's "Evangiles Synoptiques," *The Hibbert Journal* (July 1908), 926–930. A more conservative miniature of the previous articles. Important for vH's critical views at this time.

30. The announcement of Tyrrell's death in *The Times*, and *The Daily Mail*, (July 16, 1909) 13. Composed by Miss Petre and vH, signed by Miss Petre.

31. A letter in *The Tablet* (July 31, 1909), 181–182, together with one from M. Petre, to correct certain mistakes in the account of Tyrrell's death given by the Prior of Storrington. A similar letter appeared on July 27, 1909 in *Corriere della sera* and the *Giornale d'Italia*.

32. "Father Tyrrell: some memorials of the last twelve years of his life," *The Hibbert Journal* (January, 1910), 233–252. Precisions of his relationship to Tyrrell's thought and his ideas on the notion of authority.

33. "John, the Apostle," "John, Gospel of St.," "Loisy," *Encyclopoedia Britannica*, 11th edition, XV, 432–433, 452–458; XVI, 926–928. Reflecting Loisy's positions, these articles also give his ideas on the anti-Modernist decrees.

34. "The Religious Philosophy of Rudolph Eucken," *The Hibbert Journal* (April, 1912), 660–677. Differs with Eucken on his

idealism, in allowing ontological instinct to be supplanted by idealist hunger.

35. *Eternal Life: a Study of its Implications and Applications* (Edinburgh, 1912), 2nd ed. (1913); reprinted (1948), 443 pp. A study of the idea of the Eternal in philosophy and religion. Ch. XII important for attitude to authority. An important work.

36. "Petit consultation sur les difficultés concernant Dieu" (October-November 1912), published by P. Scoppola, *Crisi modernista e rinnovamento cattolico in Italia* (Bologna, 1961), appendix, 368–392. An important study of contemporary relevance. (See M. Nédoncelle, "A Recently Discovered Study of von Hügel on God," *International Philosophical Quarterly* (Feb. 1962), pp. 5–24.)

37. *Christian Commonwealth* (August 26, 1914). An interviewer's report of vH's ideas on the War and German culture.

38. *The German Soul and its Attitude towards Theism and Christianity, the State and the War* (London, 1916), 223 pp. A fine study on religion and war and a plea for a new vision for the German soul of the time. vH's own evaluation of the temperaments of his two homelands is revelatory, 125–128, 145–150.

39. "Eudoxe Irénée Mignot," *The Contemporary Review*, cxiii, (May 1918), 519–526. Abridged translation in *Revue du Clergé français*, XLIV, by L. de Lecger. At Mignot's death, an evaluation of his attitudes toward Loisy. Loisy was not totally wrong in saying that vH here wrote his own obituary. Opposes Loisy's "immanentism." P. 50, "the 'Modernist' movement—events still too recent for any ultimate appraisement."

40. *Essays and Addresses on The Philosophy of Religion*, First Series (London, 1921), 308 pp. The best introduction to vH's thought. In chronological order:
"Religion and Illusion"; and "Religion and Reality," *Cenobium*, Lugano (1909), and *The Quest* (April and July 1918).
"The Essentials of Catholicism," *Liddon House Occasional Paper* (July 1913).
"Preliminaries to Religious Belief," letter on the death of a baby (January 1914).
"The Specific Genius of Christianity," *The Constructive Quarterly* (March, December 1914).
"Progress in Religion," reprinted from F. Marvin, *Progress and History*, (1916).
"What do we mean by Heaven? And What do We mean by Hell?"

Church Quarterly Review (April 1917).

"The Convictions Common to Catholicism and Protestantism," *Homiletic Review* (N. Y., September, 1917).

"Institutional Christianity, an Address" (October 1918), to *Christian Student Movement* executives.

"The Apocalyptic Element in the Teaching of Jesus, an Address" (October 1919).

"Responsibility in Religious Belief," an address (March 1920), for *Christian Student Movement* executives.

"Christianity and the Supernatural," *The Modern Churchman* (June 1920).

41. A review of Friedrich Heiler's *Das Gebet, International Review of Missions* (April 1921), 266–270. Opposes Heiler underestimation of the senses and the sacraments. "I must remain in the crowd, not only for the crowd's sake but especially for my own." A permanent need even "for the most cultivated." Review shows a softening of his critical stand on sacramental words of Jesus.

42. A letter to *The Times Literary Supplement* (December 22, 1921), 860. Opposes being given the title "apologist." "I have long been greatly tried by the apologist's mentality."

43. A letter on Monsignor Duchesne, *The Times Literary Supplement* (May 28, 1922), 342. (Also a note correcting an error [June 1, 1922.] Says that Duchesne taught his juniors method, but did not point out its defects. Now speaks of "the precise but prudent *Lamentabili* ... and the vehement but more vague encyclical *Pascendi*."

44. A letter about G. C. Rawlinson, *The Church Times* (February 9, 1923), 158. Reminiscences on a cleric of action and writer with whom the Baron corresponded.

45. Ernst Troeltsch, *The Times Literary Supplement* (March 29, 1923), 216; translated in *Christliche Welt* (1923), #20–21. At the death of Troeltsch who was about to come to England for a lecture tour projected by the Baron.

46. Ernst Troeltsch, *Christian Thought, its History and Application*, edited, with an introduction and an index, by Baron F. von Hügel (London, 1923), reprinted Meridian Books (N. Y., 1957). Most of the translation was done by vH. See *Der Historismus und seine Ueberwindung*, 5 Vorträge, Einleitung von F.v.H. (Berlin, 1924). Appreciation of Troeltsch with a critique of his growing radical individualism in the twenty page introduction.

47. "Der Mystiker und die Kirche aus Anlass des Sadhu," *Hochland* (December 1924), 320–330. A discussion of the Sadhu's mysticism. True mysticism demands the institution, the Church.

POSTHUMOUS

48. *Essays and Addresses on the Philosophy of Religion*, second series, (London, 1926), 287 pp. (Anonymously edited by Professor Edmund Gardner, vH's literary executor.)
Listed chronologically:
"Official Authority and Living Religion," written privately in 1904 and slightly revised by Tyrrell in 1907. That the Baron would not have wished this included as representative of his later thought is suggested in a letter to M. Petre in 1920 on *EA* I, where his norm of selection was "those of recent years, all predominantly in the philosophy of Religion."
"The Place and Function of the Historical Element in Religion," an address (May 1905).
"On the Place and Function Within Religion, of the Body, of History, and of Institutions," an Address to Religious Thought Society (July 1913).
"On the Central Needs of Religion, and The Difficulties of Liberal Movements in Face of the Needs," an address (July 1914).
"The Idea of God," an address to Anglicans (September 1918).
"Morals and Religion," an address at Oxford (September 1920).
"Suffering and God," an important address to the London Society for the Study of Religion (May 1921).
"The Facts and Truths Concerning God and the Soul Which are of Most Importance in the Life of Prayer," an address (October 1921). Reprinted as a booklet.
"The Catholic Contribution to Religion," *The Student Movement* (December 1921).
"The Difficulties and Dangers of Nationality," *The Challenge* (August 4, 11, 1922).
49. *The Reality of God and Religion and Agnosticism*, being the literary remains of Baron F. von Hügel, ed., Edmund G. Gardner

(London, 1931), 264 pp. The unfinished work on the Gifford Lectures. The reality of God approached now, not so much through "objective interiority," as through cosmological design, though the first is not completely abandoned. Part II is a discussion of the agnosticism of his friend, the Orientalist, Sir Alfred L. Lyall, uncle of Bernard Holland.

50. *The Life of Prayer* (London, 1929), reprint 1960 (ed., Edmund Gardner). Reprint of *EA* II, #8.

LETTERS

51. "Some Letters of Baron Friedrich von Hügel," privately printed by F. C. (Mrs. F. R.) Lilley (Chicago, 1925). All except one short letter, p. 47, later reprinted elsewhere. Reprint of E. R. Bevan's obituary from *The Times* (January 28, 1925); her last conversations with vH.

52. *Selected Letters* (1896–1924), edited with a Memoir by Bernard Holland (London, 1927), 376 pp. Holland was Lyall's nephew and a friend of vH. A fine memoir. Indispensable work but letters must be supplemented for full view.

53. *Letters From Baron von Hügel to a Niece* (1919–1924), edited with an introduction by Gwendolen Greene (London, 1928), 201 pp. German edition, *Briefe en eine Nitchte*, tr.. von Karlheinz Schmidthüs (Freiburg, 1938). A delightful introduction to the personality and spiritual-literary direction of the Baron.

Other letters are to be found in the works of N. Abercrombie, M. Cropper, A. Loisy, R. Marlé, M. Petre, C. Tresmontant, M. Ward and W. Ward, cited in the text.

ANTHOLOGIES

Algar Thorold, *Readings from Friedrich von Hügel* (London, 1928). Introduction (from *The Edinburgh Review* [April, 1922]), by Thorold a friend of the Baron.

P. Franklin Chambers, *A Little Book of Baron von Hügel* (London, 1945).

Douglas Steere, *Spiritual Counsels and Letters of Baron Friedrich von Hügel* (London, 1964).

PRIMARY SOURCES

1. *The von Hügel-Tyrell correspondence*. Almost intact, it is preserved in the Department of Manuscripts, the British Museum, #44927–44931.

2. *Letters of von Hügel to Miss Petre*. Also preserved at the British Museum, #45361–45362. Miss Petre's letters to the Baron were apparently left in the care of his literary executor, Mr. Edmund Gardner, but I have been unable to discover their present location.

3. *The Petre papers*. Papers and letters which may be used with the permission of her sister, Mrs. Margaret Clutton.

4. *Letters of Tyrell* on questions of his situation within the Jesuit Order and some letters to the Old Catholic Archbishop Mathew. With permission open to inspection in the Jesuit archives at Farm Street, London.

5. *The Diaries of von Hügel and some letters*. 43 diaries, 1877–1879, 1884–1900, 1902–1924; letters to his wife; reduplication of part of the Wilfrid Ward-von Hügel correspondence; copies of the von Hügel letters to Petre; various clippings; in the possession of Rev. Jeremy Bunting, Cambridge, belonging to Mr. Michael de la Bedoyère. The complete Ward-von Hügel correspondence apparently has been lost.

6. *The von Hügel-Loisy correspondence*. At the Bibliothèque nationale, to be made available in 1971, 1981. Copies of von Hügel's books sent to Loisy with dedicatory greetings are kept in the work room of the Library of *L'Histoire des religions* at the Sorbonne.

7. *The von Hügel-Laberthonnière correspondence*. At the Department of Manuscripts, Bibliothèque nationale.

8. *Letters of von Hügel to his son-in-law Count Salimei*. In the possession of P. Scuppola, Rome, together with the Count's papers.

9. *Letters of von Hügel to Bremond*. Private archives. 22 letters, 30 postcards, 1899–1922.

10. *Letters of von Hügel to Archbishop Mignot*. At the archives of the Diocese of Rodez, France. See *Bulletin de Littérature Ecclésiastique*, Jan. to Dec. 1966.

KEY TO ABBREVIATIONS

AER	*American Ecclesiastic Review*
An P C	*Annalei de philosophie chrétienne*
APL	*Autour d'un petit livre*, A. Loisy, 1903.
CB	*The Church and the Bible articles*, von Hügel, 1894–1895.
CE	*Du Christ éternel et de nos christologies successives*, von Hügel, 1904.
DS	*Denzinger-Schönmetzer*, 1962 (the second reference number refers to previous editions).
EA	*Essays and Addresses*, von Hügel.
EB	*Etudes Bibliques*, collected and published 1903, A. Loisy.
EE	*L'Evangile et L'Eglise*, A. Loisy, 1902.
EL	*Eternal Life*, von Hügel, 1912.
ES	*Les Evangiles Synoptiques*, A. Loisy, 1908.
HD	*Histoire et Dogme*, M. Blondel, 1904.
IVR	*Insurrection Versus Resurrection*, Maisie Ward, 1938.
LTN	*Letters to a Niece*, ed. by Gwendolen Greene, 1928.
ME	*The Mystical Element of Religion*, von Hügel, 1908.
Mém	*Mémoires pour servir à l'histoire religieuse de notre témps*, 1930–1931, A. Loisy.
RB	*Revue Biblique*
RG	*The Reality of God and Religion and Agnosticism*, von Hügel, 1931.
R Sc Ph Th	*Revue des sciences philosophiques et théologiques*
R Sc Rel	*Recherches de science religieuse*
SL	*Selected Letters*, ed. by B. Holland, 1927.
TWW	*The Wilfrid Wards and the Transition*, Maisie Ward, 1934.

INDEX

297